Current Research on Gender Issues in Advertising

Gender stereotypes are general beliefs about sex-linked traits and roles, psychological characteristics, and behaviors, all of which contribute towards describing women and men. Gender role stereotyping in advertising has been a critical topic since the 1970s, and there is a long-lasting debate between advertisers and sociologists about the role and the social nature of advertising. Although changing role structures in the family and the labor force have brought significant variation in both male and female roles, it has been noted that there is a cultural lag in advertising, where men and women were, for a long period of time, depicted in more traditional roles.

This book extends the research on gender stereotypes in advertising over the past 20 years, highlighting key themes such as attitude towards sex and nudity in advertising; women in decorative roles; the changing roles of women and men in advertising; and the viewpoints of those advertising professionals who design campaigns.

This book was originally published as a special issue of the *International Journal of Advertising*.

Yorgos C. Zotos is Professor Emeritus of Applied Communication in the Faculty of Communication and Media Studies at Cyprus University of Technology, Cyprus.

Stacy Landreth Grau is Professor of Marketing Practice in the Neeley School of Business at Texas Christian University, USA.

Charles R. Taylor is the John A. Murphy Professor of Marketing at Villanova University, USA. He is also the Editor-in-Chief of the *International Journal of Advertising*.

Current Research on Gender Issues in Advertising

Edited by
Yorgos C. Zotos, Stacy Landreth Grau and Charles R. Taylor

LONDON AND NEW YORK

First published 2018 by Routledge

2 Park Square, Milton Park, Abingdon, Oxfordshire OX14 4RN
52 Vanderbilt Avenue, New York, NY 10017

Routledge is an imprint of the Taylor & Francis Group, an informa business

First issued in paperback 2020

British Library Cataloguing in Publication Data
A catalogue record for this book is available from the British Library

ISBN 13: 978-0-8153-8020-7 (hbk)
ISBN 13: 978-0-367-59310-0 (pbk)

Typeset in Times New Roman
by RefineCatch Limited, Bungay, Suffolk

Publisher's Note
The publisher accepts responsibility for any inconsistencies that may have
arisen during the conversion of this book from journal articles to book chapters,
namely the possible inclusion of journal terminology.

Disclaimer
Every effort has been made to contact copyright holders for their permission to
reprint material in this book. The publishers would be grateful to hear from any
copyright holder who is not here acknowledged and will undertake to rectify
any errors or omissions in future editions of this book.

Contents

Citation Information

The chapters in this book were originally published in the *International Journal of Advertising*. When citing this material, please use the original page numbering for each article, as follows:

Chapter 1
Gender stereotypes in advertising: a review of current research
Stacy Landreth Grau and Yorgos C. Zotos
International Journal of Advertising, volume 35, issue 5 (2016), pp. 761–770

Chapter 2
Attitudes toward ads portraying women in decorative roles and female competition: an evolutionary psychology perspective
Antigone G. Kyrousi, George G. Panigyrakis and Anastasios P. Panopoulos
International Journal of Advertising, volume 35, issue 5 (2016), pp. 771–798

Chapter 3
Do feminists still respond negatively to female nudity in advertising? Investigating the influence of feminist attitudes on reactions to sexual appeals
Hojoon Choi, Kyunga Yoo, Tom Reichert and Michael S. LaTour
International Journal of Advertising, volume 35, issue 5 (2016), pp. 823–845

Chapter 4
Influence of gender stereotypes on advertising offensiveness and attitude toward advertising in general
Bruce A. Huhmann and Yam B. Limbu
International Journal of Advertising, volume 35, issue 5 (2016), pp. 846–863

Chapter 5
Stereotypical or just typical: how do US practitioners view the role and function of gender stereotypes in advertisements?
Kasey Windels
International Journal of Advertising, volume 35, issue 5 (2016), pp. 864–887

For any permission-related enquiries please visit:
http://www.tandfonline.com/page/help/permissions

Notes on Contributors

Christina Boutsouki is based at the Department of Economics, School of Economics and Political Science, Aristotle's University of Thessaloniki, Greece.

Hojoon Choi is Assistant Professor at the Jack J. Valenti School of Communication, University of Houston, USA.

Alfons González is based at the Universitat Autònoma de Barcelona, Spain.

Stacy Landreth Grau is Professor of Marketing Practice in the Neeley School of Business at Texas Christian University, USA.

Leonidas Hatzithomas is Assistant Professor at the Department of Business Administration, University of Macedonia, Greece.

Bruce A. Huhmann is based at the Department of Marketing, New Mexico State University, USA.

Antigone G. Kyrousi is Academic Researcher at the Department of Business Administration, Athens University of Economics and Business, Greece.

Michael S. LaTour is based at the School of Business, Ithaca College, Ithaca, USA.

Patrícia Lázaro is based at the Universitat Autònoma de Barcelona, Spain.

Yam B. Limbu is Associate Professor of Marketing at Montclair State University, USA.

George G. Panigyrakis is Professor of Marketing at the Department of Business Administration, Athens University of Economics and Business, Greece.

Anastasios P. Panopoulos is Assistant Professor at the University of Macedonia, Greece.

Tom Reichert is Dean of the College of Information and Communications at the University of South Carolina, USA.

David Roca is based at the Universitat Autònoma de Barcelona, Spain.

Charles R. Taylor is the John A. Murphy Professor of Marketing at Villanova University, USA. He is also the Editor-in-Chief of the *International Journal of Advertising*.

Daniel Tena is based at the Universitat Autònoma de Barcelona, Spain.

Kasey Windels is Associate Professor at the Manship School of Mass Communication, Louisiana State University, USA.

Kyunga Yoo works at the KT Corporation, Seoul, Korea.

Paschalina Ziamou is based at the Department of Marketing and International Business, Zicklin School of Business, Baruch College, The City University of New York, USA.

Yorgos C. Zotos is Professor Emeritus of Applied Communication in the Faculty of Communication and Media Studies at Cyprus University of Technology, Cyprus.

Introduction: Current research on gender issues in advertising

Yorgos C. Zotos, Stacy Landreth Grau and Charles R. Taylor

Gender stereotypes in advertising: exploring new directions

Since the early 1970's, scholars have studied portrayals of women and men in advertising. Advertisers use what consumers believe about gender roles to promote products and services. As such, researchers have been interested in the cultural and social consequences of stereotyping in advertising (Hawkins and Coney 1976; Lundstrom and Sciglimpaglia 1977; McArthur and Resko 1975) especially when it comes to the role of women.

In this book, compiled from articles appearing in a special issue of the *International Journal of Advertising* we offer readers new insights on Gender Stereotypes in Advertising. The 'corpus' of research on this topic, the last five decades, provides an interesting background to current and diverse research. It offers the challenge to follow alterations in advertising stereotypes, and how and to what extent these alterations reflect the prevailing norms, beliefs, attitudes, and changes in society with respect to gender roles (Pollay 1986). The chapters presented here were recognized for their originality and scholarship on the topic of Gender Stereotypes in Advertising.

In Chapter 1 which is titled, "Gender stereotypes in advertising: a review of current research," Stacy Landreth Grau and Yorgos Zotos summarize the current state of knowledge on gender issues in advertising based on a review of studies published in four major advertising journals: *Journal of Advertising, International Journal of Advertising, Journal of Advertising Research* and *Journal of Current Issues in Research in Advertising* since 2010. The purpose of the paper is to highlight the key themes found in recent research as well as to identify several key areas for future research on this topic.

Chapter 2 by Antigone Kyrousi, George Panigyrakis, and Anastasios Panopoulos continues the theme of attitude toward ads portraying women in decorative roles. In "Attitudes toward ads portraying women in decorative roles and female competition: an evolutionary psychology perspective," the authors put forward theory that appears to cast insight on seemingly conflicting attitudes toward the portrayal of women in advertising. Drawing on the principles of evolutionary psychology, the paper proposes that women's attitudes toward ads depicting beauty and sexiness underlie the evolved and context-sensitive mechanism of intra-sexual competition. Relevant hypotheses are tested and supported via two experimental studies.

Chapter 3 is Hojoon Choi, Kyunga Yoo, Tom Reichert, and Michael LaTour's paper, "Do feminists still respond negatively to female nudity in advertising? Investigating the influence of feminist attitudes on reactions to sexual appeals." The authors test the belief that feminism and the sexualization of women in advertising stand in opposition. The study employed a large US national sample (n=1298) to examine how consumers' level of feminist attitudes differentiate and predict their ethical judgment and ad-related evaluations of sexual images of women in advertising. The findings of the study, which diverge from previous research, may indicate that contemporary feminists view sexual images of women differently than in previous decades.

Chapter 4 is titled the "Influence of gender stereotypes on advertising offensiveness and attitude toward advertising in general" by Bruce Huhmann and Yam Limbu. The authors explore the degree to which the portrayal of gender stereotypes create irritation. The chapter focuses on an understudied area: the degree to which gender stereotype-related constructs are related to Attitude toward Advertising in General (AG). The paper uses structural equation modeling to demonstrate that attitude toward sex/nudity in advertising predicts AG indirectly via the perceived offensiveness of advertising. Furthermore, the more that consumers believe that advertising portrays gender stereotypes, the less favorable their AG.

Chapter 5 is Kasey Windels' "Stereotypical or just typical: how do US practitioners view the role and function of gender stereotypes in advertisements?" This paper was motivated by the view that practitioners' perspectives on the role and function of stereotyping in advertising have remained largely unknown. The study uses qualitative interviews with 42 practitioners and details seven themes concerning professionals' perceptions of the role and function of stereotypes in advertising. Findings suggest that practitioners felt stereotypes were used most appropriately when they were subverted or challenged in advertising messages. Moreover, stereotypes were most inappropriate when they reinforced negative perceptions.

Chapter 6 is authored by Leonidas Hatzithomas, Christina Boutsouki, and Paschalina Ziamou and is titled, "A longitudinal analysis of the changing roles of gender advertising: a content analysis of Super Bowl commercials." A content analysis of 20 years of Super Bowl advertising (1990–2009) was conducted to examine whether portrayals of women have changed. The findings detect and discuss shifts in cultural notions of gender constructed in advertising messages.

Chapter 7 is authored by David Roca, Daniel Tena, Patrícia Lázaro, and Alfons González and is titled, "Is there gender bias when creative directors judge advertising? Name cue effect in ad evaluation." The paper supports the idea that creative departments in Spain have been seen as a male subculture in advertising agencies, where women experience many difficulties in their career progress. An experimental design was selected where the independent variable was authorship of the ad by gender. Although creative departments are highly male dominated in the country studied, the results of the study actually reveal an absence of gender bias where neither the gender of the ad creators, nor the creatives affected the evaluations.

We, the editors, thank our authors for their contributions and hope readers benefit from this new knowledge on gender issues in advertising.

References

Hawkins, D.I. and Coney, K.A. (1976), "Advertising and differentiated sex roles in contemporary American society," *Journal of the Academy of Marketing Science*, 4, 418–428.
Lundstrom, W.J. and Sciglimpaglia, D. (1977), "Sex role portrayals in advertising," *Journal of Marketing*, 41, 72–129.
McArthur, L.Z. and Resko, B.G. (1975), "The portrayal of men and women in American television commercials," *Journal of Social Psychology*, 97, 209–220.
Pollay, R.W. (1986), "The distorted mirror: Reflections on the unintended consequences of advertising," *Journal of Marketing*, 50, no. 2, 18–36.

Gender stereotypes in advertising: a review of current research

Stacy Landreth Grau and Yorgos C. Zotos

The purpose of this paper is to highlight the historical context of gender stereotypes in advertising and then examine the scholarship related to gender stereotypes. Gender portrayals in advertising have been examined extensively in the last five decades and still remain an important topic. Changing role structure in the family and in the labor force has brought significant variation in both male and female roles and subsequently how it is reflected in advertising. It has been noted that there is a culture lag. Sexes for a long period of time were depicted in advertising in more traditional roles. Women were presented in an inferior manner relative to their potential and capabilities, while at the same the data indicated a shift towards more positive role portrayals. The changing role of men is the area that has seen the greatest interest in the past few years. Men are depicted in advertising in 'softer' roles, while interacting with their children. Men are also shown in more egalitarian roles. The paper finally attempts to outline the future research direction of gender portrayals in advertising. First, research should focus on examining gender portrayals in online platforms, and find ways to modify current coding schemes to digital formats. Second, companies and the media are beginning to pay attention to a once largely ignored segment the lesbian/gay/bisexual/transgender (LGBT) consumer. Third, recent advertising has focused on the 'empowered' women called femvertising.

Introduction

Scholars have been interested in stereotypes – particularly of women – in advertising for more than 50 years. In that time, researchers have been interested not only in the 'what' (e.g., what stereotypes are used to portray women and men) but also the 'why' (e.g., the cultural implications of using stereotypes and advertising and the 'now what' (e.g., the social consequences of stereotypes and advertising (Hawkins and Coney 1976; Lundstrom and Sciglimpaglia 1977; McArthur and Resko 1975). The purpose of this paper is to examine research in this area since 2010 and provide direction for the next five years in a fragmented media environment.

Stereotypes are beliefs about a social category (Vinacke 1957) especially those that differentiate genders (Ashmore and Del Boca 1981). Stereotypes become problematic when they lead to expectations about one social category over another or restrict opportunities for one social category over another. Over the years, several content analyses have examined components such as physical characteristics (e.g., body size, height), occupational status, roles (e.g., leadership) and traits (e.g., self-assertion). Research has shown that women are generally presented in more decorative roles (e.g., for their beauty or body), in more family oriented roles, in fewer professional roles and in more demure roles (Uray and Burnaz 2003) while men are typically shown as more independent, authoritarian and professional with little regard to age and physical appearances (Reichert and Carpenter 2004).

That said, there is still much to be learned about the changing role of gender representations in advertising. This introduction to the *International Journal of Advertising's* special issue on Gender Stereotypes in Advertising highlights some of the historical context of gender stereotypes in advertising and then examine scholarship related to gender stereotypes since 2010 to identify the current key areas being studied.

Gender stereotypes in advertising

Gender stereotypes in advertising is a topic with more than five decades of related research. The outcome of literature was ignited by social and historical contingencies. First, the rise of feminism in the 1960s challenged equal opportunities for men and women and initiated a gradual change in occupational opportunities and domestic structures (Zotos and Lysonski 1994; Plakoyiannaki et al. 2008; Plakoyiannaki and Zotos 2009; Zotos and Tsichla 2014) especially for women. Second, changes in the labor force brought significant variation in both male and female roles and subsequently how they are reflected in advertising (Zotos and Lysonski 1994; Zotos and Tsichla 2014). Third, the changing role structure in the family has created significant variations in the female role (Zotos and Lysonski 1994) and more recently the male role. During these years, women were presented in an inferior manner relative to their potential and capabilities, while at the same time the data indicated a slow shift towards more positive role portrayals. Past literature (Lysonski 1985; Corteze 1999; Kilbourne 1999; Lazar 2006; Plakoyiannaki and Zotos 2009) has proposed that advertising contributes to gender inequality by promoting 'sexism', and distorted body image symbols as valid and acceptable. Since then, women's roles have undergone dramatic changes and there have been changes in portrayals as well.

The 'mirror' versus the 'mold' debate

There is a long-lasting debate between advertisers and sociologists, about the role and the social nature of advertising, especially when it comes to stereotypes within advertising. Two opposing points of view have been developed – the 'mirror' versus the 'mold' argument. Following the 'mirror' point of view, advertising reflects values that exist and are dominant in society. Furthermore, this view suggests that the best that advertising can succeed to do is to act as a magnified lens, which offers an extrapolated picture of a social phenomenon (Pollay 1986, 1987). A possible interpretation of this argument suggests that in the contemporary socioeconomic and political environment, which influences the value system of a society, multiple factors are interfaced and interrelated. Therefore, the impact of advertising is not valued as being significant. Hence the way that women and men presented in advertising would follow the dominant concepts held regarding gender roles (Zotos and Tsichla 2014).

In contrast, the 'mold' point of views advertising as a *reflection* of society and its prevailing values (Manstead and McCulloch 1981; Pollay 1986, 1987). Cultivation theory suggests that peoples' perception of social reality is shaped by the media (Gerbner 1998). They incorporate stereotypes presented by the media into their own system of values, ideas, and beliefs about the quality of life (Zotos and Tsichla 2014). They start creating a concept of reality, which tends to match the advertised images. At the end of a long process, individual behavior and human beings relationships are formulated in such a manner that could be characterized as a 'hybrid.' Advertising's impact is a crucial factor, which contributes to the development of this 'hybrid.' It is accepted the gender representations are socially constructed. According to this viewpoint, advertising campaigns create gender identity, based on their images, the stereotyped iconography of masculinity and femininity (Schroeder and Zwick 2004).

Based on the aforementioned analysis, it could be suggested that the 'mirror' and the 'mold' argument is a continuum. The real life examples lie in this continuum according to the social values which are promoted, and the type of the advertised products (Zotos and Tsichla 2014). Accepting advertising as a system of visual representation, which creates meaning within the framework of culture, it seems that reflects and contributes to culture (Hall 1980; Albers-Miller and Gelb 1996; Zotos and Tsichla 2014). To grasp these ideas in an integrated manner, this long-lasting debate between the 'mirror' and the 'mold' argument should reflect Kilbourne's (1999, 57–58) statement: 'Advertising is our environment. We swim in it as fish swim in the water. We cannot escape it… advertising messages are inside our intimate relationships, our home, our hearts, our heads.'

Gender stereotypes in advertising: recent research since 2010

Despite the fact that gender stereotypes in advertising have been studied for many years, the past six years have seen a robust addition to the literature. We highlighted research found in four key advertising journals: *Journal of Advertising, International Journal of Advertising, Journal of Current Issues in Research in Advertising*, and *Journal of Advertising Research* as well as other marketing communications journals. Several important themes emerged (see Table 1).

Updated trends and directions

Recent research shows that, in general, gender stereotyping in advertising still exists and is prevalent in many countries around the world. Eisend (2010) set out to explore the degree of gender stereotyping as well as any changes over the years. The primary contribution of his work is to provide a quantitative review of 64 studies in a meta-analysis on the effects of gender stereotypes in advertising. He found that some stereotyping still persists – particularly for women. Occupational status still showed the highest degree of stereotyping, despite the education, occupation and status changes earned by women over the past several years. Interestingly, Eisend (2010) also found that the degree of stereotyping has decreased over the years due mostly to improvements in high masculinity societies (such as Japan). There was no substantial decrease in low masculinity societies like Sweden.

Knoll, Eisend and Steinhagen (2011) developed a new way to measure the degree of stereotyping in advertising. They found that gender stereotyping was still prevalent in German television and that this stereotyping depends on the type of channel (public vs. private channels). Across both types of channels, Knoll et al. (2011) found that women were more likely to be younger and depicted as product users with domestic products and more likely to be portrayed at home in dependent roles. Men were more likely depicted as authoritarian and older and are more likely to be portrayed outside of the home in independent roles. These findings are in line with other studies of several other cultures. However, on public channels, stereotyping was higher for variables like role and location as well as occupational status. On private channels, stereotyping relates more to role behavior and physical characteristics. The results of stereotyping were not limited to the USA

Table 1. Gender stereotypes in advertising: research since 2010

Research	Theory	Methodology	Key findings
Baxter, Kulczynski, and Illicic (2015) *International Journal of Advertising*	Gender role ideologies	181 Australian consumers; online panel; typical *vs.* atypical caregivers	Consumers perceive in-ad gender role portrayals of males as caregivers as atypical of the current advertising environment. Those holding more egalitarian gender role ideology have more positive attitudes about advertising that challenges traditional roles.
Chu, Lee, and Kim (2016) *International Journal of Advertising*	Non-stereotypical gender role (NSGR), self-construal, need for uniqueness, perceived novelty, cognitive resistance	5 experiments with Korean consumers	The overall effects NSGR advertising depends on the self-construal and need for uniqueness. The authors found dual mediation effect of novelty perception and cognitive resistance.
Eisend (2010) *Journal of the Academy of Marketing Science*	Mirror vs. mold theory	Meta-analysis	The results show empirical support for the mirror argument over the mold argument.
Fowler and Thomas (2015) *Journal of Marketing Communications*	Traditional and contemporary gender roles	Content analysis of depictions of males between 2003 and 2008. Male depictions in lead role (2003 = 907 prime time commercials; 2008 = 961 prime time commercials in four networks	Some aspects of male depictions are counter to the changing gender roles in society while others are reflective of these changes.
Gentry and Harrison (2010) *Marketing Theory*	Hegemonic masculinity	Content analysis of ads targeted to men (1392 ads in sports programming), women (200 ads on afternoon TV) and children (225 ads on kids TV)	The research found that male portrayals still reflect a very traditional masculine perspective. They have not become more gender neutral
Eisend, Plagemann, and Sollwedel (2014) *Journal of Advertising*	Information processing theories	Content analysis & Experiment	The research finds that they way that women and men are stereotyped in advertising is dependent on humor. Specifically, traditional male stereotypes are more prevalent in humorous ads where female stereotypes are more prevalent in non-humorous ads

(continued)

Table 1. *(Continued)*

Research	Theory	Methodology	Key findings
Knoll, Eisend, and Steinhagen (2011) *International Journal of Advertising*	Stereotyping and gender equality	Content analysis of ads on public and private German TV channels; June 2008	This research provides a measure for the degree of stereotyping in advertising. It still prevails German TV and there is a difference between public and private channels.
Lee (2014) *International Journal of Advertising*	Gender stereotypes; resonance theory, negative bias, expectancy-disconfirmation theory	Experiment with voters in Taiwan	Examined gender stereotypes in political advertising context. It examines the persuasive impact of a campaign theme that is congruent or incongruent with gender stereotypes and a positive vs. negative ad style
Marshall et al. (2014) *Journal of Marketing Management*	Hegemonic masculinity	Content analysis of ads in Good Housekeeping from 1950–2010.	Family related advertising in women's magazines does little to challenge traditional roles of paternal masculinity. But is some broadening of breadwinner roles.
Rubie-Davis, Liu, and Lee (2013) *Journal of Social Psychology*	Cultivation theory	Content analysis of 3,000 TV ads in New Zealand	Men and women are less often depicted in stereotypical roles than previously reported but they found differences between white and Maori/Pacific Island people.
Shao (2014) *International Journal of Advertising*	Mirror vs. mold theory	Interviews of ad professionals in China.	This research examines how Chinese ad professionals' culture perceptions of gender influence on their work.
Van Hellemont and Van de Bulck (2012) *International Journal of Advertising*		Belgium; online survey of advertising and marketing professionals; gender equal opportunity workers and consumers	Examines differences in adherence of three sectors to 2008 EU Parliament Resolution on marketing and advertising equality. Results suggest a degree of tolerance that varies according to sector, language, gender and age.
Zawisza and Cinnirella (2010) *Journal of Applied Social Psychology*	Stereotype content model & stereo content hypothesis	2 experiments that investigate the effectiveness of ads that use (non) traditional stereotypes of women and men	The paternalistic ad strategies were more effective than envious ones. This supported the predictions the stereotype content model.
Zayer and Coleman (2015) *Journal of Advertising*	Institutional theory	Interviews of advertising professionals	Research shows professionals' perceptions about women's vulnerability and men's immunity to the negative consequences of advertising. Four themes are derived.

and Europe. Work by Rubie-Davies, Liu, and Lee (2013) found that in their examination of television advertising in New Zealand men and women were less often depicted in stereotypical roles than in the past. This research suggests progress in stereotyped portrayals in the country.

There are caveats to the consequences of stereotyping. Eisend, Plagemann, and Sollwedel (2014) found that while stereotyping does exist in advertising, consumer's perceptions about it might be less serious than expected. They examined the role of humor in advertising and its relationship to gender stereotyping. They found that gender role portrayals are less serious if they are used as sources of humor. Specifically, male stereotypes are more prevalent in humorous ads, while female stereotypes are more prevalent in non-humorous ads. This points to the influence of other variables in determining the ultimate effects of stereotypes in advertising that require additional examination. It is important to continue to track changes in gender stereotypes in advertising and examine factors that could affect consumers' reactions to these portrayals.

View from practitioners

Advertising professionals are often considered 'cultural intermediaries' (Cronin 2004) who develop messages. And yet their decision making process about gender portrayals in advertising campaigns is barely considered. Despite Grow's (2008) call for more research, little has been done on the 'gendered voice of advertising' until the past two years. Shao (2014) examined Chinese advertising practitioners and how Chinese culture impacts advertising creation. In terms of similarities and differences, Chinese advertising depicts males in more occupational and recreational roles whereas women were depicted in more decorative roles (Cheng 1997). However, Johansson (1999) found that Chinese advertising depicted women as shy and subordinate compared to stronger roles for women in the USA. But in general there are more similarities than differences in how women and men are depicted in China compared to other societies. In 26 interviews with advertising professionals, Shao (2014) found that Chinese advertising professionals do not reflect on their role in perpetuating stereotypes, claiming that they mirror reality rather than representing or distorting it. They claimed that they were simply reflecting Chinese culture.

Zayer and Coleman (2015) examined advertising professionals' perceptions of how gender portrayals impact men and women and how these perceptions influence their strategic and creative decisions. Using institutional theory as a foundation, the authors provide a more holistic viewpoint of advertising ethics. Their interview respondents claimed they also mirror the dominant viewpoints of society regarding gender stereotypes but point out that men are not immune to the gender stereotypes and call for more research on the negative impact of gender stereotypes of men in advertising as well.

Few studies have examined advertising that is viewed as unfriendly towards men or women by other stakeholders. Van Hellemont and Van de Bulck (2012) examined the views of advertising professionals in Belgium about 10 ads that were identified as potentially offensive due to their stereotypical depictions of both men and women. Interestingly, advertising professionals and consumers did not differ in their perceptions of advertising deemed potentially unfriendly to women and men. Furthermore, the study finds that advertising professionals were more tolerant of these messages than consumers. These insights can prove useful in understanding their role as cultural intermediaries and their responsibility to promote more gender equality in advertising. More research should work towards understanding the role of advertising professionals in crafting campaigns, specifically when it comes to portraying men and women.

Stereotypes in contexts

There are certain contexts where gender stereotypes play an enhanced role. In other words, the consequences are greater than enhanced sales for the product. Lee (2014) examined the role of gender stereotypes in political advertising, a unique context because of the larger implications beyond consumerism. Recently, political communication researchers have paid more attention to gender differences in political advertising and Lee's (2014) study examined the effects of gender in a fictitious Taiwanese election. The results showed that emphasizing gender stereotypes in politics is a double edged sword. Lee found that important traits and issues in campaigns are not static so candidates should emphasize or deemphasize gender based stereotypes based on positive or negative campaigning.

Role of European interventions

In the EU, advertising's self-regulatory bodies as well as the European Advertising Standard Alliance (EASA) began updating their ethical guidelines on gender portrayals following increased complaints by consumers as well as the approval of anti-discrimination laws in several European countries. In 2008, a EU resolution was adopted on how marketing and advertising affects equality between women and men. Van Hellemont and Van de Bulck (2012) argue that less restrictive (or non-restrictive) literacy programs and awards for positive advertising are more effective at reducing gender stereotyping as opposed to increased legislation and regulation. Alternatively, Knoll et al. (2011) argue that the steps taken by the European Parliament move in the right direction given the presence of gender stereotypes and that self-regulation is already current practice and has not been successful especially on German public channels.

Changing portrayal of men in advertising

The changing role of men is perhaps the area that has seen the greatest interest in the past few years. As recently as the 2015 Super Bowl, advertising from Dove Men Care showing men in much 'softer' roles while interacting with their children and was well received. Other brands have followed. Yet there is a lack of research about the stereotypes associated with men in advertising. As such, Marshall et al. (2014) examined 60 years of advertising portrayals of men in the role as a father. They found that most of the advertising in Good Housekeeping (1950–2010) does little to challenge traditional models of paternal masculinity (Marshall et al. 2014). They seem to reinforce traditional gender roles. More recently there does seem to see a wider view of the original 'breadwinner' role for men, thus updating how we view fathers. Similarly, Fowler and Thomas (2015) conducted a content analysis of television advertising in primetime from 2003 to 2008. This was one of the few studies to focus exclusively on men and provides a baseline for further research. Fowler and Thomas (2015) found that there were changes in the five-year time frame. First, they found fewer men in the lead and some suggest that male characters are being portrayed to reflect society's changing view of men and women's roles. Second, they found an increased in men portrayed as fathers, for example. However, the research showed that these trends are small.

While that research used content analysis to show the presence of stereotypes, other research examined how consumers feel about these newer portrayals of men in advertising. Chu, Lee, and Kim (2016) examined 'non-stereotypical gender role representation' (NSGR) and found that consumers do see this advertising in a positive light. NSGR is used to achieve marketing objectives like increasing attention, gaining interest and increasing sales. Chu, Lee, and Kim (2016) also found that the presence of NSGR advertising can actually lead to minor changes in society since they found a decrease in gender stereotyping after exposure to this type of advertising. Baxter, Kulczynski, and Illicic (2015) examined consumer reactions to atypical images of men (e.g., men as caregivers) and found that consumer reactions depended on whether they were traditionalists, transitionalists or egalitarians. Their findings show that while men as caregivers was seen as atypical for the current advertising environment, consumers did express positive attitudes and that while these ads do cut through the clutter, it is important to emphasize product benefits as well.

Most of the research on gender stereotypes deals with unfair depictions of women and is steeped in feminist critical scholarship. But in order to get a full picture of gender stereotypes it becomes apparent that research in masculinity theories are also appropriate. Gentry and Harrison (2010) argue that 'if scholars are to effectively challenge issues of gender roles in advertising, it is important to critically examine the discursive frameworks that shape our understanding of such topics' (90). They found that while there may be advertising that show men in more egalitarian roles, men are not likely to see them because they are typically not the target audience for them. Additionally the depictions of men in advertising also dependent on the product advertised. They call for 'father's portrayal in the media should facilitate active parenthood, not sustain the more distant perspective from the past' (91).

Future research directions

The past 50 years have proven to be pivotal in our understanding of how people – primarily women – are portrayed in television and print advertising. As we move into a more postmodern and digital age, there are several areas that warrant attention. First, most of the current research on gender stereotypes has been examined in print (e.g., magazine) and television advertising. However, both of these media have seen steady decreases in readership and viewership. At the same time, people spend more time online – with videos, social media and apps. But little research has examined gender portrayals in online platforms (Plakoyiannaki et al. 2008 is one exception). Future research should examine ways to modify current coding schemes in print and television advertising to digital formats and also work to develop completely new coding schemes that will allow researchers to truly examine the role of gender stereotypes in digital advertising, native advertising and social media advertising formats. Additionally, more research needs to examine the role of gender stereotypes in non 'paid' formats such as owned media and content marketing.

Second, companies (and the media) are beginning to pay attention to a once largely ignored segment – the lesbian/gay/bisexual/transgender (LGBT) consumer. Some companies have been more open about using same sex couples in their advertising. However, other companies have decided to use more coded representations, which may appear invisible to heterosexual consumers, but possibly be interpreted as 'gay' by LGBT consumers. This strategy known as 'gay window advertising' (Bronski 1984) stems from some advertisers' fear of alienating heterosexual consumers (Greenlee 2004; Oakenfull 2004). Future research should examine the stereotypes of LGBT consumers in advertising.

Third, recent advertising has focused on the 'empowered' women (e.g., Pantene, Always) called femvertising. The goal of this 'pro-women' messaging is to celebrate women rather than objectifying them in advertising (Bahadur 2014). In a SheKnows poll, 91% of respondents say that how women are portrayed in advertising has a direct impact on girls' self-esteem and that 51% of respondents say that these ads help break down gender equality. A key to the effectiveness of these ads is the idea of authenticity. Indeed, there is a fear that some companies are simply jumping on the bandwagon of femvertising to increase sales. Future research needs to examine femvertising in more detail and identify the elements that make it more or less effective.

Overall, while there has been major progress in examining the types of stereotypes of women and men and how portrayals have changed. Over the next five years, we hope to see new and interesting insights in these areas.

Disclosure statement

No potential conflict of interest was reported by the authors.

References

Ashmore, R.D., and F.K. Del Boca. 1981. Conceptual approaches to stereotypes and stereotyping. In *Cognitive processes in stereotyping and intergroup behavior*, ed. D.L. Hamilton, 1−35. Hillsdale: Lawrence Erlbaum Associates.

Albers-Miller, N.D., and B.D. Gelb. 1996. Business advertising appeals as a mirror of cultural dimensions: A study of eleven countries. *Journal of Advertising* 25: 57−70.

Bahadur, Nina. 2014. Femvertising ads are empowering women − and making money for brands. *Huffington Post* (October 3). http://www.huffingtonpost.com/2014/10/02/femvertising-advertis ing-empowering-women_n_5921000.html

Baxter, S.M., A. Kulczynski, and J. Illicic. 2015. Ads aimed at dads: Exploring consumers' reactions towards advertising that conforms and challenges traditional gender role ideologies. *International Journal of Advertising*, http://dx.doi.org/10.1080/02650487.2015.1077605

Bronski, M. 1984. *Culture clash: The making of gay sensibility*. Boston, MA: South End Press.

Cheng, M. 1997. Holding up half of the sky? A socio-cultural comparison of gender-role portrayals in Chinese and US advertising. *International Journal of Advertising* 16, no. 4: 295−319.

Chu, K., D-H. Lee, and J.Y. Kim. 2016. The effect of non-stereotypical gender role advertising on consumer evaluation. *International Journal of Advertising* 35, no. 1: 106−34.

Cortese, A.J. 1999. *Provocateur, images of women and minorities in advertising*. New York, NY: Rowman and Littlefield Publishers.

Cronin, A.M. 2004. Regimes of mediation: Advertising practitioners as cultural intermediaries? *Consumption, Market and Culture* 7, no. 4: 349−69.

Eisend, M. 2010. A meta-analysis of gender roles in advertising. *Journal of the Academy of Marketing Science* 38: 418−40.

Eisend, M., J. Plagemann, and J. Sollwedel. 2014. Gender roles and humor in advertising: The occurrence of stereotyping in humorous and nonhumorous advertising and its consequences for advertising effectiveness. *Journal of Advertising* 43, no. 3: 256−73.

Fowler, K., and V. Thomas. 2015. A content analysis of male roles in television advertising: Do traditional roles still hold?. *Journal of Marketing Communications* 21, no. 5: 356−71.

Gentry, J., and R. Harrison. 2010. Is Advertising a barrier to male movement toward gender change? *Marketing Theory* 10, no. 1: 74−96.

Gerbner, G. 1998. Cultivation analysis: An overview. *Mass Communication and Society* 1: 175−94.

Greenlee, T.B. 2004. Mainstream marketers advertise to gays and lesbians: Strategic issues and research agenda. In *Diversity in Advertising*, ed. J.D. Williams, W.N. Lee, and C.P. Haugtvedt, 357−67. London: Lawrence Erlbaum.

Grow, J.M. 2008. The gender of branding: Early Nike women's advertising a feminist antenarrative. *Women's Studies in Communication* 31, no. 3: 312−43.

Hall, S. 1980. Encoding/decoding. In *Culture, media, language*, ed. S. Hall, D., Hobson, A., Lowe, and P., Willis, 117−27. London: Hutchison.

Hawkins, D.I., and K.A. Coney. 1976. Advertising and differentiated sex roles in contemporary American society. *Journal of the Academy of Marketing Science* 4: 418−28.

Johansson, P. 1999. Consuming the other: The fetish of the western women in Chinese advertising and popular culture. *Postcolonial Studies: Culture, Politics, Economy* 2, no. 3: 377−88.

Kilbourne, J. 1999. *Deadly persuasion: Why women and girls must fight the addictive power of advertising.* New York, NY: The Free Press.

Knoll, S., M. Eisend, and J. Steinhagen. 2011. Gender roles in advertising: Measuring and comparing gender stereotyping on public and private TV channels in Germany. *International Journal of Advertising* 30, no. 5: 867−88.

Lazar, M. 2006. Discover the power of femininity! Analyzing global 'power femininity' in local advertising. *Feminist Media Studies* 6: 505−17.

Lee, Y.K. 2014. Gender stereotypes as a double-edged sword in political advertising: Persuasion effects of campaign theme and advertising style. *International Journal of Advertising* 33, no. 2.

Lundstrom, W.J., and D. Sciglimpaglia. 1977. Sex role portrayals in advertising. *Journal of Marketing* 41: 72−129.

Lysonski, S. 1985. Role portrayals in British magazine advertisements. *European Journal of Marketing* 19, no. 7: 37−55.

Manstead, A.S.R., and R. McCulloch. 1981. Sex-role stereotyping in British television advertisements. *British Journal of Social Psychology* 20: 171−80.

Marshall, D., T. Davis, M.K. Hogg, T. Schneider, and A. Petersen. 2014. From overt provider to invisible presence: Discursive shifts in advertising portrayals of the father in Good Housekeeping, 1950-2010. *Journal of Marketing Management* 30, no. 15−16: 1654−79.

McArthur, L.Z., and B.G. Resko. 1975. The portrayal of men and women in American television commercials. *Journal of Social Psychology* 97: 209−20.

Oakenfull, G.K. 2004. Targeting consumer segments based on sexual orientation: Can advertisers swing both ways? In *Diversity in Advertising*, ed. J.D. Williams, W.N. Lee, and C.P. Haugtvedt, 369−81. London: Lawrence Erlbaum.

Plakoyiannaki, E., and Y. Zotos. 2009. Female role stereotypes in print advertising: Identifying associations with magazine and product categories. *European Journal of Marketing* 43, no. 11−12, 1411−34.

Plakoyiannaki, E., K. Mathioudaki, P. Dimitratos, and Y. Zotos. 2008. Images of women in online advertisements of global products: Does sexism exist?. *Journal of Business Ethics* 83: 101−12.

Pollay, R.W. 1986. The distorted mirror: Reflections on the unintended consequences of advertising. *Journal of Marketing* 50, no. 2: 18−36.

Pollay, R.W. 1987. On the value of reflections on the values in 'The distorted mirror.' *Journal of Marketing* 51, no. 3: 104−09.

Reichert, T., and C. Carpenter. 2004. An update on sex in magazine advertising: 1983−2003. *Journalism & Mass Communication* 81, no. 4: 823−37.

Rubie-Davis, C., S. Liu, and K.C. K. Lee. 2013. Watching each other: Portrayals of gender and ethnicity in television advertisements. *Journal of Social Psychology* 153, no. 2: 175−95.

Schroeder, J.E., and D. Zwick. 2004. Mirrors of masculinity: Representation and identity in advertising images. *Consumption, Markets and Culture* 7: 21−52.

Shao, Y. 2014. Chinese advertising practitioners' conceptualization of gender representation. *International Journal of Advertising* 33, no. 2: 329−50.

Uray, N., and S. Burnaz. 2003. An analysis of the portrayal of gender roles in Turkish television advertising. *Sex Roles* 48, no. 1−2: 77−87.

Van Hellemont, C., and H. Van de Bulck. 2012. Impacts of advertisements that are unfriendly to women and men. *International Journal of Advertising* 31, no. 3: 623−56.

Vinacke, W.E. 1957. Stereotypes ad social concepts. *Journal of Social Psychology* 46: 229−43.

Zawisza, M., and M. Cinnirella. 2010. What matters more − breaking tradition or stereotype content? Envious and paternalistic gender stereotypes and advertising effectiveness. *Journal of Applied Social Psychology* 40, no. 7: 1767−97.

Zayer, L.T., and C. Coleman. 2015. Advertising professionals' perceptions of the impact of gender portrayals on men and women: A question of ethics?. *Journal of Advertising* 44, no. 3: 264−75.

Zotos, Y. C., and S. Lysonski. 1994. Gender representations: The case of Greek Magazine advertisements. *Journal of Euromarketing* 3, no. 2: 27−47.

Zotos, Y., and E. Tsichla. 2014. Snapshots of men and women in interaction: An investigation of stereotypes in print advertisement relationship portrayals. *Journal of Euromarketing* 23, no. 3: 35−58.

Attitudes toward ads portraying women in decorative roles and female competition: an evolutionary psychology perspective

Antigone G. Kyrousi, George G. Panigyrakis and Anastasios P. Panopoulos

The portrayal of women in advertising is a prolific research topic and extant studies have emphasized the negative attitudes of female consumers toward stereotypic depictions of women in advertising in general. However, empirical evidence regarding female consumers' responses to specific ads depicting women in decorative roles is scarce and conflicting. Drawing on the principles of evolutionary psychology, the present paper proposes that women's attitudes toward such ads are underlied by the evolved context-sensitive mechanism of intrasexual competition. Relevant hypotheses are tested through two experimental studies. The findings indicate that decorative portrayals in advertising elicit more favorable attitudes when female consumers compete through a self-promotion strategy with regard to a competitor derogation one. Additionally, the temporal orientation of self-referencing during ad processing emerges as a moderator of the influence of the motivational state elicited by the medium context on attitudes.

Introduction

Portrayals of women in advertising have long attracted researchers' interest. In particular, the depiction of women in advertising has raised societal concerns about the pressure put on women by idealized images of beauty (e.g. Bissell and Rusk 2010) and much has been said and written about the roles that advertisers prescribe to them (e.g. Debevec and Iyer 1986). Especially regarding the latter, a voluminous stream of research has focused on the examination of the phenomenon of gender stereotyping in advertising (for reviews, see Eisend 2010; Wolin 2003); it has been widely reported that female consumers disapprove of the way advertising generally represents women (e.g. Zimmerman and Dahlberg 2008). Yet, most studies on the topic have been descriptive in nature, with only limited focus on theoretical explanations of women's responses to actual ads that portray women in decorative roles with little if any relevance to the advertised product. The latter portrayals have been frequently considered to arise from preconceived notions about 'a woman's place' (cf. Courtney and Lockeretz 1971) and the media and advertising industries' reinforcement of patriarchal values (McDonagh and Prothero 1997). Contemporary advertisements, even those targeting a female audience, have not ceased to portray women in decorative roles (Taylor, Landreth, and Bang 2005), with what can be superficially considered as a blatant disregard of female consumers' indignation with the way they are depicted in advertising. However, only few empirical studies have supported the notion that women respond unfavorably to such portrayals (see Theodoridis et al. 2013). The present paper aims at addressing this apparent controversy by proposing that female responses to decorative depictions of women in advertisements are context-sensitive and can be explained via the evolved mechanism of intrasexual competition and presenting the results of two studies conducted to test the corresponding hypotheses.

Evolutionary psychology is a paradigm that seeks to account for cultural phenomena via the biological underpinnings of humans (Saad and Gill 2000); its principles can be used to explain several facets of human behavior, such as mating preferences, consumption of foods rich in salt or sugar, and fear of snakes through the identification of domain-specific psychological mechanisms which have evolved to respond to adaptive problems faced by the human species (Colarelli and Dettman 2003). As such, evolutionary psychology is not considered a sub-field of psychology by its proponents; rather, it is viewed as a meta-theoretical integrative perspective that integrates the field of psychology as a whole (Carmen et al. 2013; Duntley and Buss 2008). Thus, evolutionary psychology challenges what Tooby and Cosmides (1992, 23) refer to as the 'Standard Social Science Model,' i.e. the extant 'intellectual framework for the organization of psychology and the social sciences' which posits that human behavior is governed by 'general-purpose' and 'content-free' mechanisms, such as learning, reasoning and imitation (Cosmides and Tooby 1994, 54) and that it is principally shaped by social norms. Nonetheless, evolutionary psychology does not dismiss the influence of culture or socialization processes, as it emphasizes the interaction of evolved mechanisms with environmental context (Buss and Schmitt 2011; Campbell 2004). In essence, the debate is one of causality: evolutionary psychology advocates that different evolved mechanisms lead to psychological differences which in turn lead to different social roles and norms, while social psychology argues that different social roles lead to psychological differences (Buss 1995; Eagly and Wood 1999).[1] Even since the beginning of this century, several promising theoretical implications of evolutionary psychology for marketing have been identified and repeated calls have been made for more research on the matter (Bagozzi and Nataraajan 2000; Colarelli and Dettman 2003; Garcia and Saad 2008). Nonetheless, it has not been until very recently that relevant empirical studies started to appear (Durante et al. 2014; Griskevicius, Goldstein, et al. 2009; Hartmann and Apaolaza-Ibanez 2013; Hudders et al. 2014; Wang and Griskevicius 2014). Evolutionary psychology can offer explanations for diverse aspects of consumer behavior, including responses to advertising (Saad and Gill 2000). As for consumer responses to decorative portrayals of women in advertising, it has been theoretically argued that advertisers base their creative decisions on an almost intuitive understanding of male responses to such depictions which can be explained by the evolved mechanism of mate attraction (Saad 2004). Yet, given that advertisements that portray women in this manner often target a female audience (Michell and Taylor 1990), the examination of female responses to such depictions under the prism of evolutionary psychology represents a thus far unexploited research direction, relevant to practitioners and academicians alike.

The present paper pursues the afore-discussed direction by first briefly reviewing extant literature regarding female reactions to images of women in advertising and drawing theoretical insight from the evolutionary psychology literature focusing on the evolved and context-sensitive mechanism of intrasexual competition. Subsequently, the paper describes a series of hypotheses deriving from a synthesis of the two fields. Then, the design and findings of two studies designed to test the hypotheses are presented.

The paper concludes with an overall discussion of the results and the main conclusions, the limitations of the studies and suggestions for future research.

A brief review of the advertising literature on female responses to portrayals of women in advertising

Gender stereotypes are beliefs about the traits, characteristics, roles and behaviors that differentially characterize men and women (Ashmore and Del Boca 1981). Stereotypes have four different components: trait descriptors, physical characteristics, role behaviors and occupational status (Deaux and Lewis 1984). Within academic research in advertising, the issue of gender stereotypes has received attention for more than 40 years now (Eisend 2010; Wolin 2003); researchers' vivid interest in the topic can be justified by the extensive use of stereotypic depictions by the advertising industry and the potential social implications of this phenomenon (Gulas and McKeage 2000; Lysonski and Pollay 1990). Despite the prolificacy of this research area, surprisingly little is to date known regarding the actual responses of female consumers to stereotypic presentations of women in specific ads, for the majority of the relevant literature consists of either content analyses aiming at assessing temporal and cultural differences in relevant advertising practices (e.g. Gilly 1988) or of studies investigating general attitudes toward the phenomenon of stereotyping in advertising (e.g. Ford and LaTour 1996).

Gender stereotypes in advertising refer to the tendency of advertisements to portray central figures in conformity with pre-established feminine or masculine traits, physical characteristics, occupational status and role behaviors (Eisend 2010). Especially regarding the latter, stereotypical depictions of women in advertisements typically involve their portrayal in decorative, traditional or non-traditional roles or as being equal to men (Plakoyiannaki and Zotos 2009). Traditional portrayals involve showing women as dependent upon men and/or in the role of the typical housewife, whereas non-traditional portrayals refer to depictions of women as career-oriented or involved in activities outside the home; women can be also portrayed neutrally, as equal to men (Plakoyiannaki et al. 2008; Zotos and Lysonski 1994). Decorative portrayals refer to women being presented as concerned with their physical appearance or as sex objects (Plakoyiannaki and Zotos 2009); these depictions are consistent with what Shimp (2008, 308) terms 'sexual objectification,' which 'occurs when ads use women (or men) as decorative or attention-getting objects with little or no relevance to the product category.' Although much has changed regarding the way women are portrayed in advertising over the last decades (for detailed reviews, see Eisend 2010; Furnham and Paltzer 2010; Stern 1999; Wolin 2003), there is evidence that suggests that even in recent years, more than half a century after the surge of the feminist movement, advertisements depicting women in decorative roles remain a frequent occurrence in both general audience magazines (Plakoyiannaki and Zotos 2009) and female-oriented magazines (Lindner 2004; Michell and Taylor 1990; Taylor, Landreth, and Bang 2005).[2]

In terms of the literature concerning actual consumer responses to stereotypic ads, there seems to be considerable agreement among researchers that women tend to believe that advertising in general does not portray them in a realistic manner (Christy 2006; Ford and LaTour 1996; Harker, Harker, and Svensen 2005; Lundstrom and Sciglimpaglia 1977; Zimmerman and Dahlberg 2008). Nonetheless, the few extant studies dealing explicitly with attitudinal reactions of female consumers to specific stereotypic advertisements have come up with diverging findings, often with little theoretical justification. In fact, extant evidence indicates that stereotypic portrayals 'can be helpful or detrimental' to advertising effectiveness (Eisend, Plagemann, and Sollwedel 2014, 256). Some early studies have shown that female participants rate non-stereotyped portrayals of women in advertising more favorably in terms of liking (Duker and Tucker Jr. 1977) and preference (Leavitt 1978 as quoted in Whipple and Courtney 1985), whereas opposing results have also been reported (Bettinger and Dawson 1979 as quoted in Whipple and Courtney 1985). Moreover, Jones, Stanaland and Gelb (1998) report that women express negative attitudes toward stereotypic ads featuring a sexy female model, and Rouner, Slater and Domenech-Rodriguez (2003) state that female adolescents are critical of traditional gender role images of women in commercials. Jaffe and Berger (1994) conclude that egalitarian role portrayals are the most effective in terms of female responses to advertising, whereas Orth and Holancova (2004) have found that women have unfavorable reactions toward non-stereotypic ads that depict women as being superior to men. To further complicate matters, Orth, Malkewitz, and Bee (2010) report that female consumers experience more mixed emotions when gender roles are depicted in a way that is incongruous with their self-concept, but surprisingly express favorable attitudinal responses, while Vantomme, Geuens, and Dewitte (2005) distinguish between implicit and explicit preference and find that the former, but not the latter, is more favorable for ads portraying women in traditional, as opposed to non-traditional, roles. It has also been found that attitudes to stereotypic ads vary by individuals' age (Theodoridis et al. 2013) and gender-role orientations (Morrison and Shaffer 2003), as well as the advertised product category and its perceived 'gender' (Debevec and Iyer 1986; Whipple and Courtney 1985).

We note that most studies concerned with examining consumer responses to stereotypic ads focus on the 'role' component of stereotyping: most studies seem to contrast progressive (non-traditional) and traditional role portrayals (e.g. Debevec and Iyer 1988; Morrison and Shaffer 2003), others compare reactions to egalitarian, traditional and superwoman portrayals of female models (Jaffe and Berger 1994) and yet others differentiate between images of women in decorative, traditional and non-traditional roles (Theodoridis et al. 2013). More importantly perhaps, we observe that from a theoretical standpoint, researchers have tried to account for any differences found in women's evaluations of such ads through the socialization patterns of women (see, for instance, the explanations put forth by Orth and Holancova 2004 or Morrison and Shaffer 2003), thus adhering to the Standard Social Science Model. Nonetheless, evolutionary psychology could offer an entirely different explanation.

Insights from evolutionary psychology on the evolved mechanism of female intrasexual competition

How can evolutionary principles aid the understanding of consumer responses to female portrayals in advertising? Discussing this very question, Saad (2004) argues in favor of the evolved mechanism of mating preferences underlying men's responses to decorative representations of the opposite sex in advertisements. He posits that women in decorative roles embody desirable characteristics, such as youthfulness and physical attractiveness, eliciting favorable attitudes on the part of the male audience. Notwithstanding the fact that the paper in question broke new ground in advertising research, calling attention to the merit of evolutionary psychology for the comprehension of consumer responses to gender stereotypes in advertising, Saad's (2004) rationale does not address why women are portrayed in decorative roles not only when advertisers target male audiences, but also when there is an exclusively female audience. Thus, we turn to evolutionary psychology in search of a mechanism explaining the behavior of women toward same-sex others.

A very recent paper by Durante et al. (2014) provides evidence that female consumer behavior has a strong evolutionary basis with women's hormonal fluctuations significantly affecting their consumption patterns so as to improve their competitive standing relative to other women. In a different paper, published almost simultaneously, Hudders et al. (2014) undertake a series of studies that show a link between luxury consumption and female intrasexual competition.

Within the field of evolutionary psychology, intrasexual competition is considered as a mechanism that is closely related to the mechanisms of sexual attraction and mate selection. The latter mechanisms have long attracted researchers' interest (see Buss 1989; Feingold 1990), given that there are more differences than similarities between the two sexes in these domains (Buss and Schmitt 2011). The mechanisms of sexual attraction, apart from offering explanations for various aspects of male-to-female and female-to-male interactions, are suggested to also lie behind some behavioral predispositions toward members of one's own sex in the context of *intrasexual competition*, i.e. 'competition between members of the same sex for mating access to members of the opposite sex' (Buss 1988, 616). Evolutionary psychology considers intrasexual competition an evolved mechanism which attempts to solve the adaptive problem of scarcity of suitable mates (Campbell 2004; Geary 2000); in line with parental investment theory,[3] males, as the sex investing less in parenting, tend to express more aggression toward other competing males for access to constrained resources, with the latter resources in this case being the higher investing sex (Schmitt 2005; Trivers 1972). Consequently, evolutionary literature is replete with instances of competition and aggression among males and relevant supporting evidence (e.g. Buss 1988; Van Vugt, De Cremer, and Janssen 2007; Wilson and Daly 1985).

Although male intrasexual competition is well acknowledged ever since Darwin's era (Buss 1988), female-to-female competition is still a relatively unexplored territory, even within the realms of evolutionary psychology where it long remained a 'politically taboo subject' (Campbell 2004, 23). As of late though, a growing volume of studies provides evidence that competition also exists among women who, not unlike men, compete for access to desirable mates (Fink et al. 2014; Piccoli, Forroni, and Carnaghi 2013; Vaillancourt 2013). However, female intrasexual competition is less visible; women are less likely than men to employ directly aggressive competitive tactics, often engaging in acts of indirect or relational aggression, such as gossip or manipulation (Campbell 2004; Vaillancourt 2013). In line with the distinction between behavior and psychological mechanisms discussed by Buss (1998),[4] the manifest behavior of indirect aggression toward same-sex rivals can be viewed as the output of the evolved psychological mechanism of intrasexual competition. In stark contrast to this evolutionary view, the explanation for female competition advocated by the Standard Social Science Model is that women compete among themselves because of their internalization of patriarchal values and their tendency to conform to socially predefined gender roles (Bussey and Bandura 1999; Wood and Eagly 2002).

Returning to the fundamentals of intrasexual competition, it is interesting to note that mating preferences operate as a 'selective force' on intrasexual competition (Buss 1992, 252); in other words, members of the same sex employ competitive tactics that are closely aligned to the traits favored by the opposite sex. For instance, competing females tend to enhance their appearance more than competing males, mirroring the male tendency to favor physical attractiveness in potential mates (Buss 1992). As Campbell (2004, 19) notes, 'attractiveness appears to be the currency of female competition even when no mention is made of what the competition is about.'

Intrasexual competition can assume the form of either *self-promotion*, whereby one seeks to acquire or appear to have the traits favored by the opposite sex, or *competitor derogation*, whereby one seeks to reduce the perceived mate value of same-sex rivals (Schmitt and Buss 1996, 1187). More broadly defined, self-promotion regards 'any act used to enhance the positive qualities of oneself, relative to same-sex others,' whereas competitor derogation refers to 'any act that is used to decrease a rival's value relative to oneself' (Cox and Fisher 2008, 145). Hence, from an evolutionary psychology perspective, it would make adaptive sense for a female to either seek to (or even appear to) embody the traits favored by men, such as youth and physical attractiveness, or to derogate her same-sex 'opponents' in terms of these traits so as to enhance her own competitive standing. In the context of female competition, self-promotional tactics include the display of resources and the enhancement of one's appearance while derogatory tactics involve acts such as gossip and rumors (Buss 1992). Extant evidence from women's self-reports on the competitive tactics they use indicates that women mainly tend to attract attention to their physical appearance in the interest of self-promotion (Cashdan 1998 as quoted in Campbell 2004; Fisher and Cox 2011; Walters and Crawford 1994 as quoted in Campbell 2004). Nonetheless, intolerance of physically attractive women (Leenaars, Dale, and Marini 2008), gossip aiming at the derogation of other women (Buss and Dedden 1990) and criticism of their appearance (Fisher 2004; Fisher and Cox 2011; Vaillancourt 2013) have also been reported.[5] From an evolutionary standpoint, competition among females can vary depending on a variety of ecological factors, such as age, family status, sexual maturity, resource availability and mate value (Campbell 2004). For instance, during adolescence and early adulthood when a young women's fertility is high, indirect aggression toward other women is increased (Massar, Buunk, and Rempt 2012). It has also been reported that women in a relationship are more likely to use competitor derogation than other competitive strategies (Fisher and Cox 2011). Furthermore, Lydon et al. (1999) have found that women's level of commitment to a romantic relationship affects ratings of attractiveness of potential same-sex opponents. Some evidence also suggests that hormonal fluctuations over the course of the ovulatory cycle can affect intrasexual competition; it has been found that women with high estrogen levels are more likely to give other women lower attractiveness ratings (Baenninger, Baenninger, and Houle 1993; Fisher 2004) and to dehumanize them (Piccoli, Forroni, and Carnaghi 2013).[6]

In order to optimize the outcome of the competition and to avoid wasting resources, females as well as males tend to assess their opponents' relative mate value before competing (Sugiyama 2005). As is the case with most evolved mechanisms, which are both functional and context-sensitive (Buss 1998, 24), the mechanism of intrasexual competition is activated only in the presence of specific *immediate situational input* (Buss 1995, 11), that is, only if relevant cues exist in a certain context. Exploring the motives for same-sex aggression acts, Griskevicius, Tybur, et al. (2009) have found that both status and mating goals (*competition* and *courting* motives, respectively) triggered women's indirect aggression toward other women. Simply put, women can compete with other women even if no mention of the opposite sex is made (see also Hudders et al. 2014; Durante et al. 2011). It is hence interesting to note that acts stemming from intrasexual competition do not necessarily require immediate mating or reproductive-related motives.

Having discussed the evolutionary roots of female intrasexual competition, the paper proceeds to examine how these principles can be utilized to explain the responses of female consumers to advertisements depicting women in decorative roles. The next section of the paper presents a series of relevant hypotheses, along with their supporting rationale.

Hypotheses

From an evolutionary psychology perspective, we suggest that female attitudes toward advertisements depicting women in decorative roles can be explained via the mechanism of female competition. Hence, we essentially argue that an activation of the competition mechanism will influence the reactions of female consumers to such ads.

As discussed previously, extant research on gender stereotypes in advertising has come up with diverging evidence regarding female attitudes toward depictions of women in stereotypic roles in the context of specific ads (e.g. Jaffe and Berger 1994; Orth and Holancova 2004). When it comes to physical attractiveness which is another component of stereotypes, a distinct stream of advertising research concerned with spokespersons' physical attractiveness has established that women can have positive (for a review, see Belch, Belch, and Villareal 1987), as well as negative (e.g. Caballero, Lumpkin, and Madden 1989), affective reactions to attractive female models in advertising. Under a social comparison perspective, Bower (2001, 53) refers to the former positive reactions as the 'what is beautiful is good' effect and seeks to account for the latter negative reactions through social comparison jealousy and derogation, thus arguing that female consumers compare themselves with the model and act as 'threatened comparers' (Bower 2001, 54), experiencing negative affect.

Under an evolutionary psychology perspective, we view attractiveness as the currency of female competition (Campbell 2004) and suggest an alternate explanation of why women would derogate a female model in an advertisement; we propose that the latter is the case when women unconsciously compete with the model through competitor derogation. Women engaging in competitor derogation have been found to derogate the attractiveness of their female rivals, as previously discussed. The question that thus arises is whether it is possible for women to compete with models in advertisements. Previous evolutionary research indicates that in order for women to compete, the female rival does not necessarily have to be 'in the flesh': Durante et al. (2011) found that ovulating women tended to choose sexier clothes when primed with photos of attractive women, comparing themselves to the latter and attempting to self-promote, while Fisher (2004) reported that women presented with photos of other women derogated their attractiveness. Furthermore, it has been shown that women compare themselves with female models in advertisements (Martin and Kennedy 1993; Richins 1991) for both self-evaluation and self-improvement motives (Martin and Kennedy 1994) and can experience positive and negative affective reactions toward them (Bower 2001). In line with Buss' (1998) view of evolved mechanisms, we thus reason that if women are motivated to compete (situational input), the attitudes and attractiveness evaluations of the model will reflect the corresponding psychological mechanism, i.e. their tendency to self-promote or derogate the woman in front of them.

If female consumers are therefore motivated to engage in a competitor derogation strategy, they can be reasonably expected to evaluate other women as less attractive and by extension express unfavorable attitudes toward advertisements showing women in decorative roles. Contrarily, when women are motivated to engage in a self-promotion strategy, they will not actively derogate the model's attractiveness and resulting attitudes will be more favorable. Therefore, the following hypotheses are formulated:

H1: When women compete through self-promotion, they will evaluate a model in a decorative role as more attractive than when they compete through competitor derogation.

H2: When women compete through self-promotion, their attitudes toward an ad depicting a model in a decorative role will be more favorable than attitudes toward the same ad when women compete through competitor derogation.

We therefore propose that ads portraying women in decorative roles in female-oriented media are effective when they aid female consumers in engaging in intrasexual competition through a self-promotion strategy. However, although such favorable outcomes might reasonably be the advertisers' intention, in practice, this might not always be the case, since under different circumstances, ads showing women in decorative roles could elicit less favorable attitudes resulting from female consumers employing a competitor derogation strategy. We further posit that the aforementioned circumstances may result from situational aspects of the exposure (the motivation elicited by the medium context and the type of self-referencing). Therefore, we essentially argue that ads in female-oriented media showing women in decorative roles are likely to lead to favorable attitudinal outcomes in certain *contexts*, with context being the operative word.

Effects of motivation elicited by the medium context

While the few past studies that have examined consumer responses to stereotyped ads have only dealt with the advertising stimulus per se, we propose that media context influences female attitudes toward ads depicting models in decorative roles. Media context is defined as 'the characteristics of the content of the medium in which an ad is inserted [..], as they are perceived by the individuals who are exposed to it' (De Pelsmacker, Geuens, and Anckaert 2002, 49). Past advertising literature offers abundant evidence supporting the influence of media context on advertising effects (for a review, see De Pelsmacker, Geuens and Anckaert 2002). Media context characteristics can be subjective or objective (Van Reijmersdal, Smit, and Neijens 2010); for the purposes of the present paper, we focus on the influence of motivational state (the 'subjective mental reactions that people experience after confrontation with medium content'; Van Reijmersdal, Smit, and Neijens 2010, 281) as a subjective medium context characteristic. We posit that the motivational state (neutral or competitive) that the female audience finds themselves in after reading an article in a female-oriented magazine or a website can operate as situational input for the evolved mechanism of female intrasexual competition and that the activation of the latter mechanism will affect female consumers' attitudes toward ads depicting women in decorative roles. Such a view appears to concur both with the context-sensitive nature of the intrasexual competition mechanism (Buss 1995; Campbell 2004) and the notion that media viewing context functions as situational input for evolutionary mechanisms that explain responses to advertising (Griskevicius, Goldstein, et al. 2009). Hence, the following hypothesis is put forward:

H3: The motivational state induced by the medium context will influence attitudes toward ads depicting women in decorative roles.

Effects of type of self-referencing

Moreover, we posit that self-referencing moderates the previously hypothesized main effect. One of the mechanisms proposed to account the effect of media context is that it operates as a cognitive prime that 'activates a semantic network of related material that guides attention and determines the interpretation of the ad' (Dahlen 2005, 90). A related aspect of the interpretation of a stereotypic ad is self-referencing, which is defined as 'a cognitive process whereby individuals associate self-relevant stimulus information with information previously stored in memory to give the new information meaning' (Debevec and Iyer 1988, 74). It has been repeatedly shown that consumers relate advertisements to their own selves (e.g. Burnkrant and Unnava 1995; Hong and Zinkhan 1995), with high self-referencing leading to more positive attitudes (Chang 2005). More importantly, low self-referencing has been found to mediate the effect of stereotypic role portrayals in advertising on attitudinal responses (Debevec and Iyer 1988; Morrison and Shaffer 2003). The latter two studies have only dealt with one's general self-concept; nonetheless, the self is commonly viewed as comprising of past (existing) and future (imagined) self-concepts (see Dimofte and Yalch 2010). Moreover, it has been proposed that consumers process advertisements by referring to either autobiographical memories or imagined events (Escalas 2004). Interestingly, previous research has indicated that the temporal orientation of self-referencing (i.e. whether consumers engage in retrospective self-referencing processing the ad by referencing memories about their past selves or whether they engage in anticipatory self-referencing whereby the ad is processed with reference to their imagined or anticipated self) differentially affects ad processing (Dimofte and Yalch 2010; Krishnamurthy and Sujan 1999).

In order to predict the potential effects of anticipatory and retrospective self-referencing, we return to evolutionary principles regarding the self. Within evolutionary psychology, the *symbolic self* or one's own self-concept is defined as 'the language-based and abstract representation of one's own attributes and the use of this representation for effective functioning in affective, motivational and behavioral domains' (Sedikides and Skowronski 2002). The symbolic self is considered an adaptation which has evolved over time as a response to ecological or social pressures (Sedikides and Skowronski 2002). Self-referencing has been found to play an important role in mate selection (Allen and Hauber 2013). Campbell and Wilbur (2009) have demonstrated that the self-concepts of both women and men mirror the preferences of prospective mates.

On the basis of the aforementioned discussion, we anticipate that the temporal orientation of self-referencing (essentially thinking of the past, i.e., retrospectively vs. thinking of the future, i.e., anticipatorily) will have an impact on how positively a stereotypic ad is perceived. More specifically, we hypothesize that under *retrospective* self-referencing instructions, the activation of the competition mechanism will lead women to engage in a competitor derogation strategy which will result in less favorable attitudes toward the advertised brand. Given that ad processing under retrospective self-referencing instructions is a top-down process (Krishnamurti and Sujan 1999), we propose that women process the stereotyped ad with reference to their past 'actual' selves (Sedikides and Skowronski 2002) and compete by seeking to devalue their 'opponent,' i.e. the model in the ad. This would ultimately result in less favorable attitudes toward the ad among women. The underlying logic behind this prediction is based on the assumption that the portrayal of the female model in a decorative role is appealing to males (Saad 2004); such a portrayal suggests to female consumers that the model possesses traits favored by the opposite sex. Therefore, the following hypothesis is formulated:

H4: When the self-referencing process is retrospective, a competitive context will lead to less favorable attitudes toward ads depicting women in decorative roles with respect to a neutral context.

Conversely, we hypothesize that under anticipatory self-referencing instructions, triggering the intrasexual competition mechanism will lead women to engage in self-promotion, thereby expressing more favorable attitudes toward the advertisement. Given that ad processing under anticipatory self-referencing instructions is a bottom-up process (Krishnamurti and Sujan 1999), we propose that women implicitly reference the ad with regard to their 'symbolic self far into the future' (Sedikides and Skowronski 2002) and set corresponding goals, thus competing by seeking to improve their relative standing. The idea here is that the idealized model becomes representative of what the woman herself wants to look more like in the future. In this context, consumers will respond positively to the decorative model and have favorable attitudes toward the stereotyped ad. Hence, we hypothesize that:

H5: When the self-referencing process is anticipatory, a competitive context will lead to more favorable attitudes toward ads depicting women in decorative roles with respect to a neutral context.

Study 1: Competitive strategies and attitudes toward decorative ads

Experimental design and subjects

The purpose of the first study was to test the key assumption described above, i.e. that attitudes toward an ad showing a woman in a decorative role differ with respect to the competitive strategy employed by the female audience. To test hypotheses 1 and 2, an experimental study was conducted, with the participation of 62 female students aged between 21 and 26 years ($M = 22.66$, $SD = 1.32$). A student sample was selected in an attempt to keep participants' age relatively constant since the latter has been previously found to affect both attitudes toward stereotypical ads (Theodoridis et al. 2013) and indirect aggression toward other women (Massar, Buunk, and Rempt 2012). Subjects were randomly assigned to one of two conditions: half of the students read a scenario designed to motivate them to engage in a self-promotion strategy, whereas the remaining half read another scenario designed to motivate them to employ a competitor derogation strategy. No significant differences emerged with respect to age across the different conditions (F $(1,61) = 2.13, p = 0.150$).

Procedure, stimuli and measures

Participants completed an online questionnaire for the purposes of the study. They initially read a cover story which indicated that the experiment investigated their ability to memorize information under different instructions; it was expected that these instructions would not trigger demand effects. Participants were initially exposed to a list of six fictional brand names and were asked to study them carefully; this was a filler task intended to enhance the plausibility of the cover story. Subsequently, they saw a short scenario that primed them to engage in either a self-promotion or a competitor derogation strategy, depending on the condition. They were instructed to read it and to imagine themselves in the situation and to try to feel the emotions and feelings that the woman in the story is experiencing. The instructions were adapted from Griskevicius, Tybur, et al. (2009). The scenarios[7] were based on a story used to manipulate context in Hudders et al. (2014) and can be found in Appendix 1. Notwithstanding their artificiality, scenarios are commonly used in both evolutionary psychological research (e.g. Buss et al. 1992; Wilson and O'Gorman 2003) and experimental studies in the consumer behavior literature (e.g. Griskevicius, Goldstein, et al. 2009; Williams and Steffel 2014; Wang and Griskevicius 2014).

After reading the scenarios, the subjects answered a series of questions about how likely they were to engage in a self-promotion or competitor derogation strategy; this was intended as a manipulation check. After completing a filler recognition task, participants were shown a mock ad and then indicated their attitudes toward it and listed their thoughts. For reasons of internal validity, the mock ad referred to a fictitious brand for a new web radio. The advertised product category was selected on the basis of a pretest (12 female respondents) so as to be gender neutral[8] and non-attractiveness-enhancing, since prior studies have found that attitudes toward stereotypic ads differ with regard to the product's perceived gender (Debevec and Iyer 1986) and that the degree to which a product is seen as attractiveness-enhancing influences women's preferences for it in a competitive context (Hudders et al. 2014). The ad (Appendix 2) was designed with the use of professional photo editing software and comprised a professionally taken photo of a female model lying on a couch, the fictitious brand name (Tempo) and a tagline (The new web radio); the ad was selected on the basis of a pretest (22 female respondents).[9] Some additional filler questions and an open-ended question regarding the perceived purpose of the study followed. As intended, none of the participants guessed its true purpose. Then, participants were again presented with the target ad and evaluated the attractiveness of the model in the ad; the evaluation of attractiveness was intended as an indicator of whether the respective competition strategies had been transferred to the model in the ad. Physical attractiveness ratings have been previously been used as a proxy for competitive strategies employed by Fisher (2004, 271), in line with extant evolutionary psychological literature that links attractiveness to competitive tactics (Campbell 2004; Vaillancourt 2013). A similar indirect assessment of social comparison derogation has also been used by Bower (2001, 56). We therefore reasoned that negative model attractiveness' evaluations could be considered as evidence of competitor derogation occurring, while positive model attractiveness' evaluations could be seen as evidence of self-promotion. Finally, subjects indicated the extent to which they believed that its portrayal of women was stereotypic. The questionnaire concluded with demographics questions and the debriefing of the participants.

Table 1 presents the variables used in the study and the operationalization of each. As shown in the Table, all scales had satisfactory reliability (all Cronbach α values above 0.70).

Results

There was a significant main effect of the scenario read on participants' self-reported intention to engage in a self-promotion strategy ($F(1,60) = 243.96, p < 0.001$), with the subjects in the self-promotion condition expressing a significantly more pronounced intention to engage in self-promotion than their counterparts in the competitor derogation condition ($M_{\text{self-promotion}} = 5.34, M_{\text{competitor derogation}} = 3.30; t(60) = 15.62, p < 0.001$). The main effect of the scenario on participants' intention to derogate the competitor was also significant ($F(1,60) = 281.08, p < 0.001$); participants in the competitor derogation condition indicated that they were more likely to employ a competitor derogation strategy than those in the self-promotion condition ($M_{\text{self-promotion}} = 2.66, M_{\text{competitor derogation}} = 5.24; t(60) = -16.77, p < 0.001$). Thus, the manipulation of competitive strategy was successful.

As expected, competitive strategy was found to have a significant effect on attractiveness ratings ($F(1,60) = 42.30, p < 0.001$), with subjects engaging in self-promotion rating the model's attractiveness higher than their counterparts engaging in competitor

Table 1. Operationalization of variables in Study 1

Variable/construct	Description	Operationalization/measure	
		Items	Reliability (Cronbach's α)
Attitude toward the ad	Four-item, seven-point semantic differential scale (Mitchell and Olson 1981)	• Good/bad* • Like/dislike* • Irritating/not irritating• Interesting/uninteresting	0.90
Model attractiveness	Single item, seven-point Likert-type scale (Fisher 2004)	Extremely unattractive/extremely attractive	n/a
Intention to use a self-promotion strategy	Six-item, seven-point scale with endpoints 'definitely would not do' and 'definitely would do' (Fisher and Cox 2011)	If I sensed that another woman was competing with me for attention, I would: • try to make myself physically look more attractive • try to seem nice, caring and helpful • try to seem independent and play 'hard to get' • flirt and make eye contact • show off my body, especially one of my good features • try to hide my flaws	0.706
Intention to use a competitor derogation strategy	Seven-item, seven-point scale with endpoints 'definitely would not do' and 'definitely would do' (Fisher and Cox 2011)	If I sensed that another woman was competing with me for attention, I would: • mention to the man that the rival is immature • tell the man that the rival is promiscuous • actively put down the rival to the man • try to derogate or say something negative about the rival • tell gossip to the man • hide good things about the rival when asked about them • point out to the man some flows in the rival's appearance	0.857
Decorative/stereotypic portrayal of model in the advertisement	Two items, seven-point Likert scale	• The advertisement depicts women in a stereotyped manner. • The advertisement shows women as decorative objects.	0.70

*Recoded.

derogation ($M_{\text{self-promotion}} = 4.94$, $M_{\text{competitor derogation}} = 3.19$; $t(60) = 6.504$, $p < 0.001$), hence providing support for H1. This significant effect can be interpreted as evidence that the strategies resulting from the manipulations have been transferred to the model in the ad. Additional evidence supporting this assumption was obtained from coding participants' thoughts relating to the model according to their valence. Participants in the self-promotion condition had a significantly higher number of positive (vs. negative) thoughts about the model ($M_{\text{positive}} = 2.00$, $M_{\text{negative}} = 0.61$; $t(30) = 5.31$, $p < 0.001$), while the opposite was the case for participants in the competitor derogation condition ($M_{\text{positive}} = 0.77$, $M_{\text{negative}} = 1.81$; $t(30) = -3.46$, $p < 0.01$).

Regarding the effect of competitive strategy on attitude toward the ad, a one-way ANOVA indicated that it was significant ($F(1,60) = 110.27$, $p < 0.001$).[10] As hypothesized, the subjects in the self-promotion condition expressed more favorable attitudes toward the ad than those in the competitor derogation condition ($M_{\text{self-promotion}} = 5.12$, $M_{\text{competitor derogation}} = 3.06$; $t(60) = 10.50$, $p < 0.001$). Hence, H2 is also supported.

Study 2: Effects of motivational state elicited by the medium context and temporal orientation of self-referencing on attitudes toward decorative ads

Experimental design and subjects

To test Hypotheses 3–6, a 2 × 2 (motivational state: neutral/competitive × self-referencing: retrospective/anticipatory) between-subjects experiment was conducted, with the participation of 88 female students aged between 20 and 26 years ($M = 22.27$). Subjects were randomly assigned to one of the four conditions (22 subjects per condition) in order to minimize the potential of systematic differences in personal characteristics such as stage in the ovulatory cycle (Fisher 2004). No significant differences emerged with respect to age across the different conditions ($F(3,84) = 1.908$, $p = 0.134$).

Procedure, stimuli and measures

Participants received a link to an online questionnaire and were led to believe that they were participating in two unrelated studies. They initially read a cover story identical to the one used in Study 1 and were then asked to read an excerpt from an advice column at a women's website; they were instructed to concentrate on the story because they were to be asked about it later on and to try to feel the emotions and feelings that the woman in the story is experiencing. In reality, the excerpts were two different stories (one per condition) designed to manipulate subjects' motivation and to elicit neutral or competitive motives (Appendix 3). The stories and instructions were adapted from Griskevicius, Tybur, et al. (2009). Participants then answered a series of questions regarding their motivational state intended to check the success of the manipulation (desire to compete, desire to attract a mate, positive arousal and negative arousal) and some filler recall questions regarding the story to enhance the believability of the cover story. Subsequently, subjects were exposed to a mock ad (identical to the one used in Study 1); half of them were instructed to look carefully at the ad and try to relate it to an experience that they have had in the past (retrospective self-referencing condition), whereas the other half were told to relate the ad to an experience they may have in the future (anticipatory self-referencing condition), per Krishnamurti and Sujan (1999). Next, participants indicated their attitudes toward the ad, as well as the extent to which they engaged in self-referencing in general and in the intended type of self-referencing (past orientation, future orientation). After that, participants answered two additional filler questions and an open-ended question to assess demand bias. They were thanked for their participation in the study and were asked to answer another supposedly unrelated questionnaire regarding skepticism toward firms. On the next page, they indicated their agreement with some filler statements and indicated their attitudes toward stereotyped portrayals in advertising. The latter was included to address potential confounding effects, given that a priori attitudes toward stereotyping in advertising have been previously found to influence attitudes toward specific ads (Orth and Holancova 2004); the cover story aimed at concealing any link between the two and at discouraging the participants to use the ad stimulus as a point of reference for their answers. An open-ended question asking participants about the purpose of the study followed (as previously, participants were unsuspecting) and the participants were debriefed and thanked for their participation.

Table 2 presents the variables used in the study and the operationalization of each. As shown in the Table, all scales had satisfactory reliability (all Cronbach α values above 0.70).

Results

There was a significant main effect of the self-referencing instructions on the manipulation check for past orientation ($F(1,84) = 255.14, p < 0.001$), with the subjects in the retrospective self-referencing condition being more past oriented than those in the anticipatory self-referencing one ($M_{retrospective} = 5.77, M_{anticipatory} = 2.27; t(86) = 15.83, p < 0.001$). The main effect of self-referencing on the manipulation check for future orientation was also significant ($F(1,84) = 215.47, p < 0.001$), with the subjects in the anticipatory self-referencing condition being more future-oriented than the subjects in the retrospective self-referencing one ($M_{retrospective} = 2.50, M_{anticipatory} = 5.75; t(86) = -14.80, p < 0.001$). There were no significant differences in the subjects' degree of general self-referencing between the two conditions ($t(86) = -0.06, p = 0.956$). Regarding the manipulation of motivational state, there was a significant main effect of the type of story read on the manipulation check for desire to compete ($F(1,84) = 169.02, p < 0.001$), with the subjects in the competitive motivation condition expressing increased desire to compete with regard to the subjects in the neutral motivation condition ($M_{neutral} = 2.53, M_{competitive} = 5.08; t(86) = -13.12, p < 0.001$). Additionally, there was a significant main effect of the type of story read on the manipulation check for desire to attract a mate ($F(1,84) = 86.92, p < 0.001$), with the subjects in the competitive motivation condition expressing increased desire to attract a mate with regard to the subjects in the neutral motivation condition ($M_{neutral} = 3.17, M_{competitive} = 4.90; t(78.86) = -9.41, p < 0.001$). The story intended to elicit competitive motives evoked similar levels of positive and negative arousal (3.03 vs. 2.80, respectively; $t(43) = 1.87, p = 0.068$). Therefore, both manipulations were successful.

To test the relevant hypotheses, a two-way independent ANOVA (2 levels of motivational state × 2 levels of self-referencing) was conducted, with attitude toward the ad as the dependent variable.[11] There was a significant main effect of self-referencing type on attitude toward the ad ($F(1,84) = 30.38, p < 0.001$), with the subjects in the anticipatory self-referencing condition expressing more favorable attitudes than those in the retrospective self-referencing one ($M_{retrospective} = 3.23, M_{anticipatory} = 4.59; t(86) = -5.03, p < 0.001$). Contrary to H3, the main effect of motivational state on attitude was not significant ($F(1,84) = 0.17, p = 0.680$). However, the means plot (Figure 1) indicates a disordinal interaction between the two factors. Indeed, there was a significant interaction effect

Table 2. Operationalization of variables in Study 2.

Variable/construct	Operationalization/measure		Reliability (Cronbach's α)
	Description	Items	
Attitude toward the ad	Four-item, seven-point semantic differential scale (Mitchell and Olson 1981)	• Good/bad* • Like/dislike* • Irritating/not irritating • Interesting/uninteresting	0.93
Desire to compete	Two items, seven-point scale with endpoints 'not at all' and 'very much' (Griskevicius, Tybur, et al. 2009)	• To what extent do you feel competitive? • To what extent are you motivated to compete?	0.935
Desire to attract a mate	Two items, seven-point scale with endpoints 'not at all' and 'very much' (Griskevicius, Tybur, et al. 2009)	• To what extent do you feel romantically aroused? • To what extent are you motivated to attract a romantic partner?	0.856
Positive arousal	Two items, seven-point scale with endpoints 'not at all' and 'very much' (Griskevicius, Tybur, et al. 2009)	• To what extent do you feel enthusiastic? • To what extent do you feel excited?	0.845
Negative arousal	Two items, seven-point scale with endpoints 'not at all' and 'very much' (Griskevicius, Tybur, et al. 2009)	• To what extent do you feel frustrated? • To what extent do you feel angry?	0.893
General self-referencing	Two items, seven-point Likert-type (Krishnamurthy and Sujan 1999)	• I could relate myself to the ad. • The ad was personally relevant.	0.701
Past orientation of self-referencing (retrospective)	Single item, seven-point Likert-type (Krishnamurthy and Sujan 1999)	I had thoughts relating to my past when I saw the ad.	n/a
Future orientation of self-referencing (anticipatory)	Single item, seven-point Likert-type (Krishnamurthy and Sujan 1999)	I thought of myself in the future when I saw the ad.	n/a
General attitudes toward sex role portrayals in advertising	12-item, seven-point Likert-type scale (Lundstrom and Sciglimpaglia 1977)	• Ads which I see show women as they really are. • Ads suggest that women are fundamentally dependent upon men.*	0.870

(continued)

Table 2. (*Continued*)

Variable/construct	Operationalization/measure	
	Description	Items	Reliability (Cronbach's α)
		• Ads which I see show men as they really are. • Ads treat women mainly as sex objects.* • Ads which I see accurately portray women in most of their daily activities. • Ads suggest women make important decisions. • Ads which I see accurately portray men in most of their daily activities. • Ads suggest that women don't do important things.* • Ads suggest that a woman's place is in the home.* • I'm more sensitive to the portrayal of women in advertising than I used to be.* • I find the portrayal of women in advertising to be offensive.* • Overall I believe that the portrayal of women in advertising is changing for the better.	

*Recoded.

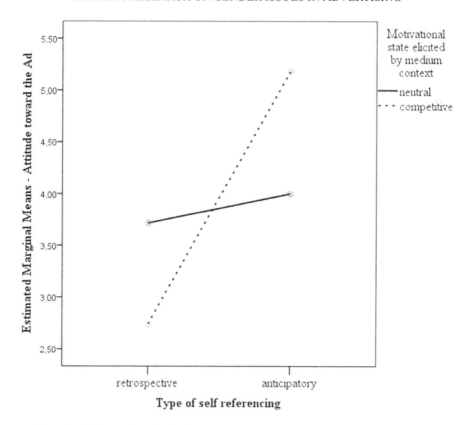

Figure 1.   Effects of motivational state and self-referencing on attitude toward the ad.

between motivational state and self-referencing type ($F(1,84) = 19.04, p < 0.001$), which indicates that the temporal orientation of self-referencing moderates the effect of motivational state on attitude toward the ad. To further investigate this interaction, a Simple Effects Analysis was performed at each level of the moderator variable (i.e. self-referencing). As recommended by Pedhazur and Schmelkin (1991, 527), we adjusted the alpha level to 0.025. There was a significant simple main effect of motivational state on attitude toward the ad at the retrospective level of self-referencing ($F(1,85) = 5.80, p < 0.025$); when they were processing the ad with reference to their past selves, subjects in the competitive motivation condition exhibited less favorable attitudes toward the ad with regard to their counterparts in the neutral motivation condition ($M_{neutral} = 3.72$, $M_{competitive} = 2.74$; $t(42) = 2.63, p < 0.025$). Hence, H4 is supported. The Simple Effect Analysis also indicated a significant simple main effect of motivational state on attitude toward the ad at the anticipatory level of self-referencing ($F(1,85) = 8.48, p < 0.01$); when they were processing the ad with reference to their future selves, subjects in the competitive motivation condition exhibited more favorable attitudes toward the ad with regard to their counterparts in the neutral motivation condition ($M_{neutral} = 4.00$, $M_{competitive} = 5.18$; $t(42) = -3.62, p < 0.01$). Thus, H5 is supported. The fact that the two opposite simple main effects seem to balance each other out accounts for the observed non-significant main effect of motivational state on attitude.

Discussion, limitations and conclusions

Researchers have long been interested in the portrayal of female roles in advertising; surprisingly though, only a scant of extant studies has examined actual responses of women toward such depictions, coming up with conflicting evidence. The continuously developing literature that stresses the importance of the evolved mechanism of female competition to the understanding of female consumption behavior has the potential to offer an alternative explanation of women's stances toward advertisements presenting women in decorative roles. Accordingly, the two studies reported in this paper began to address the need for further understanding of female attitudes toward such ads from a female competition standpoint. Since competition is activated by immediate situational input, we focused on situational characteristics of exposure to ads. In this spectrum, we investigated the effect of alternative competitive strategies employed by female consumers on attitudes toward advertisements portraying women as decorative objects. Additionally, we examined how the motivational state elicited by the medium context affects attitudes toward this type of ads and tested the hypothesis that the temporal orientation of self-referencing moderates this effect. The results of the two studies largely confirmed our hypotheses. In particular, the results of Study 1 indicate that when female consumers are primed to engage in self-promotion in the interest of competing with other females, an ad portraying a woman in a decorative role elicits favorable reactions. Contrarily, when women are primed to engage in competitor derogation, attitudes toward the focal ad substantially deteriorate. In accordance with our conceptual framework, the observed effect may be explained by the tendency of women in the latter case to perceive the female model in the ad as a rival, seek to derogate her attractiveness and thus respond unfavorably toward the ad. The results of Study 2 shed additional light into this phenomenon, indicating that when women process an ad featuring a female model in a decorative role with reference to their past selves and the competition mechanism is activated by situational input in the form of an article in the medium, attitudes toward the ad are generally negative. On the other hand, if women are encouraged to process the ad with reference to their future selves and an article in the medium motivates them to compete, attitudes toward the ad are significantly more favorable.

Some limitations of the studies represent interesting directions for future research. For instance, as is the case with most laboratory experiments, our experimental studies are characterized by an artificial design which could be a concern for external validity (DeVaus 2001, 77–78; Harris 2008, 168; Sani and Todman, 2006, 35); it would be interesting to see if similar findings emerge from future studies using different research designs. Furthermore, for reasons of feasibility, our studies have relied on small, convenience student samples. It is crucial for subsequent studies to test similar hypotheses using larger non-student probability samples, preferably including older women. Moreover, our samples were uniform in terms of their cultural background. Since evolutionary psychology emphasizes panhuman similarities (Tooby and Cosmides 1995), it is critical for future studies to check if the observed patterns are replicated cross-nationally. Given that, to the best of the authors' knowledge, the aforedescribed studies constitute the first attempt to account for female responses to decorative portrayals of women in advertisements through the evolved mechanism of female intrasexual competition, it would be important for future studies on the topic to include additional variables, such as participants' self-perceived attractiveness, self-confidence, general attitude toward advertising and relationship status, that were not examined in this paper. Since we used a single ad for only one product category with a fictitious brand name, subsequent studies could include additional product categories and existing brands to assess whether familiarity with the category or the brand influences responses to decorative portrayals. Similarly, it could be assessed whether the latter differ with regard to consumers' mood when viewing the ad, which could be influenced by their being motivated to compete. Future studies could also extend beyond retrospective and anticipatory self-referencing, including instructions that encourage thoughts related to one's present self. Furthermore, our studies have solely focused to responses to a single ad depicting a model in a decorative role; we are currently expanding our focus to juxtaposing female attitudes toward ads portraying women in decorative and non-decorative roles. Also, we are planning to examine potential differences between ads that refer to attractiveness-enhancing and non-attractiveness-enhancing products (Hudders et al. 2014).

Despite the limitations, the results of the two experimental studies viewed together have considerable theoretical implications. Although the dominant view of stereotyped portrayals of females in advertising focuses on the indignation of women toward the way they are generally presented in advertising (e.g. Ford and LaTour 1996), thus far there is only limited support of these negative a priori attitudes predicting responses to actual ads (Orth and Holancova 2004; Theodoridis et al. 2013). In this sense, our findings offer an alternative explanation of the mechanism underlying such attitudes. Previous research has provided evidence of women responding both positively and negatively to ads with attractive female models (see Bower 2001 for a review). Although attractiveness is a physical characteristic and decorative portrayal refers to role behaviors, they are both relevant to the understanding of female responses to decorative ads. In our view, this is not ultimately due to both role behaviors and physical characteristics being components of stereotypes (Eisend 2010), but due to attractiveness being 'the currency of female competition' (Campbell 2004, 19). In other words, female consumers use the female model's attractiveness as a 'weapon' in their favor when they think of her as a projection of themselves in the future, but they use this 'weapon' against the woman in the ad when they think of her as a rival to their past selves. In this regard, it is important to note that our findings enhance the understanding of the relationship between self-referencing and role portrayals of women in advertising, which has been addressed only limitedly by prior research (Debevec and Iyer 1988; Morrison and Shaffer 2003). The findings of the two studies also extend prior attempts to account for male reactions to female stereotypes in advertising through the evolutionary principles of mate attraction (Saad 2004) to explain female responses to such portrayals, thus indicating that scientific inquiry on the representation of women in advertising should further capitalize on evolutionary psychology principles in contrast to its yet interpreting this phenomenon from a 'Standard Social Science Model' (Tooby and Cosmides 1995, 23) viewpoint.

From a managerial perspective, the findings of the studies have also important practical implications, as they stress the need for advertising practitioners to closely examine the medium context in which ads showing women in decorative roles are placed. The medium context could metaphorically function as a 'double-edged sword' when it comes to the effectiveness of such advertisements; a context that motivates female consumers to compete and at the same time think about themselves in the future could be seen as an opportunity to elicit favorable attitudes, whereas a context that encourages women to derogate the model in the ad could plausibly undermine its effectiveness. We thus echo Cauberge, Geuens, and De Pelsmacker's (2011, 656) suggestion to advertising professionals to pay attention to the characteristics of the context. Given that female-oriented media are replete with content focusing on romantic relationships, as well as stories of friendship and animosity with other women, media planning should be closely aligned with creative strategy to ensure visual advertising effectiveness. Especially when it comes to online advertising, this could be achieved through the use of contextual targeting tools that rely on processing keywords or language processing algorithms to semantically analyse the verbal content of webpages. For instance, ads with female models in decorative roles should not be placed next to a website article that encourages women to think about what they have experienced in the past; our research shows that such a context might lead women to engage in competitor derogation and prove detrimental to attitudes toward the ad. For traditional media such as print where contextual targeting is not yet possible, our findings imply that ads should not be pretested outside of context, as De Pelsmacker, Geuens, and Anckaert (2002) also point out. Taking this a step further, our findings also imply that advertisers and advertising agencies need to carefully reconsider creative executions that involve female models in decorative roles in campaigns targeting female audiences, especially in the many cases when controlling for the medium context is not feasible, given that consumer responses seem to be context-sensitive. In such cases, we would recommend that they use a less risky approach. As a concluding remark, we would like to stress the fact that the present paper constitutes, to our knowledge, the first attempt to account for female consumers' responses to advertisements depicting other women from a female competition standpoint. In our view, the fact that advertising research has thus far omitted to address such a possibility can be explained by the fact that female competition is a relatively new topic; after all, it is only fairly recently that publications on this matter have appeared in the marketing literature. Nonetheless, it could also be the case that researchers are reluctant to touch this controversial issue, which has not ceased to be a 'politically taboo subject' even a decade after Campbell (2004, 23) suggested that this was the case in the past. Female intrasexual competition should be neither a priori dismissed as a 'misogynistic' or 'demeaning' idea nor in any way misinterpreted to demean women (see Welling and Nicolas 2015 for a discussion on the latter). Given the growing body of empirical evidence supporting the existence of such a mechanism, the possibility of its underlying diverse aspects of consumer behavior merits to be tested. It remains to be seen whether further studies in this nascent research area will support or challenge the notion of female competition.

Disclosure statement

No potential conflict of interest was reported by the authors.

Funding

This work was supported by the Athens University of Economics and Business [EP-2168-01].

Notes

1. Evolutionary psychology as a paradigm has received substantial criticism in terms of its explanatory power (e.g. Eagly 1997; Levy 2004; Panksepp and Panksepp 2000), the testability of its hypotheses (see Holcomb 1998; Ketelaar and Ellis 2000), and even the political views of its proponents (see Tybur, Miller, and Gangestad 2007). Given that a detailed discussion of the controversy and criticisms surrounding evolutionary psychology is beyond the scope of this paper, interested readers are encouraged to consult Confer et al. (2010), Smith, Mulder, and Hill (2001) and Welling and Nicolas (2015).

2. To explain this 'paradoxical evidence' (Plakoyiannaki et al. 2008, 104), one could argue that female models are used so as to function as role models for the target audience (Forbes et al. 2004). It has inadvertently been pointed out that such decisions are made by advertising executives who are predominantly male (McDonagh and Prothero 1997, 365); advertising has been thus seen to propagate the aesthetic of the 'white male middle-class heterosexual' (Stern 1999, 8), thus operating as a 'distorted mirror' (Pollay 1986, 18) of society, which in turn produces a number of negative social consequences (Hackley and Kitchen 1999).

3. According to parental investment and sexual selection theory (Trivers 1972), men value traits such as youthfulness and physical attractiveness in their potential mates, whereas women favor mates with a high social status (Buss 1989).

4. Buss (1998) distinguishes between evolved mechanisms and manifest behavior in the domain of sexual selection and argues in favor of formulating relevant hypotheses on the basis of inward psychological mechanisms rather than behaviors, since the latter is limited by numerous constraints.

5. For more detailed reviews of the empirical evidence in support of intrasexual competition among males and females, please see Buss (1998; 2009) and Campbell (2004).

6. Numerous studies in evolutionary psychology have indicated that hormonal fluctuations influence females' mating preferences (e.g. Anderson et al. 2010; Gangestad et al. 2004); in a meta-analytic study by Gildersleeve, Haselton, and Fales (2014), the existence of context-dependent cycle shifts in women's mate preferences has been confirmed. Drawing on the fact that mating preferences are thought to drive intrasexual competition (Buss 1988, 1989), it has been suggested that the female ovulatory cycle also affects the latter mechanism (Fisher 2004). Ovulating women have been found to dress so as to impress other women (Durante et al. 2011) and to attempt to improve their social standing with regard to other women by acquiring positional goods (Durante et al. 2014). Although the link between hormonal fluctuations and mating-related behaviors is well established, the 'ovulatory competition hypothesis' (i.e. the notion that ovulation intensifies female intrasexual competition) merits further research, as noted by Durante et al. (2014, 35).

7. A pretest (26 female respondents aged 21–25 years) indicated that both scenarios led women to engage in the intended strategies (self-promotion scenario: $M_{self\text{-}promotion} = 5.10$, $M_{competitor\ derogation} = 2.67$; competitor derogation scenario: $M_{self\text{-}promotion} = 3.17$, $M_{competitor\ derogation} = 5.09$).

8. In the pretest, participants were presented with a list of six candidate product categories (alcoholic beverage, high-end fashion, radio station, website, soft drink, mobile phone) and were asked to rate the image of each product category on a set of 10 seven-point semantic differential scales, derived from Alreck, Settle, and Belch (1982). The product category (radio station) that received an average rating closer to the scale midpoint ($M = 4.03$, $SD = 0.24$) was selected for inclusion in the study. The web radio category was chosen so as to be both familiar and of interest to the participants; recent industry data indicate that young consumers increasingly listen to Internet radio (Edison Research, 2014; Statista, 2015).

9. In the pretest, participants were shown nine mock ads with different pictures and then rated their agreement with two statements regarding each ad ('The advertisement depicts women in a stereotyped manner', 'The advertisement shows women as decorative objects') on a seven-point Likert scale. The statements were generated on the basis of the previously discussed definition of a stereotypic ad that portrays a woman in a merely decorative role. The mock ad that received the highest rating ($M = 4.84$, $SD = 0.75$) was selected for inclusion in the study. In the pretest, participants were asked to list their thoughts regarding each mock ad and the answers to this open-ended question were coded into positive or negative ad-related, product-related and brand-related thoughts. The findings indicated that they were familiar with the product category (web radio) and that their evaluations of the brand name were generally positive. Their ad-related thoughts regarding the focal stimulus also evidenced that it was perceived as realistic.

10. As a confound check, we inserted the mean score of the items used to assess the degree to which participants considered the ad to portray the female model in a decorative role in an ANCOVA as a covariate (Perdue and Summers 1986); its effect was non-significant ($F(1,59) = 1.69, p = 0.199$).

11. Prior to hypothesis testing, to dismiss the possibility of general attitudes toward sex role portrayals in advertising influencing attitude toward the ad, we inserted the former in an ANCOVA as a covariate (Perdue and Summers 1986); its effect was non-significant ($F(1,83) = 0.47, p = 0.495$).

References

Allen, K.R. and M.E. Hauber. 2013. Self-referencing and mate choice among college students: Epiphenomenon or consistent patterns of preference across populations? *Journal of Social, Evolutionary, and Cultural Psychology* 7, no. 2: 163.

Alreck, P.L., R.B. Settle, and M.A. Belch. 1982. Who responds to "gendered" ads, and how? Masculine brands versus feminine brands. *Journal of Advertising Research* 22, no. 2: 25−32.

Anderson, U.S., E.F. Perea, D.V. Becker, J.M. Ackerman, J.R. Shapiro, S.L. Neuberg, and D.T. Kenrick. 2010. I only have eyes for you: Ovulation redirects attention (but not memory) to attractive men. *Journal of Experimental Social Psychology* 46, no. 5: 804−8.

Ashmore, R.D. and F.K. Del Boca. 1981. Conceptual approaches to stereotypes and stereotyping. In *Cognitive processes in stereotyping and intergroup behavior*, ed. D. Hamilton, 1−35. Hillsdale, NJ: Erlbaum.

Baenninger, M.A., R. Baenninger, and D. Houle. 1993. Attractiveness, attentiveness, and perceived male shortage: Their influence on perceptions of other females. *Ethology and Sociobiology* 14, no. 5: 293−303.

Bagozzi, R.P. and R. Nataraajan. 2000. The year 2000: Looking forward. *Psychology & Marketing* 17, no. 1: 1−11.

Belch, G.E., M.A. Belch, and A. Villarreal. 1987. Effects of advertising communications: Review of research. In *Research in marketing*, ed. J.H. Sheth. Greenwich, CT: JAI Press.

Bettinger, C.O. and L. Dawson. 1979. Changing perspectives in advertising: The use of 'liberated' feminine life-style themes. In *Developments in marketing science*, eds. H.S. Geatlow and E.W. Wheatey, 111−4. Coral Gables, FL: Academy of Marketing Science.

Bissell, K. and A. Rask. 2010. Real women on real beauty: Self-discrepancy, internalisation of the thin ideal, and perceptions of attractiveness and thinness in dove's campaign for real beauty. *International Journal of Advertising* 29, no. 4: 643−68.

Bower, A.B. 2001. Highly attractive models in advertising and the women who loathe them: The implications of negative affect for spokesperson effectiveness. *Journal of Advertising* 30, no. 3: 51−63.

Burnkrant, R.E. and H.R. Unnava. 1995. Effects of self-referencing on persuasion. *Journal of Consumer Research* 22, no. 1: 17−26.

Buss, D.M. 1988. The evolution of human intrasexual competition: Tactics of mate attraction. *Journal of Personality and Social Psychology* 54, no. 4: 616.

Buss, D.M. 1989. Sex differences in human mate preferences: Evolutionary hypotheses tested in 37 cultures. *Behavioral and Brain Sciences* 12, no. 1: 1−14.

Buss, D.M. and L.A. Dedden. 1990. Derogation of competitors. *Journal of Social and Personal Relationships* 7, no. 3: 395−422.

Buss, D.M., R.J. Larsen, D. Westen, and J. Semmelroth. 1992. Sex differences in jealousy: Evolution, physiology, and psychology. *Psychological Science* 3, no. 4: 251−5.

Buss, D.M. 1992. Mate preference mechanisms: Consequences for partner choice and intrasexual competition. In *The adapted mind: Evolutionary psychology and the generation of culture*, eds. J. Barkow, J. Tooby, and L. Cosmides, 249−66. New York: Oxford University Press.

Buss, D.M. 1995. Evolutionary psychology: A new paradigm for psychological science. *Psychological Inquiry* 6, no. 1: 1−30.

Buss, D.M. 1998. Sexual strategies theory: Historical origins and current status. *Journal of Sex Research* 35, no. 1: 19−31.

Buss, D.M. 2009. How can evolutionary psychology successfully explain personality and individual differences? *Perspectives on Psychological Science* 4, no. 4: 359−66.

Buss, D.M. and D.P. Schmitt. 2011. Evolutionary psychology and feminism. *Sex Roles* 64, no. 9−10: 768−87.

Bussey, K. and A. Bandura. 1999. Social cognitive theory of gender development and differentiation. *Psychological Review* 106, no. 4: 676.

Caballero, M.J., J.R. Lumpkin, and C.S. Madden. 1989. Using physical attractiveness as an advertising tool: An empirical test of the attraction phenomenon. *Journal of Advertising Research* 29, no. 4: 16−22.

Campbell, A. 2004. Female competition: Causes, constraints, content, and contexts. *Journal of Sex Research* 41, no. 1: 16−26.

Campbell, L. and C.J. Wilbur. 2009. Are the traits we prefer in potential mates the traits they value in themselves? An analysis of sex differences in the self-concept. *Self and Identity* 8, no. 4: 418−46.

Carmen, R.A., G. Geher, D.J. Glass, A.E. Guitar, T.L. Grandis, L. Johnsen, M.M. Philip, R.L. New-mark, G.T. Trouton, and B.R. Tauber. 2013. Evolution integrated across all islands of the human behavioral archipelago: All psychology as evolutionary psychology. *EvoS Journal: The Journal of the Evolutionary Studies Consortium* 5, no. 1: 108–26.

Cauberghe, V., M. Geuens, and P. De Pelsmacker. 2011. Context effects of TV programme-induced interactivity and telepresence on advertising responses. *International Journal of Advertising* 30, no. 4: 641–63.

Chang, C. 2005. Ad–self–congruency effects: Self–enhancing cognitive and affective mechanisms. *Psychology & Marketing* 22, no. 11: 887–910.

Christy, T.P. 2006. Females' perceptions of offensive advertising: The importance of values, expectations, and control. *Journal of Current Issues & Research in Advertising* 28, no. 2: 15–32.

Colarelli, S.M. and J.R. Dettmann. 2003. Intuitive evolutionary perspectives in marketing practices. *Psychology & Marketing* 20, no. 9: 837–65.

Confer, J.C., J.A. Easton, D.S. Fleischman, C.D. Goetz, D.M. Lewis, C. Perilloux, and D.M. Buss. 2010. Evolutionary psychology: Controversies, questions, prospects, and limitations. *American Psychologist* 65, no. 2: 110.

Cosmides, L. and J. Tooby. 1994. Beyond intuition and instinct blindness: Toward an evolutionarily rigorous cognitive science. *Cognition* 50, no. 1: 41–77.

Courtney, A.E. and S.W. Lockeretz. 1971. A woman's place: An analysis of the roles portrayed by women in magazine advertisements. *Journal of Marketing Research* 8, no. 1: 92–5.

Cox, A. and M. Fisher. 2008. A framework for exploring intrasexual competition. *Journal of Social, Evolutionary, and Cultural Psychology* 2, no. 4: 144.

Dahlén, M. 2005. The medium as a contextual cue: Effects of creative media choice. *Journal of Advertising* 34, no. 3: 89–98.

De Pelsmacker, P., M. Geuens, and P. Anckaert. 2002. Media context and advertising effectiveness: The role of context appreciation and context/ad similarity. *Journal of Advertising* 31, no. 2: 49–61.

Deaux, K. and L.L. Lewis. 1984. Structure of gender stereotypes: Interrelationships among components and gender label. *Journal of Personality and Social Psychology* 46, no. 5: 991.

Debevec, K. and E. Iyer. 1986. The influence of spokespersons in altering a product's gender image: Implications for advertising effectiveness. *Journal of Advertising* 15, no. 4: 12–20.

Debevec, K. and E. Iyer. 1988. Self–referencing as a mediator of the effectiveness of sex–role portrayals in advertising. *Psychology & Marketing* 5, no. 1: 71–84.

Devaus, D. 2001. *Research design in social research*. London: Sage.

Dimofte, C.V. and R.F. Yalch. 2010. The role of frequency of experience with a product category and temporal orientation in self-referent advertising. *Journal of Consumer Psychology* 20, no. 3: 343–54.

Duker, J.M. and L.R. Tucker Jr. 1977. "Women's lib-ers" versus independent women: A study of preferences for women's roles in advertisements. *Journal of Marketing Research* 14, no. 4: 469–75.

Duntley, J.D. and D.M. Buss. 2008. Evolutionary psychology is a metatheory for psychology. *Psychological Inquiry: An International Journal for the Advancement of Psychological Theory* 19, no. 1: 30–4.

Durante, K.M., V. Griskevicius, S.M. Cantú, and J.A. Simpson. 2014. Money, status, and the ovulatory cycle. *Journal of Marketing Research* 51, no. 1: 27–39.

Durante, K.M., V. Griskevicius, S.E. Hill, C. Perilloux, and N.P. Li. 2011. Ovulation, female competition, and product choice: Hormonal influences on consumer behavior. *Journal of Consumer Research* 37, no. 6: 921–34.

Eagly, A.H. 1997. Sex differences in social behavior: Comparing social role theory and evolutionary psychology. *American Psychologist* 52, no. 12: 1380–3.

Eagly, A.H. and W. Wood. 1999. The origins of sex differences in human behavior: Evolved dispositions versus social roles. *American Psychologist* 54, no. 6: 408.

Edison Research. 2014. Eight in ten millennials listen to Internet radio. http://www.edisonresearch. com/eight-in-ten-millennials-listen-to-internet-radio/.

Eisend, M. 2010. A meta-analysis of gender roles in advertising. *Journal of the Academy of Marketing Science* 38, no. 4: 418–40.

Eisend, M., J. Plagemann, and J. Sollwedel. 2014. Gender roles and humor in advertising: The occurrence of stereotyping in humorous and nonhumorous advertising and its consequences for advertising effectiveness. *Journal of Advertising* 43, no. 3: 256–73.

Escalas, J.E. 2004. Imagine yourself in the product: Mental simulation, narrative transportation, and persuasion. *Journal of Advertising* 33, no. 2: 37–48.

Feingold, A. 1990. Gender differences in effects of physical attractiveness on romantic attraction: A comparison across five research paradigms. *Journal of Personality and Social Psychology* 59, no. 5: 981.

Fink, B., D. Klappauf, G. Brewer, and T.K. Shackelford. 2014. Female physical characteristics and intra-sexual competition in women. *Personality and Individual Differences* 58: 138–41.

Fisher, M.L. 2004. Female intrasexual competition decreases female facial attractiveness. *Proceedings of the Royal Society of London. Series B: Biological Sciences* 271, Suppl. no. 5: S283–5.

Fisher, M. and A. Cox. 2011. Four strategies used during intrasexual competition for mates. *Personal Relationships* 18, no. 1: 20–38.

Forbes, G.B., K. Doroszewicz, K. Card, and L. Adams-Curtis. 2004. Association of the thin body ideal, ambivalent sexism, and self-esteem with body acceptance and the preferred body size of college women in Poland and the United States. *Sex Roles* 50, no. 5–6: 331–45.

Ford, J.B. and M.S. Latour. 1996. Contemporary female perspectives of female role portrayals in advertising. *Journal of Current Issues & Research in Advertising* 18, no. 1: 81–95.

Furnham, A. and S. Paltzer. 2010. The portrayal of men and women in television advertisements: An updated review of 30 studies published since 2000. *Scandinavian Journal of Psychology* 51, no. 3: 216–36.

Gangestad, S.W., J.A. Simpson, A.J. Cousins, C.E. Garver-Apgar, and P.N. Christensen. 2004. Women's preferences for male behavioral displays change across the menstrual cycle. *Psychological Science* 15, no. 3: 203–7.

Garcia, J.R. and G. Saad. 2008. Evolutionary neuromarketing: Darwinizing the neuroimaging paradigm for consumer behavior. *Journal of Consumer Behaviour* 7, no. 4–5: 397–414.

Geary, D.C. 2000. Evolution and proximate expression of human paternal investment. *Psychological Bulletin* 126, no. 1: 55.

Gildersleeve, K., M.G. Haselton, and M.R. Fales. 2014. Do women's mate preferences change across the ovulatory cycle? A meta-analytic review. *Psychological Bulletin* 140, no. 5: 1205.

Gilly, M.C. 1988. Sex roles in advertising: A comparison of television advertisements in Australia, Mexico, and the United States. *The Journal of Marketing* 52, no. 2: 75–85.

Griskevicius, V., N.J. Goldstein, C.R. Mortensen, J.M. Sundie, R.B. Cialdini, and D.T. Kenrick. 2009. Fear and loving in Las Vegas: Evolution, emotion, and persuasion. *Journal of Marketing Research* 46, no. 3: 384–95.

Griskevicius, V., J.M. Tybur, S.W. Gangestad, E.F. Perea, J.R. Shapiro, and D.T. Kenrick. 2009. Aggress to impress: Hostility as an evolved context-dependent strategy. *Journal of Personality and Social Psychology* 96, no. 5: 980.

Gulas, C.S. and K. Mckeage. 2000. Extending social comparison: An examination of the unintended consequences of idealized advertising imagery. *Journal of Advertising* 29, no. 2: 17–28.

Hackley, C.E. and P.J. Kitchen. 1999. Ethical perspectives on the postmodern communications leviathan. *Journal of Business Ethics* 20, no. 1: 15–26.

Harker, M., D. Harker, and S. Svensen. 2005. Attitudes towards gender portrayal in advertising: An Australian perspective. *Journal of Marketing Management* 21, no. 1–2: 251–64.

Harris, P. 2008. *Designing and reporting experiments in psychology*. New York: Open University Press.

Hartmann, P. and V. Apaolaza-Ibáñez. 2013. Desert or rain: Standardisation of green advertising versus adaptation to the target audience's natural environment. *European Journal of Marketing* 47, no. 5/6: 917–33.

Holcomb, H.R. 1998. Testing evolutionary hypotheses. In *Handbook of evolutionary psychology: Ideas, issues, and applications*, eds. C. Crawford and D.R. Krebs, 303–34. Mahweh, NJ: Lawrence Erlbaum.

Hong, J.W. and G.M. Zinkhan. 1995. Self–concept and advertising effectiveness: The influence of congruency, conspicuousness, and response mode. *Psychology & Marketing* 12, no. 1: 53–77.

Hudders, L., C. De Backer, M. Fisher, and P. Vyncke. 2014. The rival wears prada: Luxury consumption as a female competition strategy. *Evolutionary Psychology* 12, no. 3: 570–87.

Jaffe, L.J. and P.D. Berger. 1994. The effect of modern female sex role portrayals on advertising effectiveness. *Journal of Advertising Research* 34, no. 4: 32–42.

Jones, M.Y., A.J. Stanaland, and B.D. Gelb. 1998. Beefcake and cheesecake: Insights for advertisers. *Journal of Advertising* 27, no. 2: 33–51.

Ketelaar, T. and B.J. Ellis. 2000. Are evolutionary explanations unfalsifiable? Evolutionary psychology and the Lakatosian philosophy of science. *Psychological Inquiry* 11, no. 1: 1–21.

Krishnamurthy, P. and M. Sujan. 1999. Retrospection versus anticipation: The role of the ad under retrospective and anticipatory self-referencing. *Journal of Consumer Research* 26, no. 1: 55–69.

Leavitt, C. 1978. Even housewives prefer working women in TV ads. *Marketing News* 11, no. 23: 10.

Leenaars, L.S., A.V. Dane, and Z.A. Marini. 2008. Evolutionary perspective on indirect victimization in adolescence: The role of attractiveness, dating and sexual behavior. *Aggressive Behavior* 34, no. 4: 404–15.

Levy, N. 2004. Evolutionary psychology, human universals, and the standard social science model. *Biology and Philosophy* 19, no. 3: 459–72.

Lindner, K. 2004. Images of women in general interest and fashion magazine advertisements from 1955 to 2002. *Sex Roles* 51, no. 7–8: 409–21.

Lundstrom, W.J. and D. Sciglimpaglia. 1977. Sex role portrayals in advertising. *The Journal of Marketing* 41, no. 3: 72–79.

Lydon, J.E., M. Meana, D. Sepinwall, N. Richards, and S. Mayman. 1999. The commitment calibration hypothesis: When do people devalue attractive alternatives? *Personality and Social Psychology Bulletin* 25, no. 2: 152–61.

Lysonski, S. and R.W. Pollay. 1990. Advertising sexism is forgiven, but not forgotten: Historical, cross-cultural and individual differences in criticism and purchase boycott intentions. *International Journal of Advertising* 9: 319–31.

Martin, M.C. and P.F. Kennedy. 1993. Advertising and social comparison: Consequences for female preadolescents and adolescents. *Psychology & Marketing* 10, no. 6: 513–30.

Martin, M.C. and P.F. Kennedy. 1994. Social comparison and the beauty of advertising models: The role of motives for comparison. In *Advances in consumer research*, eds. C.T. Allen and D. Roedder John, 365–71. Provo, UT: Association for Consumer Research.

Massar, K., A.P. Buunk, and S. Rempt. 2012. Age differences in women's tendency to gossip are mediated by their mate value. *Personality and Individual Differences* 52, no. 1: 106–9.

McDonagh, P. and A. Prothero. 1997. Leap-frog marketing: The contribution of ecofeminist thought to the world of patriarchal marketing. *Marketing Intelligence & Planning* 15, no. 7: 361–8.

Mitchell, A.A. and J.C. Olson. 1981. Are product attribute beliefs the only mediator of advertising effects on brand attitude? *Journal of Marketing Research* 18, no. 3: 318–32.

Mitchell, P.C. and W. Taylor. 1990. Polarising trends in female role portrayals in UK advertising. *European Journal of Marketing* 24, no. 5: 41–9.

Morrison, M.M. and D.R. Shaffer. 2003. Gender-role congruence and self-referencing as determinants of advertising effectiveness. *Sex Roles* 49, no. 5–6: 265–75.

Orth, U.R. and D. Holancova. 2004. Men's and women's responses to sex role portrayals in advertisements. *International Journal of Research in Marketing* 21, no. 1: 77–88.

Orth, U.R., K. Malkewitz, and C. Bee. 2010. Gender and personality drivers of consumer mixed emotional response to advertising. *Journal of Current Issues & Research in Advertising* 32, no. 1: 69–80.

Panksepp, J. and J.B. Panksepp. 2000. The seven sins of evolutionary psychology. *Evolution and Cognition* 6, no. 2: 108–31.

Pedhazur, E.J. and L.P. Schmelkin. 1991. *Measurement, design, and analysis: An integrated approach*. New York, NY: Psychology Press.

Perdue, B.C. and J.O. Summers. 1986. Checking the success of manipulations in marketing experiments. *Journal of Marketing Research* 23, no. 4: 317–26.

Piccoli, V., F. Foroni, and A. Carnaghi. 2013. Comparing group dehumanization and intra-sexual competition among normally ovulating women and hormonal contraceptive users. *Personality & Social Psychology Bulletin* 39, no. 12: 1600–9.

Plakoyiannaki, E., K. Mathioudaki, P. Dimitratos, and Y. Zotos. 2008. Images of women in online advertisements of global products: Does sexism exist? *Journal of Business Ethics* 83, no. 1: 101–12.

Plakoyiannaki, E. and Y. Zotos. 2009. Female role stereotypes in print advertising: Identifying associations with magazine and product categories. *European Journal of Marketing* 43, no. 11–12: 1411–34.

Pollay, R.W. 1986. The distorted mirror: Reflections on the unintended consequences of advertising. *Journal of Marketing* 50, no. 2: 18.

Richins, M.L. 1991. Social comparison and the idealized images of advertising. *Journal of Consumer Research* 18, no. 1: 71–83.

Rouner, D., M.D. Slater, and M. Domenech-Rodriguez. 2003. Adolescent evaluation of gender role and sexual imagery in television advertisements. *Journal of Broadcasting & Electronic Media* 47, no. 3: 435–54.

Saad, G. 2004. Applying evolutionary psychology in understanding the representation of women in advertisements. *Psychology & Marketing* 21, no. 8: 593–612.

Saad, G. and T. Gill. 2000. Applications of evolutionary psychology in marketing. *Psychology and Marketing* 17, no. 12: 1005–34.

Sani, F. and J.B. Todman. 2006. *Experimental design and statistics for psychology: A first course.* Oxford: Blackwell.

Schmitt, D.P. 2005. Fundamentals of human mating strategies. In *The handbook of evolutionary psychology*, ed. D.M. Buss, 258–91. Hoboken, NJ: John Wiley.

Schmitt, D.P. and D.M. Buss. 1996. Strategic self-promotion and competitor derogation: Sex and context effects on the perceived effectiveness of mate attraction tactics. *Journal of Personality and Social Psychology* 70, no. 6: 1185.

Sedikides, C. and J.J. Skowronski. 2002. Evolution of the symbolic self: Issues and prospects. In *Handbook of self and identity*, eds. M.R. Leary and J.P. Tangney, 594–609. New York, NY: The Guilford Press.

Shimp, T. 2008. Ed. *Advertising, promotion, and other aspects of integrated marketing communications.* New York, NY: Harcourt.

Smith, E.A., M.B. Mulder, and K. Hill. 2001. Controversies in the evolutionary social sciences: A guide for the perplexed. *Trends in Ecology & Evolution* 16, no. 3: 128–35.

Statista. 2015. Share of individuals listening to web radio on the internet in selected European countries in 2014. http://www.statista.com/statistics/386341/online-web-radio-consumption-in-european-countries/.

Stern, B.B. 1999. Gender and multicultural issues in advertising: Stages on the research highway. *Journal of Advertising* 28, no. 1: 1–9.

Sugiyama, L.S. 2005. Physical attractiveness in adaptationist perspective. In *The handbook of evolutionary psychology*, ed. D.M. Buss, 292–343. Hoboken, NJ: John Wiley.

Taylor, C.R., S. Landreth, and H.-K. Bang. 2005. Asian Americans in magazine advertising: Portrayals of the "model minority." *Journal of Macromarketing* 25, no. 2: 163–74.

Theodoridis, P.K., A.G. Kyrousi, A.Y. Zotou, and G.G. Panigyrakis. 2013. Male and female attitudes towards stereotypical advertisements: A paired country investigation. *Corporate Communications: An International Journal* 18, no. 1: 135–60.

Tooby, J. and L. Cosmides. 1992. The psychological foundations of culture. In *The adapted mind: Evolutionary psychology and the generation of culture*, eds. J. Barkow, L. Cosmides, and J. Tooby, 19–136. New York, NY: Oxford University Press.

Tooby, J. and L. Cosmides. 1995. The psychological foundations of culture. In *The adapted mind: Evolutionary psychology and the generation of culture*, eds. J. Barkow, L. Cosmides, and J. Tooby, 19–136. New York: Oxford University Press.

Trivers, R.L. 1972. Parental investment and sexual selection. In *Sexual selection and the descent of man*, ed. B. Campbell, 136–79. Chicago, IL: Aldine.

Tybur, J.M., G.F. Miller, and S.W. Gangestad. 2007. Testing the controversy. *Human Nature* 18, no. 4: 313–28.

Vaillancourt, T. 2013. Do human females use indirect aggression as an intrasexual competition strategy? *Philosophical Transactions of the Royal Society B: Biological Sciences* 368, no. 1631: 80–7.

Van Reijmersdal, E., E. Smit, and P. Neijens. 2010. How media factors affect audience responses to brand placement. *International Journal of Advertising* 29, no. 2: 279–301.

Van Vugt, M., D. De Cremer, and D.P. Janssen. 2007. Gender differences in cooperation and competition the male-warrior hypothesis. *Psychological Science* 18, no. 1: 19–23.

Vantomme, D., M. Geuens, and S. Dewitte. 2005. How to portray men and women in advertisements? Explicit and implicit evaluations of ads depicting different gender roles. https://lirias.kuleuven.be/bitstream/123456789/122707/1/0536.pdf

Wang, Y. and V. Griskevicius. 2014. Conspicuous consumption, relationships, and rivals: Women's luxury products as signals to other women. *Journal of Consumer Research* 40, no. 5: 834–54.

Welling, L.L. and S.C. Nicolas. 2015. The Darwinian mystique? Synthesizing evolutionary psychology and feminism. In *Evolutionary perspectives on social psychology*, eds. V. Zeigler-Hill, L.L.M. Welling, and T. Shackelford, 203–14. Cham: Springer.

Whipple, T.W. and A.E. Courtney. 1985. Female role portrayals in advertising and communication effectiveness: A review. *Journal of Advertising* 14, no. 3: 4–17.

Williams, E.F. and M. Steffel. 2014. Double standards in the use of enhancing products by self and others. *Journal of Consumer Research* 41, no. 2: 506–25.

Wilson, M. and M. Daly. 1985. Competitiveness, risk taking, and violence: The young male syndrome. *Ethology and Sociobiology* 6, no. 1: 59–73.

Wilson, D.S., and R. O'Gorman. 2003. Emotions and actions associated with norm-breaking events. *Human Nature* 14, no. 3: 277–304.

Wolin, L.D. 2003. Gender issues in advertising – an oversight synthesis of research: 1970–2002. *Journal of Advertising Research* 43, no. 1: 111–29.

Wood, W. and A.H. Eagly. 2002. A cross-cultural analysis of the behavior of women and men: Implications for the origins of sex differences. *Psychological Bulletin* 128, no. 5: 699.

Zimmerman, A. and J. Dahlberg. 2008. The sexual objectification of women in advertising: A contemporary cultural perspective. *Journal of Advertising Research* 48, no. 1: 71.

Zotos, Y.C. and S. Lysonski. 1994. Gender representations: The case of Greek magazine advertisements. *Journal of Euromarketing* 3, no. 2: 27–47.

Appendix 1.   Scenarios – Study 1

Scenario 1 (Self-promotion)

Last night, I went to this party that my friend had been organizing for ages. The minute I walked in, I saw that this handsome guy that was in one of my classes was also there. I don't really know him, but he seems smart and funny and he is so good-looking that heads turn when he passes by. He was sitting alone, looking around and I guess that he looked a little bored. Maybe he didn't know any of the people there. I realized that a lot of other girls were checking him out. I knew that it wouldn't be long until any of them tried to attract his attention. So, I quickly made up my mind to go and talk to him. As I was walking across the room, I kept thinking about what to say to him to set myself apart in his eyes.

Scenario 2 (Competitor derogation)

Last night, I went to this party that my friend had been organizing for ages. I found myself standing next to this handsome guy and soon we started talking. I realized that he was not only good-looking, but also very smart and funny and, to be honest, I liked him a lot. We had been talking for more than an hour when I realized I hadn't yet got a drink, so I just went across to the bar to get one. Of course, the bar was crowded and it took me a few minutes to get my drink. As I was walking back, I saw him talking to this other girl, one of my classmates. She is this really annoying and unlikeable type, all full of herself. The minute I got there, someone approached her, telling her to move her car because it was blocking the entrance and she left in a hurry. So, I found myself again alone with the guy thinking about what to say to him.

Appendix 2.   Ad stimulus – Studies 1 and 2

Appendix 3.   Stories – Study 2

Story 1 (Neutral motivation)

Lately, I think I have trouble focusing on something for more than a few minutes. It's not just studying, although sometimes I can't read more than a few sentences without my mind drifting away or without getting up to have a snack. Thinking back, I think that sometimes I can't watch a whole movie without pausing. I find it hard to concentrate on anything and, because of this, I constantly forget where I put stuff. I keep looking for my keys and last week, I was under the wrong impression that I had lost my wallet. I went shopping in the afternoon and I took out my wallet in order to pay. I clearly remember putting it back and then walking home, thinking about all sorts of stuff on the way. It was not until the following morning that I saw that my wallet was not in my handbag. I started looking everywhere, even in sock drawers. I had turned the whole apartment upside down when I opened the fridge to get a glass of water and I saw my wallet there. I don't really remember how or when I put it there, and I am a little worried about this. What do you think I should do?

Story 2 (Competitive motivation)

From the first time I saw P., I knew that he was not like other guys. We first met at a big party and we found ourselves sitting next to each other and started talking. I could easily tell he liked me. At some point, I got up to get a drink and when I came back, he wasn't there. I asked my close friends but they didn't seem to know him. A month passed by and I was still thinking about him. During an evening out with my friend, I saw him across the room hanging out with a group of guys and girls, but it was too crowded and he didn't notice me. Fortunately, a few minutes later, my friend and I managed to move closer. But before I had a chance to say anything to him, one of the girls in his group started dancing and flirting with him in a very obvious way. I instantly recognized her, we were attending a couple of classes together. I asked around to find out whether they were a couple and apparently they are not, though someone said that there might be something there. My friend says that we should go to that place again and that I should talk to him and tell him how I feel about him before something happens with this other girl. What do you think I should do?

Do feminists still respond negatively to female nudity in advertising? Investigating the influence of feminist attitudes on reactions to sexual appeals

Hojoon Choi, Kyunga Yoo, Tom Reichert and Michael S. LaTour

To test the belief that feminism and sexualization of women in advertising stand in opposition, this study employed a large US national sample ($N = 1298$) to examine how consumers' feminist attitudes differentiate and predict their ethical judgment and ad-related evaluations of sexual images of women in advertisements. The results indicate that (1) consumers with higher feminist attitudes evaluated sexual ads more favorably than those having lower feminist attitudes, and (2) consumers' feminist attitudes positively predict ad-related evaluations with full mediation of ethical judgment. These findings, which diverge from previous research, may indicate that contemporary feminists view sexual images of women differently than in previous decades. Theoretical and practical implications are described.

Introduction

Since the 1960s, researchers have investigated the effects of sexual appeals in advertising. In general, findings reveal that sexual content brings attention to the ad (Sparks and Lang 2015), but can evoke divergent evaluations based on audience factors (e.g., gender; see Reichert, LaTour, and Kim 2007). Also, due to its controversial nature, academic research has generally cautioned advertisers about the negative consequences of employing sexual content. Although sexual ad content can manifest as a variety of cues (e.g., sounds, text, images of sexual behavior; see Davies 2011), sexualized images of females represent the vast majority of sexual content in advertising (Reichert 2002; Soley and Reid 1988). For that reason, and given the nature of the questions addressed in this study, sexual content primarily pertains to sexual images of female models in various stages of undress.

Based on the relationship between sexual appeal and its effects in advertising, recent studies have attempted to determine the conditions of when and for whom the sexual appeal is more effective or problematic (Chang 2006; Reichert, LaTour, and Kim 2007; Feiereisen, Broderick, and Douglas 2009; Chang and Tseng 2013). These studies are valuable because they can help advertisers appropriately gauge messages to communicate effectively with consumer segments and be aware of thresholds related to sexual appeals. Biological gender (LaTour 1990), sexual self-schema (Reichert, LaTour, and Kim 2007),

41

and sensation seeking (Chang and Tseng 2013) are some of the representative examples of individual differences shown to influence the effects of sexual appeals in advertising.

Within this context, this study examines a potentially important individual belief – attitude towards feminism – and tests to what extent it influences the effects of female nudity on advertising evaluation. Traditionally, it has been known that feminists dislike the sexualization of women in advertising because such sexual depictions are demeaning and limiting, and portray women within a negative gender-role (see Ford and LaTour 1993; Mackay and Covell 1997). As time has passed, however, people's general perceptions about feminism have changed, as well as their thoughts on sexual imagery in advertising (Aronson 2003; Gill and Arthurs 2006; Zimmerman and Dahlberg 2008). For example, female sexuality and sexual expression for third-wave feminists are bolder and less restrictive than that of second-wave feminists. Provocative dress and behavior can be viewed as sources of resistance and agency to objectification and prescribed roles for women (Snyder 2008). Perhaps sexual images of women in media today may evoke more positive reactions than the negative reactions reflected in previous studies. For these reasons, it is important to determine if consumers' feminist attitudes continue to positively or negatively influence their evaluations to sexual depictions of women in advertising in the patterns observed in previous research.

Thus, employing Fassinger's (1994) attitude toward feminism scale, we observe how individuals' overall feminist attitudes moderate their ethical judgment and responses to advertising that contains sexual images of women, and whether the effect interacts with respondent gender (LaTour 1990). Furthermore, we also test a consumer information-processing model to determine if ethical judgment mediates the relationship between individuals' feminist attitude and ad responses. Previous studies found that, as the sexual content in advertising is perceived culturally or morally unacceptable, it induces negative ethical judgment among consumers (LaTour and Henthorne 1994), and sequentially predicts negative ad-related evaluations (Henthorne and LaTour 1995). However, previous studies have not examined how ethical judgment is influenced by consumers' cultural/moral/ideological beliefs, such as attitude towards feminism. In that sense, this study places attitude toward feminism as an antecedent variable and observes how feminism predicts ethical judgment and ad responses in turn. As such, this study not only updates literature in this area but offers a more robust model of consumer response to these controversial appeals.

Literature review

The effects of sex in advertising

Although sex in advertising is a controversial subject, its use has become the norm for hedonic products as cosmetics, fashion accessories, and perfume. In magazine advertising, for example, the proportion of sexualized women rose from less than one-third in 1964 to one-half in 2003 (Soley and Reid 1988; Reichert and Carpenter 2004; Nelson and Paek 2005; Reichert, Childers, and Reid 2012). Recently, any issue of *Cosmopolitan, Elle,* or *Glamour,* or a vast array of other women's (and men's) magazines, contain a high percentage of sexually charged advertisements that depict the physiques of female models in various levels of dress (Pham et al. 2014). In prime-time network commercials, up to 18% of actors dress or behave provocatively (Lin 1998), and sexual content is considerably higher in advertising in network program promotions (Walker 2000), and in ads on mainstream websites (Ramirez 2006). Indeed, employing the media options above as well as social media channels, Abercrombie & Fitch brand increasingly used sexual content in its marketing communication from 1997 to 2013 (Pham et al. 2014).

Beyond prevalence, there are generalizations that can be made about the effects of sex in advertising. With regard to advertising processing, studies indicate that the sexual content in advertising attracts consumers' attention, increases their attitude toward the ad, and also facilitates their interest toward the advertised brand (Belch, Belch, and Villarreal 1987; LaTour 1990; MacInnis, Moorman, and Jaworski 1991; Percy and Rossiter 1992; Reichert, LaTour, and Kim 2007; Sparks and Lang 2015). Alternately, sexual ad content has also been shown to distract viewers by directing attention toward the ad's executional elements at the expense of brand information (Grazer and Keesling 1995). Additionally, sexual ads are evaluated less favorably if there is little relevance of sexual content to the product category (MacInnis, Moorman, and Jaworski 1991). Professionally, it is important to note that sex in advertising is strategically used in light of these effects: enhancing awareness, creating favorability to the ad, communicating utility, creating identification with consumers, and branding and positioning (Gould 1994; Reichert, LaTour, and Kim 2007).

Ethical judgments of sex in advertising

Despite its use and potential effects, academic research has also cautioned advertisers about the negative consequences of employing graphic sexual content in advertising. For example, Courtney and Whipple (1983) forwarded the caveat: 'advertisers would be well advised to avoid overtly seductive, nude, or partially clad models' (p. 118). Gould (1994) also explained that the use of sexual appeals in advertising often is not appealing to some viewers and may result in a boomerang effect. That is, the use of sexual appeals can be met with disdain and negative evaluations, as consumers judge the appeal to be morally wrong (Gould 1994; Maciejewski 2004; Morrison and Sherman 1972; Sciglimpaglia, Belch, and Cain 1979; Alexander and Judd 1986; LaTour 1990).

Evidence from numerous studies does suggest that ethical judgment of sexual content in advertising is a construct that predicts advertising responses (LaTour and Henthorne 1994; Henthorne and LaTour 1995; Reichert, Latour, and Ford 2011). Based on Reidenbach and Robin's Multidimensional Ethics Scale (1990), ethical judgment has two dimensions: Moral Equity/Relativism and Contractualism. In the present context, the Moral Equity/Relativism dimension refers to the extent a sexual appeal is judged to be right or wrong according to an individual's moral equity and social guideline (LaTour and Henthorne 1994). Guidelines are formalized through life and heavily influenced by social institutions (e.g., family, religion, school; also see Reichert, Latour, and Ford 2011). That is, the Moral Equity/Relativism dimension assesses to what extent the morality of sexual advertising exceeds or fall into the parameter or guideline manifested by social institutions (see LaTour and Henthorne 1994; Reichert, Latour, and Ford 2011). The Contractualism dimension refers to the extent a sexual appeal violates an unspoken/unwritten social contract between the individual and society (LaTour and Henthorne 1994; Reidenbach and Robin 1990). When predicting consumers' responses to sexual ads, studies consistently show that Moral Equity/ Relativism is a much stronger dimension than Contractualism because the former dimension reflects consumers' feelings about the degree of appropriateness in advertising while the latter dimension is unrelated to ad-specific ethical evaluations (LaTour and Henthorne 1994; Reichert, Latour, and Ford 2011). These studies also show that unfavorable ethical judgments about sexual content in advertising also negatively influence advertising evaluations, such as attitude toward the ad, brand interest, and purchase intension.

The influence of gender

Researchers also have sought to identify individual differences that can influence the effects of sexual content in advertising. Among them, biological gender, or sex of respondent, has been a primary focus of attention. Almost without fail, research shows a cross-sex bias, meaning that respondents rate sexual images of the opposite sex more positively. Regarding reactions by audience gender to sexual images advertising, LaTour (1990) found that female respondents generated more tension and negative feelings towards explicit female nudity in print ads than men, while men were more energized and positive in their feelings about such ads. An extension (Reichert, LaTour, and Kim 2007) tested responses to three types of sexual stimuli in commercials: ads featuring women, men, or both women and men. Overall, affective and attitudinal responses were most favorable to opposite-sex stimuli, followed by mixed-sex stimuli, with same-sex imagery evaluated least favorably. Putrevu (2008) found this gender effect to be influenced by congruence (strong or weak fit) between the sexual appeal and its link to the brand. Sengupta and Dahl (2008) also found that males generally exhibited more positive ad attitude to unnecessarily explicit sex appeals than females. In sum, gender reactions to sexual content suggest that congruence between sex of the model and sex of the viewer play an important role in ad evaluation that can be moderated by secondary factors, such as product and message relevance.

The influence of psychological attitudes

Although biological sex is a relevant variable related to sexual content in advertising, researchers in advertising, marketing, and psychology also indicate the importance of individuals' psychological propensities (Chang 2006; Feiereisen, Broderick, and Douglas 2009). These researchers explain that, even individuals of the same gender have a variety of levels of psychological traits, knowing such psychological traits helps advertisers to identify appropriate consumer segments and ad placements. For example, Feiereisen, Broderick, and Douglas (2009) reported that the congruity between psychological gender trait (femininity vs. masculinity) and advertising appeal predicted enhancement of consumers' ad-related evaluations. Chang (2006) also tested self-rated masculinity and femininity as an individual difference factor and found that the congruency between ad portrayals and self-rated dimensions of masculinity or femininity predicted increased attitudes toward advertisement.

Furthermore, several studies indicate that consumers favorably evaluate sexual content in advertising as their psychological propensities are more favorable to sexually arousing lifestyles or behaviors. A study by Reichert, LaTour, and Kim (2007) revealed that individuals' sexual self-schema can be a significant antecedent variable predicting female's affective reactions to commercials featuring opposite-sex models and couples. Chang and Tseng (2013) also found that sensation seeking moderates the effect of sexual appeals in advertising. Additionally, Mittal and Lassar (2000) reported a positive relationship between consumer's sexual liberalism and sexual ad evaluations.

Feminism and sex in advertising

In this context, the current study offers feminist supportive attitudes as a potentially use-ful variable to help explain responses to sexually explicit images of women in advertising. Specifically, it is expected that feminist supportive attitudes serve as both a moderator and predictor of response. Feminism, defined as beliefs supportive of gender equality, espe-cially in the political, economic, cultural, personal, and social rights arenas (Offen 1988; Beasley 1999; Hawkesworth 2006), has long been an important movement and ideology that influences people's judgments and attitudes (also see Messer-Davidow 2002; Zimmerman and Dahlberg 2008). From the standpoint of feminism, sexualizing women in advertising is an example of gender stereotyping with potentially harmful short- and long-term consequences (Hall and Crum 1994; Rossi and Rossi 1985). Several research-ers have found that sexual images of women in advertising result in less favorable equal-ity attitudes (see MacKay and Covell 1997; Lavine, Sweeney, and Wagner 1999). Findings also indicate that viewers with feminist supportive attitudes respond negatively to sexual portrayals of women in advertising. For example, Lavine, Sweeney, and Wagner (1999) found that feminists tended to show more negative attitudes toward sexist ads than non-sexist ads (1999). Ford and LaTour (1993) also found that feminists are both more conscious of the portrayal of women and more critical of the sexual objectification within ads.

However, as the meaning and focus of feminism has evolved over the last few decades, research should seek to determine if contemporary feminist attitudes toward sexual images of women in ads evokes a similar pattern of responses. Historically, the feminist movements have three significant 'waves': first-wave feminism between the nineteenth and early twentieth centuries, second-wave feminism in the mid-twen-tieth century, and third-wave feminism ranging from the late twentieth century today (see Humm 1995; Freedman 2003). While first-wave feminism mainly focused on women's equal property and voting rights, second-wave feminism extended the equality issue to sexuality, family, work, among other things (see Freedman 2003). Regarding sexuality, second-wave feminists emphasized the notion of women as vic-tims of a male-dominant society (Paglia 1992; Krolokke and Sorensen 2005). Adher-ents were vocal against stereotypical femininity and sexual practices, and criticized the depiction of women's sexuality in media as 'sexist pop culture' and 'instruments of oppression' (Arrow 2007; Baumgardner and Richards 2010; Williams and Jovanovic 2015).

Contemporary feminism, referred to as 'third-wave feminism', embraces women's sexuality (see Gill and Arthurs 2006; Krolokke and Sorensen 2005; Zimmerman and Dahlberg 2008; Holt and Cameron 2010). While second-wave feminism treated women's sexual desire and pleasure as 'unfeminist', third-wave feminists advocate desire and plea-sure as a natural part of femininity (Williams and Jovanovic 2015). In this sense, third-wave feminism is more open and positive toward women's sexuality and sexual practices because women use sexual self-efficacy to communicate their sexual needs and indepen-dence (Curtin et al. 2011). Namely, third-wave feminism reflects sexuality as a means of female empowerment (Gill and Arthurs 2006; Holt and Cameron 2010), and empowered sexuality contributes to female sexual liberation while rejecting conventional norms of sexuality (Zimmerman and Dahlberg 2008; Williams and Jovanovic 2015). Indeed, Bay-Cheng and Zucker (2007) found that feminists showed more positive and affective atti-tudes toward sexual stimuli, were more sexually assertive, and reported higher levels of sexual satisfaction than non-feminists.

Considering third-wave feminism's positive standpoint toward sexuality and sexual liberation, this study posits that consumers' feminist attitudes will positively influence their evaluations to advertisements depicting sexual images of women. Several researchers have argued that within the third-wave feminism context, ads that represent women sexually could be a 'girlish offense' against men who try to regain their power as the dominant sex (Paglia 1992; Labi 1998; Zimmerman and Dahlberg 2008). Indeed, according to previous studies, sexually liberal consumers tend to evaluate ads with high sexual content more positively than their counterparts (Mittal and Lassar 2000), and women with liberal sexual attitudes showed a preference for a sexual ad vs. a non-sexual ad (Sengupta and Dahl 2008). Furthermore, a replication study by Zimmerman and Dahlberg (2008) reported that female college students viewing objectifying ads with women saw the ads as sexually objectifying, but their attitudes of the ads were significantly more positive than in the original study published almost 20 years earlier (Ford, LaTour, and Lundstrom 1991). The researchers further argued that the positive perception of sexuality represented by third-wave feminism might have cultivated others in society, such as older and male consumers (also see Ryan and David 2003). Indeed, since the beginning of third-wave feminism, Americans' values and attitudes toward non-conventional sexual relationships (e.g., premarital sex, gay or lesbian relations, and having a child outside of marriage) have been increasingly favorable regardless of age (Rudman and Fairchild 2007; Rudman and Phelan 2007; Wilke and Saad 2013). Overall, there is evidence to suggest that evaluations of sexually explicit ads featuring images of women are not as harshly evaluated as in the past.

Hypotheses and research question

In consideration of the literature described thus far, the following hypotheses and research questions are proposed.

H1: Consumers' feminist attitudes will moderate the effects of advertising that contains sexual images of women.

H1a: Consumers having higher feminist attitudes will show more favorable ethical judgment toward the advertisements depicting sexual images of women than consumers having lower feminist attitudes.

H1b: Consumers having higher feminist attitudes will show more favorable ad-related evaluations toward advertisements depicting sexual images of women than consumers having lower feminist attitudes.

H2: Consumers' feminist attitudes will predict the effects of advertising that contains sexual images of women. Specifically when consumers process the advertisements depicting such images:

H2a: Consumers' feminist attitudes will positively predict their ethical judgment.

H2b: Consumers' ethical judgment will positively predict their attitude toward ad and brand interest (ad-related evaluations) in turn.

H2c: Consumers' ethical judgment will mediate the relationship between their feminist attitudes and attitude towards ad.

R1: Does gender difference moderate the predictive relationship between feminist attitudes and ethical judgment, and between ethical judgment and attitude toward the ad?

Considering recent wave of feminism's perspective on sexuality, the first hypothesis (H1) posits the moderating role of feminist attitudes. Although previous studies provide findings that lead to inferences, the studies either did not examine the moderating role of

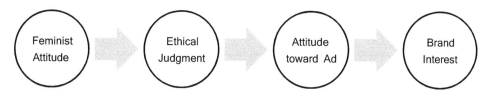

Figure 1.   Prediction model of feminist attitude to ad evaluations.

feminist attitudes directly (Mittal and Lassar 2000; Sengupta and Dahl 2008) or tested a limited sample (e.g., female student sample in Zimmerman and Dahlberg 2008). Therefore, H1 will provide evidence that will validate the impact of feminist attitudes on sexual ad evaluations.

The second hypothesis (H2) tests the predicting role of feminist attitude on consumers' ethical judgment and ad-related evaluations. In addition to the predictive relationship between the ethical judgment and sexual ad evaluations, which has been established in previous studies (Henthorne and LaTour 1995; Reichert, Latour, and Ford 2011; also see Machleit, Allen, and Madden 1993), this study postulates that feminist attitudes operate as an antecedent variable. Taking into account that consumers' ethical judgment is influenced by various cultural, communal, and educational institutions manifested by society (Reichert, Latour, and Ford 2011), their feminist attitudes will become a cultural, educational, or ideological parameter which influences ethical judgment and ad responses in turn (see Messer-Davidow 2002; Zimmerman and Dahlberg 2008). Thus, this study tests a prediction model assessing advertising effects in consideration of feminist attitude, ethical judgment, attitude toward ad, and brand interest (see Figure 1).

In addition to the proposed hypotheses, this study poses a research question to test whether the effects of feminist attitude interact with and are moderated by gender difference, which is known as a primary factor influencing sexual advertising effects (see LaTour 1990; Reichert, LaTour, and Kim 2007). The answer will help reveal if the influence of feminist-supportive attitudes is consistently across gender.

Method

A 2 (higher vs. lower feminism attitude) × 2 (male vs. female respondent) experimental design was used to test the two hypotheses and one research question. In the current study, respondents viewed one of seven ad conditions (six sexual ads + one control ad). For the following analysis, the control condition was excluded from the analysis and all six sexual ad conditions were pooled together. Sample, procedure, ad stimuli, and variables are explained as follows.

Sample

A marketing research firm with expertise in online sampling and surveying administered the experiment. From the firm's national online panel, 1298 male and female respondents were solicited and received an incentive for participation. Ages within the sample ranged from 18 to 65 ($M = 35.7$, $SD = 13.02$), and full demographic information is explained in Table 1.

Table 1.   Sample's demographic characteristics.

Category	Percentage
Gender	
Male	46.3
Female	53.7
Ethnicity	
Caucasian	74.9
African-American	7.8
Hispanic	7.4
Asian	6.5
Other	3.4
Current relationship	
Married	48.30
Divorced	6.70
Widowed	1.50
Never married	31.9
Separated	1.2
Unmarried couple	10.3
Household income	
Less than $20,000	12.6
$20,000–$39,999	26.1
$40,000–$59,999	21.9
$60,000–$99,999	24.2
More than $100,000	10.5
Did not answer	4.7

Procedure

Following recruitment, respondents began the survey by answering demographic questions and completing other measures not reported here. Afterward, they were randomly assigned to view one of six advertisements for Tom Ford cologne. Working from two original Tom Ford ads originally published in 2007, a graphic artist employed Adobe Photoshop to create four additional ads to represent distinctively single-female, sexual ad stimuli to represent the range of female nudity typically present in advertising and relevant research (nudity, partially clad, and demure; LaTour 1990; Soley and Reid 1988). Particularly for the ad stimuli, Tom Ford was chosen because the brand is known for its use of sexual appeal (Wasilak 2015). Also, testing responses to an actual brand can increase the external validity of an experiment more than a fictitious brand (see Choi et al. 2013). Moreover, cologne is a value-expressive product used in related research (LaTour 1990, Shavitt 1990).

Following exposure, subjects first registered their perceptions about the degree of sexual content to the ad stimulus (manipulation check). Then, the subjects were asked to complete items for ethical judgment, attitudinal measures about the ad and brand, as well as for feminist attitude. Preceding this, analysis of the main study consisted of two parts. First, the pooled data were analyzed to test the mean differences of attitudes between consumers having high and low feminist attitude (testing H1). Second, the prediction model of feminist attitude in Figure 1 was tested using structural equation modeling (SEM).

Variables

Perceived sexual content

For the manipulation check, respondents indicated their perceptions of the ads' sexual content with one item: 'This ad contained sexual content' on a five-point scale (1 = strongly disagree, 5 = strongly agree; from Reichert, Heckler, and Jackson 2001).

Ethical judgment

To measure ethical judgment, respondents were asked to evaluate the ad on six items of Moral Equity/Relativism (just, fair, traditionally acceptable, culturally acceptable, morally right, acceptable to my family; $\alpha = .91$), derived from the Reidenbach–Robin inventory, using a seven-point scale ranging from 1 = extremely to 7 = not at all (LaTour and Henthorne 1994). All items were re-coded so that higher numbers represent more favorable ethical judgment of the ad.

Attitude toward ad

Attitude toward ad was measured using five bipolar seven-point question items (good/ bad, like/dislike, favorable/unfavorable, interesting/uninteresting, appealing/unappealing; Muehling and McCann 1993; $\alpha = .96$). Although means for ad attitude varied from 3.73 to 5.08 (see Table 2), means were near the midpoint of this seven-point scale.

Brand interest

Brand interest was measured with four items on a five-point scale (1 = strongly disagree, 7 = strongly agree) that indicated interest in the advertised brand (e.g., 'I want to know more about the advertised brand'; $\alpha = .90$; Machleit, Allen, and Madden 1993).

Feminist attitude

Developed by Fassinger (1994), 'the Attitudes toward Feminism and the Women's Movement (FWM)' scale was used to measure individuals' feminist attitude. This measurement assesses individuals' cultured or educated attitudes about women's roles and rights in society, so it can measure a range of individuals' feminist position and attitudes (Fassinger 1994). Overall, people who support feminist ideals (e.g., equal pay and career opportunities) score high on the scale whereas those who score low are less supportive of feminism and the movement for equality. The measure has been frequently used in

Table 2. Mean differences.

		N	Ethical judgment	Attitude toward ad	Brand interest
High feminist attitude	Male	196	4.66 (1.26)	5.08 (1.88)	3.49 (1.16)
	Female	303	3.91 (1.30)	4.14 (1.86)	3.16 (1.23)
Low feminist attitude	Male	243	4.20 (1.28)	4.87 (1.78)	3.26 (1.11)
	Female	220	3.67 (1.23)	3.73 (1.83)	2.84 (1.17)

Note: Higher scores are indicative of higher/more positive attitude toward the dependent variables.

feminism studies in psychology for a long time (Fischer et al. 2000; Zucker and Stewart 2007; Bettencourt, Vacha-Haase, and Byrne 2011; Yoder, Tobias, and Snell 2011), because it accurately measures individuals' pro-feminist attitudes over a range of age and feminism positions, with brief and straight-forward assessment (Fassinger 1994; Bettencourt, Vacha-Haase, and Byrne 2011). Although notions of feminism may change over time, since the measurement assesses respondents' subjective feelings toward feminism in general, the questionnaire is consciously non-specific to political or philosophical feminist trends (Fassinger 1994, 391; also see Anastosopoulos and Desmarais 2015).

The FWM was measured using 10 items anchored on five-point scales ranging from 1 (strongly disagree) to 5 (strongly agree) (see Fassinger 1994). Some of these 10 items were reverse-coded so higher numbers represent more favorable attitudes toward women's roles and rights in society ($\alpha = .83$). The mean of FWM among respondents was 3.31 ($SD = .68$). The FWM was not correlated with respondent age ($r = -.01, p > .05$)

Covariates

Since Tom Ford is a real brand targeting specific consumer groups, respondents' different age and brand familiarity could affect the results of this experiment. Thus, they were added as covariates to control out and observe their potential external influences. To measure the brand familiarity, respondents were asked to evaluate how strongly they agree the question item 'I am familiar with this brand' (1 = strongly disagree, 5 = strongly agree; Machleit, Allen, and Madden 1993).

Results

Hypothesis 1 testing

Manipulation check

Analyses using respondents' perceived sexual content on ad stimuli revealed that respondents perceived all ad stimuli as having sexual content. According to One-Sample *T*-tests, the manipulation check was successful because demure, partially clad, and nude conditions were all significantly higher than the mid-point value 'Neither Agree Nor Disagree (3)' ($M_{demure} = 3.48$ (1.24), $t(431) = 8.13, p < .001$; $M_{partially\ clad} = 3.84$ (1.17), $t(432) = 14.99, p < .001$; $M_{nude} = 4.19$ (1.00), $t(432) = 24.82, p < .001$). Additionally, respondents differently perceived the sexual content between the ad conditions ($F (2, 1295) = 41.71, p < .001$), but there were no significant main effects on attitude toward ad ($F (2, 1295) = 1.77, p > .05$) and brand interest ($F (2, 1295) = .01, p > .05$). Thus, the researchers pooled across all ad conditions as planned.

High and low feminist groups

After the manipulation check, samples were divided into respondents having high feminist attitude and low feminist attitude. Among 1298 respondents, those in the upper 33% of FWM distribution were categorized into high feminist attitude group ($N = 499$), while those in lower 33% distribution were categorized into low feminist attitude group ($N = 463$). The mean value of FWM was significantly different between the two groups ($M_{high} = 3.98$ vs. $M_{low} = 2.63$, $t(960) = 52.19, p < .001$), and each group's mean value was significantly higher or lower than the median point '3' (for high feminist group: $t (498) = 18.63, p < .001$; for low feminist group: $t(462) = 18.63, p < .001$). The FWM scale and gender were significantly correlated ($r = .16, p < .001$), so female respondents tended to have higher feminist attitude. Additionally, perceived sexual content on pooled ad stimuli between high and low feminist groups was not significantly different ($F (1, 960) = 1.79, p > .05$), nor was respondent age ($M_{high} = 36.49$ vs. $M_{low} = 36.11, F (1, 960) = .20, p > .05$).

MANCOVA results

Using the described data, two-way multivariate analysis of covariance (MANCOVA) was used to address the first hypothesis. The assumption tests for MANCOVA reported that (1) Box's M test conforms the equality of covariance matrices (Box's $M = 23.53, F = 1.30, p > .05$); (2) Levene's test for each dependent variable satisfied the equality of error variances across groups ($p > .05$); and (3) skewness and kurtosis of each variable satisfied the assumption of normality (less than ± 1.96; see George and Mallery 2010). Thus, respondents' gender and feminist attitude were compared on their ethical judgment, attitude toward ad, and brand interest.

As shown in Tables 2 and 3, analysis of the data found significant main effects of gender and feminist attitude on all the dependent variables (see Table 3). Whereas male respondents evaluated ethical judgment, attitude toward ad, and brand interest more favorably than female respondents, the high feminist group evaluated these dependent variables more favorably than low feminist group (see Table 2). These mean differences were statistically significant ($p < .01$). According to *post hoc* tests, for female respondents, the high feminist attitude group showed significantly more favorable ethical judgment, $F (1, 519) = 5.83, p < .05$, attitude toward ad, $F (1, 519) = 7.14, p < .01$, and

Table 3. The results of MANCOVA and univariate F-values.

Multivariate statistics:	Pillai's trace	F-values
Main and interaction effects		
Feminist attitude	0.20	6.36***
Gender	0.78	26.81***
Feminist attitude × gender	0.03	0.95
Covariate/blocking variable		
Age	0.06	2.07
Brand familiarity	0.46	15.49***

		F-values	
Univariate statistics:	Ethical judgment	Attitude toward ad	Brand interest
Main and interaction effects			
Feminist attitude	14.17***	7.26**	13.87***
Gender	57.62***	66.94***	24.02***
Feminist attitude × gender	0.27	0.92	0.33
Covariate/blocking variable			
Age	0.75	0.56	1.11
Brand familiarity	45.90***	22.45***	13.70***

Note: MANCOA df = 3/954, Univariate df = 1/1294.
**$p < .01$, ***$p < .001$.

brand interest, $F (1, 519) = 9.62, p < .01$, than the low feminist attitude group. Consistently, for male respondents, the high feminist attitude group showed significantly more favorable ethical judgment, $F (1, 435) = 8.55, p < .01$, and brand interest, $F (1, 435) = 4.75, p < .05$, than the low feminist attitude group. Attitude toward ad was not statistically significant ($F (1, 435) = 1.38, p > .05$). Thus, the first hypothesis, including H1a and H1b, was generally supported. However, the interaction effect between gender and feminist attitude was not significant across all dependent variables ($p > .05$).

Additionally, as shown in Table 3, brand familiarity was a significant covariate for the dependent variables (for ethical judgment: $\eta^2 = .046$; for attitude toward ad: $\eta^2 = .023$; for brand interest: $\eta^2 = .014$). When the relations were observed in detail, brand familiarity is significantly and positively related to the dependent variables (for ethical judgment: $r = .22, p < .001$; for attitude toward ad: $r = .17, p < .001$; for brand interest: $r = .17, p < .001$). However, age was not a significant covariate for the dependent variables ($p > .05$).

Hypothesis 2 and research question 2 testing

To test the second hypothesis and first research question, SEM analysis was conducted to determine the overall relationship structure of the four latent variables (i.e., FWM, ethical judgment, attitude toward ad, and brand interest). For the analysis, we used the original pooled data before separating high and low feminist attitude respondents. Following the two-step approach of Anderson and Gerbing (1988), a confirmatory factor analysis (CFA) of the measurement model was first conducted, and then the structural model was estimated (see Close et al. 2006, 426). In addition, bootstrap analyses were conducted to investigate the mediating relationships in the model.

Assumption check

Prior to the main SEM analysis, several underlying assumptions were checked: sampling adequacy, no extreme multicollinearity, and normality (Hair et al. 1998). The sample size ($N = 1298$) satisfied sampling adequacy (Hoelter 1983). Since extracted communalities were $-.805$ to $.844$ across all our measurement items, there was no extreme multicollinearity among the measurement items. The normality assumption was satisfied because all skewness and kurtosis values associated with each item were within the range of ± 1.96 ($-.805 <$ all skewness values $< -.095$; $-1.184 <$ all kurtosis values $< -.085$).

Measurement model

As mentioned above, before fitting our proposed model, we performed a CFA using the AMOS 22.0 program. We first assessed our CFA with several goodness-of-fit measures, such as chi-square, root-mean-square-error of approximation (RMSEA), Tucker–Lewis index (TLI), goodness-of-fit-index (GFI), adjusted goodness-of-fit-index (AGFI), normed fit index (NFI), standardized root mean square residual (SRMR), and comparative fit index (CFI) (see Hu and Bentler 1995; Kline 2005).

Our four latent variables were included in the measurement model. After inspecting factor loadings of each observed variable to its proposed latent variables, we took out problematic items in the process of CFA (Hair et al. 1998). Overall, six items for ethical judgment, six items for feminist attitude, four items for attitude toward ad, and three items

Table 4. Measurement items and factor loadings.

Constructs	Measurement items	Factor loadings
Ethical judgment ($\alpha = .92$)	(1) Generally, I believe the ad I just saw to be fair	.85
	(2) Generally, I believe the ad I just saw to be culturally acceptable	.71
	(3) Generally, I believe the ad I just saw to be morally right	.86
	(4) Generally, I believe the ad I just saw to be acceptable to my family	.80
	(5) Generally, I believe the ad I just saw to be just	.83
	(6) Generally, I believe the ad I just saw to be traditionally acceptable	.77
Feminist attitude ($\alpha = .81$)	(1) The leaders of the women's movement may be extreme, but they have the right idea	.42
	(2) More people would favor the women's movement if they knew more about it.	.48
	(3) The women's movement has positively influenced relationships between men and women	.44
	(4) The women's movement has made important gains in equal rights and political power for women	.42
	(5) Feminist principles should be adopted everywhere	.42
	(6) I am overjoyed that women's liberation is finally happening in this country	.59
Attitude toward Ad ($\alpha = .97$)	(1) Please rate your feelings toward the advertisement you just saw good/bad	.94
	(2) Please rate your feelings toward the advertisement you just saw like/dislike	.96
	(3) Please rate your feelings toward the advertisement you just saw favorable/unfavorable	.95
	(4) Please rate your feelings toward the advertisement you just saw appealing/unappealing	.92
Brand interest ($\alpha = .90$)	(1) Are you intrigued by the advertised brand	.89
	(2) Would you like to know more about the advertised brand	.84
	(3) Are you little curious about the brand	.88

for brand interest were employed (see Table 4). The final measurement model showed good fit, with x^2 (146) = 480.44 ($p < .001$), TLI = .98, GFI = .96, AGFI = .95, NFI = .97, CFI = .98, RMSEA = .042, SRMR = .024.

Reliability and validity

Following the verification of overall model fit, convergent and discriminant validities of the latent variables were examined. First, as indicated in Table 3, all the question items significantly ($p < .001$) loaded to the intended factors within an acceptable range (from .42 to .96), indicating good convergent validity (see Sujan, Weitz, and Kumar 1994). Second, examination of correlations in Table 5 showed that all measures had higher correlation with the items of the corresponding latent variable than with items of the other latent variables, demonstrating discriminant validity (Fornell and Larcker 1981). Plus, regarding

Table 5. Correlation matrix of measurement items.

	EJ1	EJ2	EJ3	EJ4	EJ5	EJ6	Aad4	BI1	Aad1	BI3	BI2	Aad3	Aad2	AFSM6	AFSM5	AFSM4	AFSM3	AFSM2	AFSM1
EJ1	1.000																		
EJ2	.442	1.000																	
EJ3	.427	.459	1.000																
EJ4	.416	.448	.432	1.000															
EJ5	.415	.446	.431	.420	1.000														
EJ6	.493	.530	.512	.499	.498	1.000													
Aad4	.059	.063	.061	.059	.059	.070	1.000												
BI1	.043	.046	.045	.044	.043	.052	.616	1.000											
Aad1	.060	.065	.063	.061	.061	.072	.866	.634	1.000										
BI3	.042	.046	.044	.043	.043	.051	.609	.780	.626	1.000									
BI2	.041	.044	.042	.041	.041	.049	.585	.749	.602	.740	1.000								
Aad3	.061	.065	.063	.062	.061	.073	.872	.639	.897	.631	.606	1.000							
Aad2	.061	.066	.064	.062	.062	.074	.879	.644	.904	.636	.611	.911	1.000						
AFSM6	.069	.075	.072	.070	.070	.083	.476	.348	.490	.344	.331	.493	.497	1.000					
AFSM5	.077	.083	.080	.078	.078	.093	.532	.390	.547	.385	.370	.551	.556	.628	1.000				
AFSM4	.072	.078	.075	.073	.073	.087	.495	.363	.509	.358	.344	.513	.517	.585	.654	1.000			
AFSM3	.079	.085	.082	.080	.080	.095	.541	.396	.557	.392	.376	.561	.566	.639	.715	.665	1.000		
AFSM2	.064	.069	.066	.065	.064	.076	.438	.321	.450	.317	.304	.454	.457	.517	.578	.538	.588	1.000	
AFSM1	.080	.086	.083	.081	.080	.096	.547	.401	.563	.396	.380	.567	.572	.646	.723	.673	.736	.595	1.000

Note: EJ = ethical judgment, BI = brand interest, Aad = attitude toward ad, AFSM = feminist attitude.

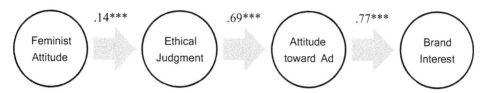

Figure 2.   Overall relationship of the prediction model.

internal reliability, results indicated that all the scales were considered to be reliable Cronbach's alpha value (see Table 4).

Hypothesis 2 and research question 1 testing

After all model and measurement verification procedures, we estimated our proposed model by performing SEM analysis. To test H2 and RQ1, each structural path coefficient was examined with fit indices of the proposed model in Figure 1. Overall, the fit indices showed a good fit for the model x^2 (149) = 542.11 ($p < .001$), TLI = .98, GFI = .96; AGFI = .94; NFI = .97; CFI = .98; SRMR = .0373; RMSEA = .045).

As shown in Figure 2, each of the path coefficients was statistically significant in the predicted direction ($p < .001$). Feminist attitude was found to have positive impact on ethical judgment (coefficient = .14, $p < .001$), while ethical judgment positively predicted attitude toward ad (coefficient = .69, $p < .001$). Attitude toward the ad also positively predicted brand interest (coefficient = .77, $p < .001$).

The mediating role of ethical judgment between feminist attitude and attitude toward the ad was also tested. First, without ethical judgment, Attitudes toward FSM significantly influenced Aad (coefficient = .09, $p < .01$). However, when ethical judgment was included in the model, the relationship between feminist attitudes and attitude toward the ad disappeared, confirming full mediation of ethical judgment (coefficient = .00, $p > .10$). This mediation role was also confirmed by a bootstrap analysis. The results indicated that the indirect effect did not include 0 (.0492 to .2655) within the 95% confidence interval (see Zhao, Lynch, and Chen 2010 for detail). Thus, the second hypothesis including H2a, H2b, and H2c was fully supported.

Additionally, for the first research question asking about the moderating role of gender in the prediction model, the results of the moderation test revealed that gender did not moderate both the relationships between feminist attitude and ethical judgment ($x^2 = 1.255$, df = 1, $p > .10$) and between ethical judgment and attitude toward ad ($x^2 = .476$, df = 1, $p > .10$).

Discussion

The purpose of this study is to examine how recent feminist attitudes moderate and predict consumers' ethical judgment and ad-related evaluations of sexually explicit images of women in advertisements. In addition, this study explores whether respondents' biological gender influences the effects of feminist attitude on ethical judgment and ad-related evaluations. To test these hypotheses and research question, MANCOVA and SEM analysis were employed to deeply examine diverse respondents' ad responses.

Overall, the proposed hypotheses were supported. Respondents' feminist attitudes significantly moderated the effects of sexual imagery. That is, respondents having higher feminist attitude showed more favorable ethical judgment and ad-related evaluations of sexually explicit advertisements containing images of women than respondents with less supportive feminist attitudes. Moreover, when respondents process the ad, their feminist attitudes positively predict their ad-related evaluations, whereas respondents' ethical judgment serves as an important mediator between their feminist attitudes and ad-related evaluations. Regarding the research questions pertaining to the influence of biological gender, there was a main effect on the dependent variables but it did not significantly moderate the predictive effects of feminist attitude and ethical judgment. These findings provide the following important theoretical and practical implications.

Theoretical implications

As for theoretical implications, first, this study found that feminist attitudes positively moderate the effects of female nudity on ethical judgment and ad-related evaluations. This result may be somewhat surprising since previous studies before the early 2000s indicated the negative relationship between consumers' feminist attitude and the sexual depiction of women in advertising (Ford and LaTour 1993; Mackay and Covell 1997; Lavine, Sweeney, and Wagner 1999). However, considering recent studies explaining the positive relationship between the third-wave feminism and sexuality (see Curtin et al. 2011; Rudman and Fairchild 2007; Rudman and Phelan 2007), the results of this study reflect current social attitudes. Because third-wave feminism positively perceives women's sexuality as a tool to empower femininity (Gill and Arthurs 2006; Zimmerman and Dahlberg 2008), sexual images of women in advertising may be more positively evaluated as consumers have more feminist supportive attitudes. Moreover, compared to the anticipation of Zimmerman and Dahlberg (2008) that third-wave feminism would cultivate a wide range of consumers to evaluate sexualized females in advertising more positively, this study provides empirical evidence via a large national sample of the positive function of feminist attitudes. The cultivation explanation is supported by this study in that the degree of feminist attitudes was not related to age of respondent.

Furthermore, this study also found that the ethical judgment of the high feminist attitude group was more positive than that of low feminist attitude group. Also, ethical judgment fully mediated the predictive relationship between feminist attitude and ad-related evaluations. Taking into account that feminism is an ideology influencing people's judgments and attitudes (Messer-Davidow 2002; Zimmerman and Dahlberg 2008), these results suggest that consumers' feminist attitudes may be one of the important factors influencing ethical judgment, and subsequently enhanced the evaluations of sexually explicit ads. Traditionally, the construct of ethical judgment has been used as a dependent or predicting variable to assess consumers' responses to sexual content in advertising (LaTour and Henthorne 1994; Henthorne and LaTour 1995). In the current study, however, the relationship between feminist attitude and ad-related evaluations can be fully explained by consumers' ethical judgments about the female sexual image. This is a new theoretical contribution to the literature of sex in advertising. Although previous studies emphasized the influences of various psychological attitudes, such as sexual liberation (Mittal and Lassar 2000; Sengupta and Dahl 2008), sexual self-schema (Reichert, Latour, and Ford 2011), and sensation seeking (Chang and Tseng 2013), research has not examined how the influences are explained and by what mechanism the influences function within the consumer. In that sense, the result of this study suggests that individuals' psychological attitude (feminist attitude) influences their ethical judgment, which then influences ad evaluation and related responses. In other words, as respondents have more positive attitudes toward feminism, their ethical judgment about the ad increases, and it predicts higher attitude toward ad and brand interest in sequence. Conversely, as respondents have less positive attitudes toward feminism, their ethical judgment about the ad is relatively less influential, and it sequentially predicts lower attitude toward ad and brand interest.

In addition, the current study found that biological gender difference produced significant main effects, which moderate the effects of sexual advertising on ethical judgment and ad-related evaluations. However, gender did not produce significant interaction effects with feminist attitudes. Regarding the prediction model of this study, none of the predictive paths were moderated by gender: The predictive path from feminist attitude to ethical judgment, or the path from ethical judgment to attitude toward the ad. Overall, these results can be interpreted such that gender is still a primary factor moderating the effects of sexual advertising on dependent variables, but it does not appear to influence the effect of feminist attitude. In other words, sexually explicit advertisements of females are evaluated by male viewers more favorably than female viewers, as previous studies (LaTour 1990; Reichert, LaTour, and Kim 2007) indicate. Regardless of respondent gender, however, consumers with more positive feminist attitudes are more likely to favorably evaluate ads with sexual images of females. Similar to other psychological attitudes that influence the ad evaluations of sexual advertising, such as sexual self-schema (Reichert, LaTour, and Kim 2007) and sensation seeking (Chang and Tseng 2013), this study provides another important psychological attitude that can be used to moderate and predict the ethical judgment, attitude toward ad, and brand interest on sexual advertising.

It should be noted, however, that feminism is a multi-faceted concept with adherents holding a range of views about female sexuality and representation. For this reason, expected reactions to sexual content cannot be overly simplified to be uniformly positive (see Williams and Wittig 1997; Liss et al. 2001). In this study, only sexual images of women were tested. If the advertisements used another stereotypical depiction of females, such as women in a primarily decorative and subservient role (Ford and LaTour 1993; Dahl, Sengupta, and Vohs 2009), the results may have been quite different. Therefore, a distinction needs be drawn between sexual and decorative content in advertising. Whereas ads can contain both types of content, ads that are blatantly decorative and sexual are likely to evoke negative reactions from pro-feminists, while ads that are sexual can evoke a more positive range of responses. In a related sense, pro-feminists value free expression so they should be more accepting of provocative ad content than non-feminists (see Liss et al. 2001). Moreover, pro-feminists are more progressive and liberal-minded than non-feminists (Liss et al. 2001; Williams and Wittig 1997), so pro-feminists should show more favorable reactions to diverse sexual stimuli (Bay-Cheng and Zucker 2007). In sum, we interpret the positive relationship between feminist attitudes and ethical judgment to be the result of consumers having more positive attitudes toward feminism and women's movement. Also, feminists are now more likely to accept sexual ads, which positively affects consumers' ad-related evaluations, and vice versa. Indeed, taking into account that two important determinants categorizing feminist are 'not conservative' and 'liberal' (Liss et al. 2001), the interpretation makes sense.

Practical implications

Based on the theoretical implications, several implications are also extended to advertising practitioners. First of all, the results of this study provide new information about the use of female sexuality in advertising. Based on past research, advice has been to avoid targeting women or feminists with images of sexual images of women (LaTour 1990; Ford and LaTour 1993). The findings of this study suggest that female sexuality in advertising can result in positive effects for marketers to those consumer groups.

For example, intimate wear marketer Victoria's Secret has achieved much success with sexualized promotional messages targeted to a broad cross-section of women. The results of this study suggest that women with feminist supportive attitudes are more likely to consider Victoria's Secret's ads as ethical – and thus more likeable – than women with non-feminist supportive attitudes. The same may be true for fragrance and apparel marketers. Overall, conclusions from the present research support the approach taken by Victoria's Secret and these other marketers to use sexual imagery to appeal to women – though research would need to verify – have feminist supportive attitudes. However, as previous studies have indicated, practitioners should be careful when depicting women's sexuality in advertising. Since sexual liberation and women's rights are closely related under the third-wave of feminism (Bay-Cheng and Zucker 2007; Curtin et al. 2011), to be more inclusive sexual depictions of women in advertising should encourage sexual independence and equality while avoiding submissive poses and nuances (also see Dahl, Sengupta, and Vohs 2009).

In a related sense, a practical reason for studying the effects of individual differences on responses to sexual appeals is to determine appropriate target audiences and ad placements (Reichert, LaTour, and Kim 2007; Chang and Tseng 2013). As consumers have more favorable ethical judgments about sexual appeals, their attention and emotional arousal can lead to better advertising responses (see LaTour and Henthorne 1994; Reichert, LaTour, and Kim 2007).

Within this context, this study provides another key determinant that can anticipate the result of sexual appeal in advertising. Since consumers have diverse psychological propensities, the challenge for advertising practitioners is to have the accurate information about the audience's psychological segmentation relevant to sexual appeal. For this purpose, this study found individuals' feminist attitude as a key determinant that can be used in segmenting audience groups and pre-testing to anticipate the possible results. Advertisers are encouraged to include the feminist attitude items included in this study when they test the usage patterns and psychographic profile of their primary consumers.

Additionally, measurement of feminist attitudes is less obtrusive than other personality variables. Reichert and his colleagues (2007) indicated that some questionnaires assessing consumers' sex-related personality, such as sex guilt (Smith et al. 1995) and erotophobia/philia (Helweg-Larsen and Howell 2000), contain explicit question items that can offend respondents or reveal the purpose of the questions which can lead to social desirability bias. The items in the attitudes toward feminism scale are not related to respondents' sexual life style and behavior, so they are much less obtrusive and are less likely to sensitize respondents.

Limitations and suggestions for future research

As with any investigation, this study has several limitations that should be noted. First, this study only manipulated visual sexuality of female in ad stimuli, not sexual innuendo or verbal exchanges. Thus, future research should test a variety of stimuli to gain more generalizable external validity. In the same way, replication studies should also consider employing other indicators of feminism. Although this study employed Fassinger's FWM scale because of its use in other contexts and brevity, there are other scales that assess individuals' feminist attitude, such as the Feminist Identity Development Scale (Bargad and Hyde 1991) and the Feminist Identity Scale (Rickard 1989). In future research it would be worthwhile to examine whether the results are consistent across these different feminist measurements, and to determine which one has an advantage related to predictable measurement of sexual ad evaluations.

Second, only gender difference and feminist attitude were examined as influencing factors in this study. Considering that other individual propensities can influence the effects of sexual appeals in advertising (see Reichert, Latour, and Ford 2011; Chang and Tseng 2013), and feminism and sexual liberation are closely related (Mittal and Lassar 2000; Bay-Cheng and Zucker 2007; Curtin et al. 2011), future studies should compare these variables together in a prediction model of sexual advertising. In doing so, it would be able to figure out which variable is more or less important variable to predict the effect of sexual advertising. Moreover, future research also needs to explore other individual propensities which can possibly influence sexual ad responses. For example, religious commitment (Michell and Al-Mossawi 1999; Taylor, Halstead, and Haynes 2010) or sexual conservatism (Cui et al. 2012) can be potential variables to predict consumers' ethical judgment on sexual advertising.

Third, this study examines only one product category (fragrance), so the findings could differ depending to product categories. For example, Chang and Tseng (see also Putrevu 2008) reported that the effects of implicit and explicit sex appeals are different by sexually relevant or irrelevant product categories. Thus, future research needs to consider employing more product categories.

In sum, the present research provides new theoretical and practical insights into the role of feminist attitudes on evaluation and reaction to sexual ads containing images of women. The study also illuminates the path of the role of feminist-supportive attitudes on ethical judgments that ultimately influence attitudes and evaluations about the ad and brand. Alternately, findings confirm that while the mechanism may be steadfast, reactions to images in advertising – as with any major media (e.g., film, programming, online video) – are influenced by cultural norms and social shifts in opinion and attitudes. As demonstrated in the current study, viewers with feminist-supportive attitudes are more accepting of sexualized images of women than in the recent past. It is hoped that this study provides a new dimension for analyzing the effects of sexual ad content and demonstrates that culturally relevant findings in published research need to be updated to ensure generalizations are accurate.

Acknowledgements
This article is dedicated to our co-author Michael S. LaTour, who passed away in 2015. He was a prolific scholar, always energized by ideas and advancing knowledge, and a first-rate collaborator. We miss his enthusiasm, his insights, and keen sense of humor.

Disclosure statement
No potential conflict of interest was reported by the authors.

References
Alexander, M.W., and B. Judd Jr. 1986. Differences in attitudes toward nudity in advertising. *Psychology* 23 (January): 27–9.
Anastosopoulos, V., and S. Desmarais. 2015. By name or by deed? Identifying the source of the feminist stigma. *Journal of Applied Social Psychology* 45, no. 4: 226–42.

Anderson, J.C., and D.W. Gerbing. 1988. Structural equation modeling in practice: A review and recommended two-step approach. *Psychological Bulletin* 10: 411–23.

Aronson, E. 2003. *The social animal.* New York, NY: Worth Publishers.

Arrow, M. 2007. 'It has become my personal anthem' 'I am woman', Popular culture and 1970s feminism*. *Australian Feminist Studies* 22, no. 53: 213–30.

Bargad, A., and J.S. Hyde. 1991. A study of feminist identity development in women. *Psychology of Women Quarterly* 15: 181–201.

Baumgardner, J., and A. Richards. 2010. *Manisfesta: Young women, feminism, and the future.* New York, NY: Farrar, Straus, and Giroux.

Bay–Cheng, L.Y., and A.N. Zucker. 2007. Feminism between the sheets: Sexual attitudes among feminists, nonfeminists, and egalitarians. *Psychology of Women Quarterly* 31, no. 2: 157–63.

Beasley, C. 1999. *What is feminism? An introduction to feminist theory.* London: Sage.

Belch, G.E., M.A. Belch, and A. Villarreal. 1987. Effects of advertising communications: Review of research. *Research in Marketing* 9: 59–117.

Bettencourt, K.E.F., T. Vacha-Haase, and Z.S. Byrne. 2011. Older and younger adults' attitudes toward feminism: The influence of religiosity, political orientation, gender, education, and family. *Sex Roles* 64, nos. 11–12: 863–74.

Chang, C. 2006. The influence of masculinity and femininity in different advertising processing contexts: An accessibility perspective. *Sex Roles* 55, nos. 5–6: 345–56.

Chang, C.T., and C.H. Tseng. 2013. Can sex sell bread? The impacts of sexual appeal type, product type and sensation seeking. *International Journal of Advertising* 32, no. 4: 559–85.

Choi, H., K. Yoo, T.H. Baek, L.N. Reid, and W. Macias. 2013. Presence and effects of health and nutrition-related (HNR) claims with benefit-seeking and risk-avoidance appeals in female-orientated magazine food advertisements. *International Journal of Advertising* 32, no. 4: 587–616.

Close, A.G., R.Z. Finney, R.Z. Lacey, and J.Z. Sneath. 2006. Engaging the consumer through event marketing: Linking attendees with the sponsor, community, and brand. *Journal of Advertising Research* 46: 420–33.

Courtney, A.E., and T.W. Whipple. 1983. *Sex, stereotyping and advertising.* Lexington, MA: Heath.

Cui, G., X. Yang, H. Wang, and H. Liu. 2012. Culturally incongruent messages in international advertising. *International Journal of Advertising* 31, no. 2: 355–76.

Curtin, N., M. Ward, A. Merriwether, and A. Caruthers. 2011. Femininity ideology and sexual health in young women: A focus on sexual knowledge, embodiment, and agency. *International Journal of Sexual Health* 23, no. 1: 48–62.

Dahl, D.W., J. Sengupta, and K.D. Vohs. 2009. Sex in advertising: Gender differences and the role of relationship commitment. *Journal of Consumer Research* 36, no. 2: 215–31.

Davies, J.J. 2011. TV ratings and verbal and visual sexual content in promotional ads. *Journal of Promotion Management* 17: 378–95.

Fassinger, R.E. 1994. Development and testing of the attitudes toward feminism and the women's movement (FWM) scale. *Psychology of Women Quarterly* 18, no. 3: 389–402.

Feiereisen, S., A.J. Broderick, and S.P. Douglas. 2009. The effect and moderation of gender identity congruity: Utilizing "Real Women" advertising images. *Psychology & Marketing* 26, no. 9: 813–43.

Fischer, A.R., D.M. Tokar, M.M. Mergl, G.E. Good, M.S. Hill, and S.A. Blum. 2000. Assessing women's feminist identity development: Studies of convergent, discriminant, and structural validity. *Psychology of Women Quarterly* 24, no. 1: 15–29.

Ford, J.B., and M.S. LaTour. 1993. Differing reactions to female role portrayals in advertising. *Journal of Advertising Research* 33: 43–52.

Ford, J.B., M.S. LaTour, and W.J. Lundstrom. 1991. Contemporary women's evaluation of female role portrayals in advertising. *Journal of Consumer Marketing* 8, no. 1: 15–27.

Fornell, C., and D.F. Larcker. 1981. Evaluating structural equation models with unobservable variables and measurement error. *Journal of Marketing Research* 18: 39–50.

Freedman, E.B. 2003. *No turning back: The history of feminism and the future of women.* New York, NY: Ballantine Books.

George, D., and M. Mallery. 2010. *SPSS for windows step by step: A simple guide and reference 17.0 update.* 10a ed. Boston, MA: Pearson.

Gill, R., and J. Arthurs. 2006. Editors' introduction: New femininities? *Feminist Media Studies* 6, no. 4: 443–51.

Gould, S.J. 1994. Sexuality and ethics in advertising: A framework and research agenda. *Journal of Advertising* 23, no. 3: 73–80.

Grazer, W.F., and G. Keesling. 1995. The effect of print advertising's use of sexual themes on brand recall and purchase intention: A product specific investigation of male responses. *Journal of Applied Business Research* 11, no. 3: 47–58.

Hair, J., F. Joseph, R.E. Anderson, R.L. Tatham, and W.C. Black. 1998. *Multivariate data analysis.* 5th ed. Upper Saddle River, NJ: Prentice Hall.

Hall, C.C., and M.J. Crum. 1994. Women and "Body-isms" in television beer commercials. *Sex Roles* 31: 329–37.

Hawkesworth, M.E. 2006. *Globalization and feminist activism.* Lanham, MD: Rowman & Littlefield.

Helweg-Larsen, M., and C. Howell. 2000. Effects of erotophobia on the persuasiveness of condom advertisements containing strong or weak arguments. *Basic and Applied Social Psychology* 22: 111–7.

Henthorne, T.L., and M.S. LaTour. 1995. A model to explore the ethics of erotic stimuli in print advertising. *Journal of Business Ethics* 14, no. 7: 561–9.

Hoelter, J.W. 1983. The analysis of covariance structures: Goodness-of-fit indices. *Sociological Methods and Research* 11: 325–44.

Holt, D., and D. Cameron. 2010. *Cultural strategy: Using innovative ideologies to build breakthrough brands.* Oxford: Oxford University Press.

Hu, L.T., and P. Bentler. 1995. Fit indices in covariance structure modeling: Sensitivity to underparameterized model misspecification. *Psychological Methods* 3, no. 4: 424–53.

Humm, M. 1995. *The dictionary of feminist theory.* Columbus, OH: Ohio State University Press.

Kline, R.B. 2005. *Principles and practice of structural equation modeling.* 2nd ed. NewYork, NY: Guilford Publications.

Krolokke, C., and A. Sorensen. 2005. *Gender communication theories and analysis: From silence to performance.* Thousand Oaks: CA: Sage Publications.

Labi, N. 1998. Feminism: Girl Power. *Time* 151, no. 25: 60–2.

LaTour, M.S. 1990. Female nudity in print advertising: An analysis of gender differences in arousal and ad response. *Psychology and Marketing* 7 (Spring): 65–81.

LaTour, M.S., and T.L. Henthorne. 1994. Ethical judgments of sexual appeals in print advertising. *Journal of Advertising* 23, no. 3: 81–90.

Lavine, H., D. Sweeney, and S.H. Wagner. 1999. Depicting women as sex objects in television advertising: Effects on body dissatisfaction. *Personality and Social Psychology Bulletin* 25, no. 8: 1049–58.

Lin, C.A. 1998. Uses of sexual appeals in prime-time television commercials. *Sex Roles* 38 (March): 461–75.

Liss, M., C. O'Connor, E. Morosky, and M. Crawford. 2001. What makes a feminist? Predictors and correlates of feminist social identity in college women. *Psychology of Women Quarterly* 25, no. 2: 124–33.

Machleit, K.A., C. Allen, and T.J. Madden. 1993. The mature brand and brand interest: An alternative consequence of ad-evoked affect. *Journal of Marketing* 57 (October): 72–82.

Maciejewski, J.J. 2004. Is the use of sexual and fear appeals ethical? A moral evaluation by generation Y college students. *Journal of Current Issues & Research in Advertising* 26, no. 2: 97–105.

MacInnis, D.J., C. Moorman, and B.J. Jaworski. 1991. Enhancing and measuring consumers' motivation, opportunity, and ability to process brand information from ads. *Journal of Marketing* 55 (October): 32–53.

MacKay, N.J., and K. Covell. 1997. The impact of women in advertisements on attitudes toward women. *Sex Roles* 36, nos. 9–10: 573–83.

Messer-Davidow, E. 2002. *Disciplining feminism: From social activism to academic discourse.* Durham, NC: Duke University Press.

Michell, P., and M. Al-Mossawi. 1999. Religious commitment related to message contentiousness. *International Journal of Advertising* 18, no. 4: 427–43.

Mittal, B., and W.M. Lassar. 2000. Sexual liberalism as a determinant of consumer response to sex in advertising. *Journal of Business and Psychology* 15, no. 1: 111–27.

Morrison, B.J., and R.C. Sherman. 1972. Who responds to sex in advertising? *Journal of Advertising Research* 12 (March/April): 15–9.

Muehling, D., and M. McCann. 1993. Attitude toward the ad: A review. *Journal of Current Issues and Research in Advertising* 15, no. 2: 25−58.

Nelson, M., and H. Paek. 2005. Predicting cross-cultural differences in sexual advertising contents in a transnational women's magazine. *Sex Roles* 53 (September): 371−83.

Offen, K. 1988. Defining feminism: A comparative historical approach. *Signs* 14 (Autumn): 119−57.

Paglia, C. 1992. *Sex, art, and American culture*. New York, NY: Vintage Books.

Percy, L., and J.R. Rossiter. 1992. A model of brand awareness and brand attitude advertising strategies. *Psychology & Marketing* 9, no. 4: 263−74.

Pham, C.N., R.A. Ozdemir, H.H. Pham, and N. Wang. 2014. Is sex still effective in fashion clothing? Understanding the changing dynamics of heavily using sexual appeals in current fashion marketing context via abercrombie & fitch case. *Paper presented at 18th Annual Western Hemispheric Trade Conference*. Laredo, TX, April 24−25, 2014. http://freetrade.tamiu.edu/pdf/18Conference.pdf#page=309 (accessed December 21, 2015).

Putrevu, S. 2008. Consumer responses toward sexual and nonsexual appeals: The influence of involvement, need for cognition (NFC), and gender. *Journal of Advertising* 37 (Summer): 57−69.

Ramirez, A. 2006. Sexually oriented appeals on the internet: An exploratory analysis of popular mainstream websites. In *Sex in consumer culture: The erotic content of media and marketing*, ed. T. Reichert and J. Lambiase, 141−57. Mahwah, NJ: LEA.

Reichert, T. 2002. Sex in advertising research: A review of content, effects, and functions of sexual information in consumer advertising. *Annual Review of Sex Research* 13: 241−73.

Reichert, T., and C. Carpenter. 2004. An update on sex in magazine advertising, 1983 to 2003. *Journalism & Mass Communication Quarterly* 81 (Winter): 823−37.

Reichert, T., C.C. Childers, and L.N. Reid. 2012. How sex in advertising varies by product category: An analysis of three decades of visual sexual imagery in magazine advertising. *Journal of Current Issues & Research in Advertising* 33, no. 1: 1−19.

Reichert, T., S.E. Heckler, and S. Jackson. 2001. The effects of sexual social marketing appeals on cognitive processing and persuasion. *Journal of Advertising* 30 (Spring): 13−27.

Reichert, T., M.S. LaTour, and J.B. Ford. 2011. The naked truth revealing the affinity for graphic sexual appeals in advertising. *Journal of Advertising Research* 51, no. 2: 436−48.

Reichert, T., M.S. LaTour, and J. Kim. 2007. Assessing the influence of gender and sexual self-schema on affective responses to sexual content in advertising. *Current Issues and Research in Advertising* 29 (Fall): 63−77.

Reidenbach, R.E., and D.P. Robin. 1990. Toward the development of a multidimensional scale for improving evaluations of business ethics. *Journal of Business Ethics* 9: 639−53.

Rickard, K.M. 1989. The relationship of self-monitored dating behaviors to level of feminist identity on the feminist identity scale. *Sex Roles* 20, nos. 3−4: 213−26.

Rossi, S.R., and J.S. Rossi. 1985. Gender differences in the perception of women in magazine advertising. *Sex Roles* 12: 1033−9.

Rudman, L.A., and K. Fairchild. 2007. The F word: Is feminism incompatible with beauty and romance?. *Psychology of Women Quarterly* 31, no. 2: 125−36.

Rudman, L.A., and J.E. Phelan. 2007. The interpersonal power of feminism: Is feminism good for romantic relationships?. *Sex Roles* 57, nos. 11−12: 787−99.

Ryan, M.K., and B. David. 2003. Gender differences in ways of knowing: The context dependence on attitudes toward thinking and learning survey. *Sex Roles* 49, nos. 11−12: 693−9.

Sciglimpaglia, D., M.A. Belch, and R.F. Cain. 1979. Demographic and cognitive factors influencing viewers' evaluations of 'Sexy' ADVertisements. In *Advances in Consumer Research*, ed. W.L. Wilkie, Vol. 6, 62−5. Miami, FL: Association for Consumer Research.

Sengupta, J., and D.W. Dahl. 2008. Gender-related reactions to gratuitous sex appeals in advertising. *Journal of Consumer Psychology* 18, no. 1: 62−78.

Shavitt, S. 1990. The role of attitude objects in attitude functions. *Journal of Experimental Social Psychology* 26, no. 2: 124−48.

Smith, S.M., C. Haugtvedt, J. J., and M. Anton 1995. Understanding responses to sex appeals in advertising: An individual difference approach. In Advances in *consumer research*, ed. F. Kardes and M. Sujan, Vol. 22, 735−9. Ann Arbor, MI: Association for Consumer Research.

Snyder, R. 2008. What is third-wave feminism? A new directions essay. *Signs* 34 (Autumn): 175−96.

Soley, L., and L.N. Reid. 1988. Taking it off: Are models in magazine ads wearing less? *Journalism and Mass Communication Quarterly* 65 (Winter): 960–6.

Sparks, J.V., and A. Lang. 2015. Mechanisms underlying the effects of sexy and humorous content in advertisements. *Communication Monographs* 82, no. 1: 134–62.

Sujan, H., B.A. Weitz, and N. Kumar. 1994. Learning orientation, working smart, and effective selling. *Journal of Marketing* 58: 39–52.

Taylor, V.A., D. Halstead, and P.J. Haynes. 2010. Consumer responses to Christian religious symbols in advertising. *Journal of Advertising* 39, no. 2: 79–92.

Walker, J.R. 2000. Sex and violence in program promotion. In *Research in media promotion*, ed. S. T. Eastman, 101–26. Mahwah, NJ: LEA.

Wasilak, S. 2015. Is Cara Delevingne's Tom Ford ad degrading to women? *POPSUGAR*. http://www.popsugar.com/fashion/Cara-Delevingne-Tom-Ford-Ad-Banned-UK-37390105 (accessed May 29, 2015).

Wilke, J., and L. Saad. 2013. Older Americans' moral attitudes changing, *Gallup*. http://www.gallup.com/poll/162881/older-americans-moral-attitudes-changing.aspx (accessed June 3, 2015).

Williams, J.C., and J. Jovanovic. 2015. Third wave feminism and emerging adult sexuality: Friends with Benefits Relationships. *Sexuality & Culture* 19, no. 1: 157–71.

Williams, R., and M.A. Wittig. 1997. "I'm not a feminist, but…": Factors contributing to the discrepancy between pro-feminist orientation and feminist social identity. *Sex Roles* 37, nos. 11–12: 885–904.

Yoder, J.D., A. Tobias, and A.F. Snell. 2011. When declaring "I am a Feminist" matters: Labeling is linked to activism. *Sex Roles* 64, nos. 1–2: 9–18.

Zhao, X., J.G. Lynch, and Q. Chen. 2010. Reconsidering Baron and Kenny: Myths and truths about mediation analysis. *Journal of Consumer Research* 37, no. 2: 197–206.

Zimmerman, A., and J. Dahlberg. 2008. The sexual objectification of women in advertising: A contemporary cultural perspective. *Journal of Advertising Research* 48, no. 1: 71–9.

Zucker, A.N., and A.J. Stewart. 2007. Growing up and growing older: Feminism as a context for women's lives. *Psychology of Women Quarterly* 31, no. 2: 137–45.

Influence of gender stereotypes on advertising offensiveness and attitude toward advertising in general

Bruce A. Huhmann and Yam B. Limbu

Although considerable research has examined attitude toward advertising in general (AG), little is known about AG's determinants. This study investigates gender stereotype-related constructs whose relationship with AG is understudied and unclear. Structural equation modeling demonstrates that attitude toward sex/nudity in advertising predicts AG indirectly through the perceived offensiveness of advertising. Also, the more consumers believe that advertising portrays gender stereotypes, the less favorable their AG. Multi-group analyses, however, demonstrate that offensiveness harms AG for men, but not women. Also, gender-stereotype attitudes harm AG for female and younger consumers, but do not harm AG for male or older consumers. These results have important implications for advertisers in message targeting and advertisement execution strategies. Also, because unfavorable AG increases demands for governmental oversight and interference, the advertising industry should strengthen self-regulation. This self-regulation should proscribe traditional gender stereotypes and excessively erotic ads that may offend consumers, even if those consumers are outside an advertiser's target market.

Introduction

Gender stereotypes remain an important advertising research topic. A review of major advertising and marketing journals found 37 articles on this topic published between 2005 and 2015. However, this research stream has evolved since the 1970s. In prior decades, research investigated gender role accuracy and sexism, primarily in the United States (US; e.g., Courtney and Lockeretz 1971; Lundstrom and Sciglimpaglia 1977; Sciglimpaglia, Lundstrom, and Vanier 1979) or in US versus non-US samples (e.g., DeYoung and Crane 1992; Ford, LaTour, and Honeycutt 1997; Lysonski and Pollay 1990). Recent research has shifted to mostly non-US samples. Only four articles between 2005 and 2015 focused exclusively on US samples. Most focused on Europe (e.g., Knoll, Eisend, and Steinhagen 2011; Theodoridis et al. 2013; Van Hellemont and Van den Bulck 2012), Asia (e.g., Lee 2014; Liu, Cheng, and Li 2009), or non-US Anglosphere countries, such as Britain, New Zealand, or Australia (e.g., Martin and Gnoth 2009; Plakoyiannaki and Zotos 2009; Rubie-Davies, Liu, and Lee 2013). One common stereotype is the female decorative model in sex appeals (Plakoyiannaki et al. 2008). Recently, advertising sex appeal research has expanded to include men's responses toward sex/nudity, male decorative models, and consumer evaluations of sex/nudity's appropriateness in advertising (e.g., Liu, Cheng, and Li 2009; Martin and Gnoth 2009; Van Hellemont and Van den Bulck 2012).

Research has long documented the conflicting views of consumers with egalitarian values who oppose 'sexist' traditional gender stereotypes and inaccurate gender role portrayals in advertising versus consumers espousing a return to 'family values' who prefer advertising with traditional gender stereotypes (Lin 2008; Lysonski and Pollay 1990; Sciglimpaglia, Lundstrom, and Vanier 1979). Also, despite mainstream consumers' receptivity (Liu, Cheng, and Li 2009; Zimmerman and Dahlberg 2008), demographic changes (e.g., increasing numbers of Moslems in Western European and evangelical Christians in the US) have heightened sensitivity to advertising featuring liberated female/inept male portrayals and sex/nudity due to its presumed influence on society's sexual mores, especially among youth (Putrevu and Swimberghek 2013; Veloutsou and Ahmed 2005).

Additionally, new media have become a double-edged sword for advertisers. The Internet and social media allow advertisers to 'narrowcast' advertising messages and tailor them to specific audiences. However, they also allow consumers to share advertisements peer to peer. Consumers upload advertisements via many social media platforms (e.g., YouTube, Twitter, Pinterest, Instagram, Facebook, blogs, etc.). Through such peer-to-peer sharing, advertisements featuring gender portrayals appropriate for one target audience may now be viewed by consumers outside the intended audience (i.e., other countries, cultures, subcultures, and lifestyle or market segments with different gender role expectations and beliefs). This increasing difficulty in limiting exposure to specific audiences can result in negative backlash for advertisers. For example, the Swedish Women's Lobby uses social media to publicly shame advertisers employing traditional gender stereotypes (Sveriges Kvinnolobby 2013).

Attitude toward advertising in general (AG) has also long interested advertising researchers (Bauer and Greyser 1968; Durvasula et al. 1993; Jin and Lutz 2013; Manceau and Tissier-Desbordes 2006; Muehling 1987; Nan 2006; Shavitt, Lowrey, and Haefner 1998; Shavitt, Vargas, and Lowey 2004). But research has primarily compared AG across cultural or demographic segments or examined AG's consequences. For example, AG affects involvement with, memory for, and attitudes toward specific advertisements, which ultimately influences consumer brand attitudes and behavioral intentions (Bauer and Greyser 1968; Bush, Smith, and Martin 1999; Defever, Pandelaere, and Roe 2011; Jin and Lutz 2013; Tan and Chia 2007). Also, favorable AG among the general public helps advertisers avoid further limitations and regulation of advertising practices (Jin and Lutz 2013). Thus, broader understanding of AG's determinants is critical for advertisers.

Unfortunately, relatively little attention has been devoted to AG's determinants (Durvasula et al. 1993; Nan 2006). Those examining AG's predictors have focused primarily on economic and social factors such as product information, advertising's societal role, consumer socialization, and media dislike (Alwitt and Prabhaker 1994; Bauer and Greyser 1968; Bush, Smith, and Martin 1999; Tan and Chia 2007).

Because advertising commonly uses gender stereotypes and sex appeals (e.g., Ganahl, Prinsen, and Netzley 2003; Grau, Roselli, and Taylor 2007; Knoll, Eisend, and Steinhagen 2011; Plakoyiannaki et al. 2008; Plakoyiannaki and Zotos 2009; Rouner, Slater, and Domenech-Rodriguez 2003), advertisers should understand their impact on AG. Scholars recognize that a paucity of research assesses gender stereotyping's impact on global evaluations of advertising (Kumari and Shivani 2012). Thus, research is required to ascertain gender-stereotype and sex/nudity attitudes' influence on advertising offensiveness evaluations and AG. Our purpose is to examine these constructs as potential predictors of offensiveness and AG among a US adult sample. Furthermore, because reactions toward gender stereotypes and sex/nudity in advertising differ across men versus women and younger versus older consumers (Eisend, Plagemann, and Sollwedel 2014; Jones and Reid 2010; Maciejewski 2004; Manceau and Tissier–Desbordes 2006; Wyllie, Carlson, and Rosenberger 2014), we also explore demographic differences in the effects of gender-stereotype and sex/nudity attitudes on offensiveness and AG.

Conceptual framework and hypotheses

This study proposes and empirically tests a conceptual model of hypothesized relationships (see Figure 1) among four latent constructs: (1) gender-stereotype attitudes include both sexism – the belief that advertising portrays women as inferior relative to men in their capabilities and potential (Plakoyiannaki and Zotos 2009) – and role inaccuracy – the belief that advertising portrays men and women unrealistically (DeYoung and Crane 1992; Sciglimpaglia, Lundstrom, and Vanier 1979), (2) sex/nudity attitudes – reactions to nudity and erotic material in advertising (Manceau and Tissier-Desbordes 2006; Treise et al. 1994), (3) offensiveness – the perception that advertising executions are frequently irritating, rude, or provocative and cause displeasure or resentment (Alwitt and Prabhaker 1992, 1994), and (4) AG – an overall positive or negative learned predisposition or reaction to the practice of advertising (Manceau and Tissier-Desbordes 2006).

Proposed construct relationships are based on the theoretical framework which suggests that criticisms of advertising focus on either (1) methods and techniques used by advertisers (i.e., advertising as an instrument) or, (2) more broadly, at advertising's negative role in society (i.e., advertising as an institution; Bauer and Greyser 1968). Based on this theory, individual beliefs or attitudes toward advertising instruments, such as gender stereotypes and sex/nudity, should influence AG (Jin and Lutz 2013; Muehling 1987). For example, Shavitt, Vargas, and Lowey (2004) found that advertisements with techniques that garnered the greatest attention had the most impact on AG. The conceptual model also captures reactions to advertising's role as a societal institution through advertising offensiveness.

Structural equation modeling (SEM) tests whether the a-priori model of construct relationships fits the data (Jöreskog 1993). Multi-group analyses compare whether or not the conceptual model fits equally well across groups, such as male versus female or younger versus older respondents. The next sections review the literature and hypothesize construct relationships.

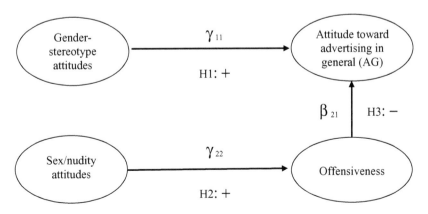

Figure 1.   Conceptual model.

Relationship between gender-stereotype attitudes and AG

Advertisements continue to portray women in traditional or decorative roles (Ganahl, Prinsen, and Netzley 2003; Kumari and Shivani 2012; Paek, Nelson, and Vilela 2011; Plakoyiannaki et al. 2008; Rouner, Slater, and Domenech-Rodriguez 2003). Compared to men, women are stereotypically portrayed as younger, in decorative roles, and more likely to be unemployed or employed in traditional female occupations (e.g., homemakers and child caretakers), be shoppers or product users, appear in domestic settings, and promote products used at home (Courtney and Lockeretz 1971; Ganahl, Prinsen, and Netzley 2003; Knoll, Eisend, and Steinhagen 2011; Plakoyiannaki and Zotos 2009; Robinson and Hunter 2008; Sheehan 2014). Courtney and Lockeretz's seminal work suggests four gender-stereotype dimensions: (1) a woman's place is in the home, (2) women do not make important decisions, (3) women are dependent on men, and (4) women are depicted primarily as sex objects.

Consumers report that advertising inaccurately portrays both genders (Lundstrom and Sciglimpaglia 1977; Rouner, Slater, and Domenech-Rodriguez 2003; Zimmerman and Dahlberg 2008). Three-quarters of US and Canadian women believe that advertising unrealistically portrays women and 63% also believe it inaccurately portrays men (DeYoung and Crane 1992; Sciglimpaglia, Lundstrom, and Vanier 1979). A recent study found almost 80% of male advertising portrayals to be inaccurate (Sheehan 2014). Men are often depicted as powerful and authoritative protagonists (Rouner, Slater, and Domenech-Rodriguez 2003). Tolerance for advertising portrayals that fail to mirror the prevalence of actual gender roles in society shapes gender-stereotype attitudes.

Gender-stereotype attitudes influence attitudes toward individual advertisements, firms, and products; brand attitudes; and purchase intentions (Eisend, Plagemann, and Sollwedel 2014; Lysonski and Pollay 1990; Orth and Holancova 2004). Although much research has focused on gender-stereotype attitudes, their impact on AG is not well documented.

Theoretically, response to instrumental practices used in advertising (e.g., gender stereotypes) should influence AG (Jin and Lutz 2013). Consumers with more traditional values have demonstrated more positive AG (Dutta-Bergman 2006); likely, this is because advertising continues to portray traditional gender stereotypes consistent with those values (Ganahl, Prinsen, and Netzley 2003; Paek, Nelson, and Vilela 2011; Rouner, Slater, and Domenech-Rodriguez 2003). However, Anglosphere cultures (e.g., US, Canada, Britain, Ireland, Australia, and New Zealand) have witnessed great concern over inaccurate advertising gender roles and criticism of traditional gender stereotypes (DeYoung and Crane 1992; Ford, LaTour, and Honeycutt 1997; Jones and Reid 2010; Plakoyiannaki and Zotos 2009; Putrevu and Swimberghek 2013; Rouner, Slater, and Domenech-Rodriguez 2003; Sciglimpaglia, Lundstrom, and Vanier 1979). Because the current sample is drawn from mainstream US adults, their low acceptance of gender stereotypes should negatively impact AG. This leads to the following hypothesis.

H1: As gender-stereotype attitudes become more negative, AG becomes less favorable.

Relationship between sex/nudity attitudes and offensiveness

Advertising increasingly and widely uses sex appeals for all sorts of products and models. For example, a content analysis found that 81% of female athlete models in magazine advertisements were partially nude or dressed suggestively (Grau, Roselli, and Taylor 2007). Sex appeals can appear in visual, audio, or verbal advertising elements and vary in intensity or suggestiveness (Manceau and Tissier-Desbordes 2006; Nelson and Paek

2008; Sheehan 2014; Wyllie, Carlson, and Rosenberger 2014). Sex/nudity attitudes are a function of exposure frequency, socialization, and beliefs about sex appeals' influence, especially on young people (Christy 2006; Liu, Cheng, and Li 2009).

Sex/nudity attitudes should influence advertising offensiveness evaluations. Research suggests support for this relationship especially in Anglosphere cultures. US consumers categorize sex appeals as offensive advertising executions (Barnes and Dotson 1990; Dudley 1999; Treise et al. 1994). US teens counter-argue against sex appeals in commercials (Rouner, Slater, and Domenech-Rodriguez 2003). However, US youths are becoming less offended by sex/nudity (Zimmerman and Dahlberg 2008). Therefore, we hypothesize the following.

H2: As objections to sex/nudity in advertising increase, advertising offensiveness increases.

Relationship between offensiveness and AG

Barnes and Dotson (1990) propose two forms of advertising offensiveness based on (1) the advertised product or (2) creative executions violating social norms. Degree of offensiveness (i.e., embarrassment, distaste, disgust, irritation, or outrage) depends on the perceiver's characteristics and the viewing atmosphere, such as higher offensiveness perceptions when viewing commercials with others rather than alone (Barnes and Dotson 1990; Sheehan 2014; Waller 2005).

Research suggests that offensiveness may harm AG. For example, advertising irritation predicts AG (Haghirian and Madlberger 2005; Shavitt, Lowrey, and Haefner 1998; Shavitt, Vargas, and Lowey 2004). Furthermore, consumers who find commercials offensive negatively evaluate television advertising in general (Alwitt and Prabhaker 1992, 1994; Shavitt, Vargas, and Lowey 2004). Based on implications from prior research, consumers who generally find advertising offensive should have unfavorable AG. Therefore, we predict the following relationship.

H3: As offensiveness increases, AG becomes more unfavorable.

Demographic differences

This study extends the literature by examining demographic differences in gender-stereotype and sex/nudity attitudes on offensiveness and AG. Research has documented gender difference in responses to some of these constructs individually, but not their construct relationships.

Compared to men, women more negatively evaluate and find less credible advertisements with gender stereotypes (Eisend, Plagemann, and Sollwedel 2014) or sex/nudity (Jones and Reid 2010; Manceau and Tissier–Desbordes 2006). Female Generation Y college students are more critical of overt or demeaning sexual appeals (Jones and Reid 2010; Maciejewski 2004), however, both men and women express serious concerns over overtly sexual advertisements (Dudley 1999; Treise et al. 1994). Higher advertising effectiveness occurs with mild sex/nudity among female students, but with explicit sex/nudity among male students (Wyllie, Carlson, and Rosenberger 2014). Women who reject gender stereotypes approve less of individual advertisements' gender role portrayals and intend to purchase advertised brands less than men (Orth and Holancova 2004). Women report lower AG but higher offensiveness and inclinations toward advertising regulation than men (Shavitt, Lowrey, and Haefner 1998, Shavitt, Vargas, and Lowey 2004). In fact, gender is the strongest predictor of support for advertising regulation (Dutta-Bergman 2006).

Age differences in AG require further exploration due to conflicting results (Dutta-Bergman 2006). Younger adults are more accepting of nudity in advertising (Manceau and Tissier–Desbordes 2006), are less offended and insulted by advertising (Shavitt, Lowrey, and Haefner 1998; Shavitt, Vargas, and Lowey 2004), and report more favorable AG than older adults (Alwitt and Prabhaker 1992). Older adults support greater advertising regulation but also view advertising as a more useful information source than younger adults (Dutta-Bergman 2006).

This initial investigation into demographic differences in these construct relationships explores the following two research questions.

RQ1: Does gender alter relationships among the gender-stereotype, sex/nudity, offensiveness, and AG constructs?

RQ2: Does age alter relationships among these constructs?

Method

Participants and data collection procedures

Respondents were adults residing in a Southwestern US metropolitan area. Social and volunteer organizations engaged in community service unaffiliated with any religious groups were contacted to obtain membership lists. From these lists, 500 participants were randomly selected and mailed paper questionnaires with prepaid return envelopes. Non-respondents received follow up reminders. As an incentive, each participant was offered a $5 donation to their community organization.

After discarding cases due to largely incomplete information or careless response patterns, the final sample ($n = 247$) was 49.6% female and ranged from 19 to 63 years of age (mean $= 29$). Two-fifths (39.9%) were married and 5.2% were divorced/widowed. Children under 18 years old live at home with 34.0% of them. Among respondents, 61.6% had college or graduate degrees and 38.0% had high school diplomas. The sample size is far larger than Hair et al.'s (2010) minimum recommendation for a model having four constructs of three or more items and with item communalities .6 or higher.

Measures

Existing measures assessed all constructs (see Table 1). Respondents rated agreement with each item on a nine-point scale (1 = strongly disagree and 9 = strongly agree). The literature offers no consensus on the best AG measure (Tan and Chia 2007). For consistency, we used both Sciglimpaglia, Lundstrom, and Vanier's (1979) attitudes toward sex role portrayals (gender stereotypes) and AG scales. AG items were reverse coded so higher scores indicate more favorable AG. Treise et al.'s (1994) four-item scale assessed sex/nudity attitudes. Alwitt and Prabhaker's (1994) four-item scale measured offensiveness.

Internal reliability for each construct was adequate (all coefficient alphas > .70). Composite reliability was higher than the acceptable .60 cut-off (Bagozzi and Yi 1988). Convergent validity for all measures was attained as composite reliability exceeded average variance extracted (AVE) and AVE $\geq$ .5, except for gender-stereotype attitudes. However, AVE for all constructs exceeded squared correlation estimates, which indicates discriminant validity (Hair et al. 2010). Also, discriminant

Table 1. Parameter values, internal reliability (coefficient α), composite reliability (CR), and AVE.

Constructs and measurement items	Estimate	t-value	α	CR	AVE
Gender-stereotype attitudes			.71	.71	.45
Advertisements suggest that a woman's place is in the home.	0.90	+4.78****			
Ads which I see show women as they really are.	0.56	+5.74****			
Ads suggest that women are fundamentally dependent on men.	0.79	+5.04****			
Ads which I see show men as they really are.	0.57	+6.00****			
Ads which I see accurately portray women in most of their daily activities.	0.37	+4.98****			
Ads which I see accurately portray men in most of their daily activities.	0.27	+4.41****			
Advertisements suggest that women do not do important things.	1.00				
I am more sensitive to the portrayal of women in advertising than I used to be.	0.42	+4.01****			
I find the portrayal of women in advertising to be offensive.	0.86	+5.38****			
If a new product is introduced with advertising that portrays women offensively, I might not buy it even if it offers other benefits which I find attractive.	0.21	+1.92*			
Sex/nudity attitudes			.78	.79	.50
Tastefully done, there is nothing wrong with using sexy ads to sell some kinds of products. [r]	0.54	+7.31****			
There are too many sex appeals in today's advertising.	1.00				
Nudity in print advertising is not appropriate for general interest magazines.	0.75	+11.94****			
Sexy ads play a role in a teenager's decision to become sexually active.	0.73	+10.68****			
Offensiveness			.77	.81	.54
There is too much sex in advertising.	1.00				
There is too much violence in advertising.	0.80	+12.65****			
Most ads are in poor taste.	0.47	+ 7.20****			
Ads are more offensive than they used to be.	0.57	+8.53****			
Attitude toward advertising in general			.80	.80	.58
I really do not enjoy television commercials. [r]	0.91	+9.25****			
Overall, advertising annoys me. [r]	1.00				
On the whole, advertising is not believable. [r]	0.77	+9.10****			

Note: *p-value ≤ 0.05; **p-value ≤ 0.01; ***p-value ≤ 0.005; ****p-value ≤ 0.001; [r] = reverse coded.

validity was exhibited as within-construct item correlations generally exceeded those between items measuring different constructs. The initial measurement model showed significant loadings of all items on their constructs except for one gender-stereotype attitudes item, 'Advertisements suggest that women make important decisions' ($t = +1.59$, ns). This item was dropped from subsequent analyses. Measurement model fit was adequate (see Table 2).

Table 2. Summary of fit statistics.

Fit indices	Measurement model	Conceptual model	Gender multi-group analysis	Age multi-group analysis
Chi-Square (*df*)	327.24**** (175)	330.55**** (177)	573**** (376)	562.24**** (376)
Contribution to chi-square			Women: 53.77% Men: 46.23%	29 or younger: 58.76% 30 or older: 41.24%
RMSEA	0.058	0.059	0.065	0.064
SRMR	0.08	0.08	Women: 0.10 Men: 0.10	29 or younger: 0.09 30 or older: 0.11
NNFI	0.93	0.92	0.90	0.90
CFI	0.94	0.94	0.91	0.91
IFI	0.94	0.94	0.91	0.91
GFI	0.89	0.89	Women: 0.81 Men: 0.83	29 or younger: 0.80 30 or older: 0.83

Note: *p-value ≤ 0.05; **p-value ≤ 0.01; ***p-value ≤ 0.005; ****p-value ≤ 0.001.

Results

Statistical power

Statistical power, the probability of correctly rejecting a false statistical null hypothesis, is critical for SEM because it directly influences the confidence with which test results can be interpreted (McQuitty 2004). All models analyzed exhibit very high power (i.e., Π = .9) with a medium sample size and degrees of freedom. All models have more than the desired level of power (i.e., Π = .8) recommended by Hair et al. (2010).

Tests of model fit

SEM using LISREL 8.80 tested the construct relationships predicted in the conceptual model. Model parameters were estimated with covariance matrices and the maximum likelihood estimation method. Because the study employs continuous data, covariance matrices are preferable as they provide greater information than correlation matrices (Hair et al. 2010).

Overall, conceptual model fit indices in Table 2 are acceptable. The chi-square test is biased against large samples, which accounts for its significance. Thus, chi-square is not the best fit indicator with this sample (Hair et al. 2010). However, the normed chi-square (χ^2/df) is below Fornell and Larcker's (1981) cut-off of 3 for the measurement, conceptual, and multi-group models, which indicates an acceptable fit. Most other fit indices are also acceptable. Root mean square error of approximation (RMSEA) is moderate (i.e., .05−.10) for the measurement, conceptual, and multi-group models (Hu and Bentler 1999). Standardized root mean residual (SRMR) for the measurement and conceptual models shows reasonable fit at less than .08 (Hair et al. 2010). Good fit is also evident for the measurement, conceptual, and multi-group models because the Non-Normed Fit Index (NNFI), Comparative Fit Index (CFI), Incremental Fit Index (IFI), and Goodness of Fit Index (GFI) are near or above .90 (Hair et al. 2010; Hu and Bentler 1999). Model fit and goodness of fit statistics must be considered in light of statistical power. These fit indices may be interpreted in a more relaxed manner due to high power (Π > .9; McQuitty 2004).

Hypothesis tests

The measurement model's loading estimates in Table 1 are all large and significant. Structural model results are presented in Table 3 with path coefficients and t-values for each hypothesized relationship. Table 4 shows the latent constructs' covariance matrix.

H1 predicts that negative gender-stereotype attitudes harm AG. Results in Table 3 support H1. This suggests that the more US consumers dislike advertising gender stereotypes, the less favorable their global evaluation of the practice of advertising.

H2 predicts that consumers with negative reactions to sex/nudity in advertising also find advertising offensive. Furthermore, H3 posits that as offensiveness increases, AG grows more unfavorable. Relationships predicted in both H2 and H3 are observed.

Multi-group analyses

Multi-group analyses investigated if the conceptual model worked equally well for men as women (RQ1) and for younger as older consumers (RQ2). Free path coefficients determined if construct relationships in the conceptual model differed across groups.

The gender multi-group analysis in Table 3 reveals interesting differences between men and women that are obscured in the aggregate results. For men, gender-stereotype attitudes do not affect AG, but all other factor loadings and path coefficients are supported. The presence of a gender-stereotype attitudes−AG relationship for women is consistent with earlier findings that show women more ardently support regulating advertising stereotypes than men (Dutta-Bergman 2006; Shavitt, Lowrey, and Haefner 1998). Conversely, the offensiveness-AG path coefficient was significant only for men. Thus, AG is not a function of offensiveness for women. Modification indices do not suggest any alternate relationships between constructs than those in the conceptual model.

The gender multi-group analysis also reveals a lack of invariance for some factor loadings on the gender-stereotype construct. 'If a new product is introduced with advertising that portrays women offensively, I might not buy it even if it offers other benefits which I find attractive' loaded on the gender-stereotypes construct for men (t-value = +2.36, $p \leq .01$), but not women (t-value = −0.13, ns). Interestingly, women agreed more with this item than men. Furthermore, two items related to gender role accuracy ('Ads which I see accurately portray women in most of their daily activities' and 'Ads which I see accurately portray men in most of their daily activities') loaded on the gender-stereotype construct for men (t-values $\geq$ +5.22, $p \leq .001$), but not women (t-values = −1.49 and +0.59, respectively, ns). Additionally, women viewed sex/nudity in advertising more negatively than men (see Table 4).

Looking at the age multi-group analysis in Table 3, factor loadings and path coefficients associated with the gender-stereotype attitudes−AG relationship are supported for younger respondents. The unsupported gender-stereotype attitudes−AG path coefficient for older respondents indicates that AG is only a function of younger respondents' gender-stereotype attitudes. However, older respondents' AG is influenced by advertising offensiveness, which is a function of their sex/nudity attitudes. Additional analysis show older respondents have more negative sex/nudity attitudes, are more offended by advertising, and hold more unfavorable AG than younger respondents. However, gender-stereotype attitudes appear similar across age groups (see Table 4).

72

Table 3. Comparison of structural model path coefficients and t-values.

Hypothesis	Path	Conceptual model	Gender multi-group analysis – women	Gender multi-group analysis – men	Age multi-group analysis – 29 and younger	Age multi-group analysis – 30 and older
H1	Gender stereotypes → AG (γ_{11})	−0.40 ($t = -3.70^{***}$)	−0.50 ($t = -2.99^{**}$)	−0.07 ($t = -0.56$)	−0.67 ($t = -3.30^{***}$)	−0.18 ($t = -1.59$)
H2	Sex/nudity → Offensiveness (γ_{22})	0.87 ($t = +16.65^{***}$)	.80 ($t = +12.28^{***}$)	0.83 ($t = +12.91^{***}$)	1.02 ($t = +12.13^{***}$)	0.83 ($t = +10.35^{***}$)
H3	Offensiveness → AG (β_{21})	−0.27 ($t = -3.87^{***}$)	−0.15 ($t = -1.54$)	−0.34 ($t = -3.84^{***}$)	−0.23 ($t = -3.00^{**}$)	−0.23 ($t = -3.00^{**}$)

Note: $^{*}p$-value ≤ 0.05; $^{**}p$-value ≤ 0.01; $^{***}p$-value ≤ 0.005; $^{****}p$-value ≤ 0.001.

Table 4. Mean scale scores and covariance matrix of latent constructs, including the phi matrix among the latent independent constructs.

| | Means | | | | | Covariance matrix | | Phi matrix | |
	Overall	Men	Women	Younger	Older	AG	Offensiveness	Gender-stereotype attitudes	Sex/nudity attitudes
AG	5.17	5.05	5.26	5.64	4.74	3.20			
Offensiveness	5.40	5.37	5.44	5.17	5.69	−1.16	3.92		
Gender-stereotype attitudes	4.32	4.41	4.26	4.31	4.34	−0.94	0.31	2.13	
Sex/nudity attitudes	5.31	5.16	5.45	5.09	5.57	−1.20	3.99	0.35	4.57

Discussion

This study represents the first investigation into gender stereotyping-related constructs' influence on AG. Results show that AG decreases as consumers hold increasingly negative gender-stereotype attitudes. Also, unfavorable attitudes toward sex/nudity in advertising lead to greater advertising offensiveness. As advertising offensiveness increases, AG becomes more unfavorable.

Demographic differences

Demographic differences were observed in predicted relationships between constructs. Gender-stereotype attitudes exerted an influence on AG for women, but not men. Women also indicated lower purchase intentions toward advertising with female role portrayals that they find offensive. This concurs with research in which women were less willing to buy a new product advertised with offensive female portrayals (Lundstrom and Sciglimpaglia 1977), more favorable toward non-traditional portrayals (Eisend, Plagemann, and Sollwedel 2014), less tolerant of offensive gender stereotypes (Van Hellemont and Van den Bulck 2012), and in another context displayed greater advertising avoidance than men (Rosa-Mendez, Davies, and Madran 2009).

Also, women less favorably evaluated sex/nudity in advertising than men, which affected women's offensiveness perceptions. However, offensiveness failed to impact women's AG. For women, AG was purely a function of gender-stereotype attitudes. This may mean women's decorative role in sex appeals is less important than their general treatment by advertisers in determining AG.

For older consumers, the gender-stereotype attitudes−AG relationship is absent. However, offensiveness influences older consumers' AG. This corresponds with prior research that found older consumers exhibited less consensus regarding gender stereotypes in specific advertisements (Theodoridis et al. 2013), were less tolerant of offensive advertising (Van Hellemont and Van den Bulck 2012), and more likely to discontinue using a product or service if it adopts an offensive advertising campaign than younger consumers (Lundstrom and Sciglimpaglia 1977).

Sex/nudity attitudes influence offensiveness for both younger and older consumers, but younger consumers hold more positive sex/nudity attitudes and find advertising less offensive than older consumers. This concurs with earlier findings that younger consumers viewed ads with sex/nudity more favorably (Liu, Cheng, and Li 2009) and was less negative toward offensive advertising executions than older consumers (Van Hellemont and Van den Bulck 2012). Younger consumers also have more positive AG than older consumers.

In a striking difference from the 1970s in which older consumers held more positive gender-stereotype attitudes than younger consumers (Lundstrom and Sciglimpaglia 1977), no difference exists in gender-stereotype attitudes between younger and older consumers today. This is likely a cohort difference. Older consumers in Lundstrom and Sciglimpaglia's sample reached maturity before the late 1960s and 1970s women's liberation movement; however, both younger and older consumers in our sample reached maturity and received gender-role socialization in a post-feminist environment.

Theoretical contributions

Applying the two theoretical types of AG-related antecedents (Jin and Lutz 2013), we investigated advertising instruments through gender-stereotype and sex/nudity attitudes and advertising's institutional role through advertising offensiveness. Similar to research on other antecedents (e.g., Durvasula et al. 1993), both attitudes–instruments and attitudes–institution antecedents predict AG.

A strength of this study is its sample of US adults. Much AG (e.g., Andrews, Lysonski, and Durvasula 1991; Defever, Pandelaere, and Roe 2011; Dianoux and Linhart 2010; Durvasula et al. 1993; Jin and Lutz 2013; Muehling 1987; Nan 2006; Tan and Chia 2007) and gender-stereotype research (e.g., Eisend, Plagemann, and Sollwedel 2014; Lysonski and Pollay 1990; Martin and Gnoth 2009; Zimmerman and Dahlberg 2008) used student samples. Interestingly, predicted relationships based on this prior literature held for younger, but not older (30 or older) consumers. Overall, the advantage of an adult sample is greater confidence in the findings and their generalizability to the general population.

Findings support and extend prior research. Sex/nudity attitudes predict advertising offensiveness for US consumers. This is consistent with previous surveys in which Asian consumers found sex appeals in advertising to be an offensiveness execution (Kasamsetty, Khisar, and Shruthi 2014; Prendergast, Ho, and Phau 2002). Offensiveness predicts AG, consistent with Alwitt and Prabhaker's (1992, 1994) finding that viewers who find TV advertising offensive dislike AG. Current results extend these findings by indicating that AG also grows more unfavorable as offensiveness increases. Sex/nudity and offensiveness results extend the literature by documenting that sex/nudity attitudes indirectly influence AG through offensiveness. This is an important contribution, because sex appeals commonly appear in advertising (Plakoyiannaki and Zotos 2009; Rouner, Slater, and Domenech-Rodriguez 2003).

Managerial implications

Advertisers should investigate their target market's gender-stereotype attitudes. Over time, advertising has featured fewer stereotypical and more non-traditional gender roles with greater gender balance (Eisend 2010; Mager and Helgeson 2011; Wolin 2003). Given our results, this may partially explains why AG is becoming less unfavorable (Alwitt and Prabhaker 1992; Muehling 1987; Shavitt, Lowrey, and Haefner 1998; Shavitt, Vargas, and Lowey 2004).

The advent of peer-to-peer sharing has created strategic marketing opportunities to enhance brand reputation relative to competitors. Advertisers may encourage sharing competitors' ads that consumers find sexist or offensive or sharing the brand's ads that align with a particular target audience's gender stereotyping preferences.

Despite fewer stereotypes, advertising continues to feature traditional gender role portrayals (Ganahl, Prinsen, and Netzley 2003; Kumari and Shivani 2012; Paek, Nelson, and Vilela 2011; Plakoyiannaki et al. 2008; Rouner, Slater, and Domenech-Rodriguez 2003). Thus, consumers tend to hold unfavorable AG if they dislike gender stereotypes, but more favorable AG if they prefer gender stereotypes. The observed negative gender-stereotype attitudes—AG relationship suggests that US consumers remain disenchanted with advertising gender roles and this continues to diminish their AG. This is more applicable to women than men and inapplicable to older consumers who appear to have already formed global predispositions toward advertising. Strategically, advertisers should downplay gender stereotypes in advertisements, especially among younger consumers whose AG may be more malleable. Future research should investigate AG's malleability across age.

Sex/nudity results also have implications for advertisers. Advertisers should be concerned that target audiences who negatively view sex/nudity may develop unfavorable AG with continual exposure to adverting sex/nudity. Thus, advertisers should avoid exposing such consumers to sex/nudity to lessen individual ad and brand rejection and unfavorable global advertising evaluations. Unfavorable AG diminishes return on advertising investment, because AG shapes reactions to individual advertisements (Defever, Pandelaere, and Roe 2011; Jin and Lutz 2013).

Consumer welfare and public policy implications

The overall negative stereotypes-AG and offensiveness-AG path coefficients suggests that advertising gender roles and offensiveness remain such a negative experience for many consumers that they undermine AG. Gender-stereotype attitudes exert a negative influence on AG for women, not men. Despite less reliance on traditional stereotypes in advertising, women's reaction to such portrayals implies that advertisers' short-term goals of attracting attention and generating favorable ad responses among their target audiences may be harming long-term consumer welfare. The societal impact of advertising gender roles is great; they impact gender equality by reinforcing or undermining stereotypes and socializing men and women by establishing behavioral norms (Paek, Nelson, and Vilela 2011). Women also bear the consequences of advertising gender stereotypes in their daily lives (Eisend, Plagemann, and Sollwedel 2014).

Advertisers determine gender portrayals by the creative message, advertised product, and preferences related to the target market's gender and age (Ganahl, Prinsen, and Netzley 2003; Orth and Holancova 2004; Plakoyiannaki and Zotos 2009; Van Hellemont and Van den Bulck 2012). Unfortunately, ad viewing by those outside the target market can have serious consequences as influential activists bring negative social pressure to bear (Crosier and Erdogan 2001). For example, Coca-Cola test-marketed an advertising campaign for Fairlife milk targeted toward 25–39 year old women in three cities. However, Coca-Cola dropped this campaign after peer-to-peer sharing via Twitter of advertisements featuring women wearing only splashes of milk, including one with a woman weighing herself, led to international criticism (Nessif 2014). Given the increased likelihood that provocative advertisements will be seen by unintended audiences due to peer-to-peer sharing on Internet and social media sites, it is in advertisers' best interest to continue moving away from gender role portrayals that some consumers might consider sexist or offensive. Advertisers as a whole should consider strengthening self-regulation in this area to avoid increased governmental interference. Public-policy-makers have shown that they are prepared to act in response to complaints about advertising's societal role in gender stereotyping (Knoll, Eisend, and Steinhagen 2011; Van Hellemont and Van den Bulck 2012).

Limitations and future research

Generalizability may be limited as the sample consisted of community organization members in a Southwestern US metropolitan area rather than a national or international sample. Future research should examine US regional or cross-cultural invariance of our model's relationships via multi-group analysis. Consumer responses to sex appeals, gender role portrayals, and AG can vary across cultures and sub-cultures (e.g., Andrews, Lysonski, and Durvasula 1991; Durvasula et al. 1993; Nelson and Paek 2008). For example, if consumers view sex/nudity as highly offensive as they do in India (Kasamsetty, Khisar, and Shruthi 2014), our model suggests increased advertising offensiveness and reduced AG in comparison with US consumers. Alternatively, Taiwanese women with traditional values prefer stereotyped gender roles in advertising and reject career-oriented and feminist depictions of women (Lin 2008). Our model suggests that with such a population, the gender-stereotype attitudes–AG relationship may be positive rather than the negative relationship observed with US adults.

Second, this study limited its investigations to gender stereotyping-related antecedents of offensiveness and AG. However, other constructs (e.g., reactions to violence, provocative/shocking visuals, crude language, some humorous appeals, unnecessary fear, culturally insensitive depictions, overly personal topics, or negative emotional appeals) may also influence advertising offensiveness evaluations and, in turn, indirectly influence AG. Future research should investigate these potential antecedents' direct influence on offensiveness and indirect influence on AG. Interestingly, some potential determinants of offensiveness may be more invariant across target markets than sex/nudity attitudes. For example, consumers can be offended if an advertisement implies indecent language, even if such language is not explicitly stated. This effect was invariant across gender or ethnic subcultures (Huhmann and Mott-Stenerson 2008).

Third, this study found problems with some gender-stereotype items. Others have also not used Sciglimpaglia, Lundstrom, and Vanier's (1979) full scale with more recent samples (e.g., Zimmerman and Dahlberg 2008), possibly due to similar problems. Future research should develop a new measure of gender-stereotype attitudes. Internal reliability with the current administration of Sciglimpaglia et al.'s (1979) measure was near the .70 cut-off rather than the coefficient alpha of .87 reported in Sciglimpaglia, Lundstrom, and Vanier's (1979) initial scale development. This may indicate societal changes in the item wording's connotation or an inability to replicate the scale's internal reliability in other samples. Also, as one reviewer indicated, item wording may prejudice responses and affect validity. However, advances in scale development techniques should be able to produce a measure with enhanced reliability and validity.

Conclusion

In conclusion, advertising practitioners and researchers should continue to consider AG due to its influence on the effectiveness of individual advertisements and campaigns as well as its role in promoting or discouraging further regulation. A study of US adults found gender-role and sex/nudity attitudes to be important antecedents of advertising offensiveness and AG. Thus, consumers who are more tolerant of gender stereotypes or sex appeals find advertising less offensive and have more positive AG than other consumers. But advertisers must consider their target audience's demographics when creating ads with gender stereotypes and sex appeals. For women, sex/nudity attitudes predict offensiveness, not AG. But for men, sex/nudity attitudes predict both. Also, gender-stereotype attitudes predict AG for younger, but not older consumers. Overall, these results highlight important connections between gender stereotyping and global advertising evaluations.

Disclosure statement
No potential conflict of interest was reported by the authors.

References

Alwitt, L.F., and P.R. Prabhaker. 1992. Functional and belief dimensions of attitudes to television advertising: Implications for copytesting. *Journal of Advertising Research* 32, no. 5: 30−42.

Alwitt, L.F., and P.R. Prabhaker. 1994. Identifying who dislikes television advertising: Not by demographics alone. *Journal of Advertising Research* 34, no. 6: 17−29.

Andrews, C.J., S. Lysonski, and S. Durvasula. 1991. Understanding cross-cultural student perceptions of advertising in general: Implications for advertising educators and practitioners. *Journal of Advertising* 20, no. 2: 15−28.

Bagozzi, R.P., and Y. Yi. 1988. On the evaluation of structural equation models. *Journal of the Academy of Marketing Science* 16, no. 1: 74−94.

Barnes, J.H., and M.J. Dotson. 1990. An exploratory investigation into the nature of offensive television advertising. *Journal of Advertising* 19, no. 3: 61−9.

Bauer, R.A., and S.A. Greyser. 1968. *Advertising in America: The consumer view.* Boston, MA: Harvard University.

Bush, A.J., R. Smith, and C. Martin. 1999. The influence of consumer socialization variables on attitude toward advertising: A comparison of African Americans and Caucasians. *Journal of Advertising* 28, no. 3: 13−24.

Christy, T.P. 2006. Females' perceptions of offensive advertising: The importance of values, expectations, and control. *Journal of Current Issues and Research in Advertising* 28, no. 2: 15−32.

Courtney, A.E., and S.W. Lockeretz. 1971. Woman's place: An analysis of the roles portrayed by women in magazine advertisements. *Journal of Marketing Research* 8, no. 1: 92−5.

Crosier, K., and B.Z. Erdogan. 2001. Advertising complainants: Who and where are they? *Journal of Marketing Communications* 7, no. 2: 109−20.

Defever, C., M. Pandelaere, and K. Roe. 2011. Inducing value-congruent behaviour through advertising and the moderating role of attitude toward advertising. *Journal of Advertising* 40, no. 2: 25−37.

DeYoung, S., and F.G. Crane. 1992. Females' attitudes toward the portrayal of women in advertising: A Canadian study. *International Journal of Advertising* 11, no. 3: 249−55.

Dianoux, C., and Z. Linhart. 2010. The effectiveness of female nudity in advertising in three European countries. *International Marketing Review* 27, no. 5: 562−78.

Dudley, S.C. 1999. Consumer attitudes toward nudity in advertising. *Journal of Marketing Theory & Practice* 7, no. 4: 89−96.

Durvasula, S.J., C. Andrews, S. Lysonski, and R.G. Netemeyer. 1993. Assessing the cross-national applicability of consumer behavior models: A model of attitude toward advertising in general. *Journal of Consumer Research* 19, no. 4: 626−36.

Dutta-Bergman, M.J. 2006. The demographic and psychographic antecedents of attitudes toward advertising. *Journal of Advertising Research* 45, no. 1: 102−12.

Eisend, M. 2010. A meta-analysis of gender roles in advertising. *Journal of the Academy of Marketing Science* 38, no. 4: 418−40.

Eisend, M., J. Plagemann, and J. Sollwedel. 2014. Gender roles and humor in advertising: The occurrence of stereotyping in humorous and nonhumorous advertising and its consequences for advertising effectiveness. *Journal of Advertising* 43, no. 3: 256−73.

Ford, J.B., M. LaTour, and E.D. Honeycutt. 1997. An examination of cross-cultural female response to offensive sex role portrayals in advertising. *International Marketing Review* 14, no. 6: 409−23.

Fornell, C., and D. Larcker. 1981. Evaluating structural equations models with unobserved variables and measurement error. *Journal of Marketing Research* 18, no. 1: 39−50.

Ganahl, D.J., T.J. Prinsen, and S.B. Netzley. 2003. A content analysis of prime time commercials: A contextual framework of gender representations. *Sex Roles* 49, no. 9/10: 545−51.

Grau, S.L., G. Roselli, and C.R. Taylor. 2007. Where's Tamika Catchings? A content analysis of female athlete endorsers in magazine advertisements. *Journal of Current Issues and Research in Advertising* 29, no. 1: 55−65.

Haghirian, P., and M. Madlberger. 2005. Consumer attitude toward advertising via mobile devices − An empirical investigation among Austrian users. In *Proceedings of the 13th European Conference on Information Systems*, ed. D. Bartmann, 1−12. Regensburg: University of Regensberg.

Hair, J.F., W.C. Back, B.J. Babin, R.E. Anderson, and R.L. Tatham. 2010. *Multivariate data analysis.* Upper Saddle River, NJ: Prentice Hall.

Hu, L., and P.M. Bentler. 1999. Cutoff criteria for fit indexes in covariance structure analysis: Conventional criteria versus new alternatives. *Structural Equation Modeling* 6, no. 1: 1−55.

Huhmann, B.A., and B. Mott-Stenerson. 2008. Controversial advertisement executions and involvement on elaborative processing and comprehension: Controlling attitude toward the advertisement and other potential confounds. *Journal of Marketing Communications* 14, no. 4: 293−313.

Jin, H.S., and R.J. Lutz. 2013. The typicality and accessibility of consumer attitudes toward television advertising: Implications for the measurement of attitudes toward advertising in general. *Journal of Advertising* 42, no. 4: 343−57.

Jones, S.C., and A. Reid. 2010. The use of female sexuality in Australian alcohol advertising: public policy implications of young adults' reactions to stereotypes. *Journal of Public Affairs* 10, no. 1−2: 19−35.

Jöreskog, K.G. 1993. Testing structural equation models. In *Testing structural equation models*, ed. K.A. Bollen and J.S. Long, 294−316. Newbury Park, CA: Sage.

Kasamsetty, S., P.M.K. Khisar,, and M.T. Shruthi. 2014. Portrayal of women in media and its impact on young generation: A perception analysis. *South Asian Journal of Marketing & Management Research* 4, no. 8: 28−37.

Knoll, S., M. Eisend, and J. Steinhagen. 2011. Gender roles in advertising: Measuring and comparing gender stereotyping on public and private TV channels in Germany. *International Journal of Advertising* 30, no. 5: 867−88.

Kumari, S., and S.A. Shivani. 2012. A study on gender portrayals in advertising through the years: A review report. *Journal of Research in Gender Studies* 2, no. 2: 54−63.

Lee, Y.-K. 2014. Gender stereotypes as a double-edged sword in political advertising. *International Journal of Advertising* 33, no. 2: 203−34.

Lin, C.-L. 2008. Sexual issues: The analysis of female role portrayal preferences in Taiwanese print ads. *Journal of Business Ethics* 83, no. 3: 409−18.

Liu, F., H. Cheng, and J. Li. 2009. Consumer responses to sex appeal advertising: a cross-cultural study. *International Marketing Review* 26, no. 4/5: 501−20.

Lundstrom, W.J., and D. Sciglimpaglia. 1977. Sex role portrayals in advertising. *Journal of Marketing* 41, no. 3: 72−9.

Lysonski, S., and R.W. Pollay. 1990. Advertising sexism is forgiven, but not forgotten: Historical, cross-cultural and individual differences in criticism and purchase boycott intentions. *International Journal of Advertising* 9, no. 1: 317−29.

Maciejewsk, J.J. 2004. Is the use of sexual and fear appeals ethical? A moral evaluation by Generation Y college students. *Journal of Current Issues & Research in Advertising* 26, no. 2: 97−105.

Mager, J., and J.G. Helgeson. 2011. Fifty years of advertising images: Some changing perspectives on role portrayals along with enduring consistencies. *Sex Roles* 64, no. 3−4: 238−52.

Manceau, D., and E. Tissier-Desbordes. 2006. Are sex and death taboos in advertising? *International Journal of Advertising* 25, no. 1: 9−33.

Martin, B., and J. Gnoth. 2009. Is the Marlboro man the only alternative? The role of gender identity and self-construal salience in evaluations of male models. *Marketing Letters* 20, no. 4: 353−67.

McQuitty, S. 2004. Statistical power and structural equation models in business research. *Journal of Business Research* 57, no. 2: 175−83.

Muehling, D.D. 1987. An investigation of factors underlying attitudes-towards-advertising-in-general. *Journal of Advertising* 16, no. 1: 32−40.

Nan, X. 2006. Perceptual predictors of global attitude toward advertising: An investigation of both generalized and personalized beliefs. *Journal of Current Issues and Research in Advertising* 28, no. 1: 31−44.

Nelson, M.R., and H.-J. Paek. 2008. Nudity of female and male models in primetime TV advertising across seven countries. *International Journal of Advertising* 27, no. 5: 715−44.

Nessif, B. 2014. Coca-Cola's "sexist" milk ads won't be used for their national campaign following backlash. December 2. http://www.eonline.com/news/602804/coca-cola-s-sexist-milk-ads-won-t-be-used-for-their-national-campaign-following-backlash.

Orth, U.R., and D. Holancova. 2004. Men's and women's responses to sex role portrayals in advertisements. *International Journal of Research in Marketing* 21, no. 1: 77−88.

Paek, H.-J., M.R. Nelson, and A.M. Vilela. 2011. Examination of gender-role portrayals in television advertising across seven countries. *Sex Roles* 64 , no. 3/4: 192−207.

Plakoyiannaki, E., K. Mathioudaki, P. Dimitratos, and Y. Zotos. 2008. Images of women in online advertisements of global products: Does sexism exist? *Journal of Business Ethics* 83, no. 1: 101−12.

Plakoyiannaki, E., and Y. Zotos. 2009. Female role stereotypes in print advertising: Identifying associations with magazine and product categories. *European Journal of Marketing* 43, no. 11/12: 1411−34.

Prendergast, G.P., B. Ho, and I. Phau. 2002. A Hong Kong view of offensive advertising. *Journal of Marketing Communications* 8, no. 3: 165−77.

Putrevu, S., and K. Swimberghek. 2013. The influence of religiosity on consumer ethical judgments and responses toward sexual appeals. *Journal of Business Ethics* 115, no. 2: 351−65.

Robinson, B.K., and E. Hunter. 2008. Is mom still doing it all? Reexamining depictions of family work in popular advertising. *Journal of Family Issues* 29, no. 4: 465−86.

Rosa-Mendez, J.I., G. Davies, and C. Madran. 2009. Universal differences in advertising avoidance behavior: A cross-cultural study. *Journal of Business Research* 62, no. 10: 947−54.

Rouner, D., M.D. Slater, and M. Domenech-Rodriguez. 2003. Adolescent evaluation of gender role and sexual imagery in television advertisements. *Journal of Broadcasting & Electronic Media* 47, no. 3: 435−54.

Rubie-Davies, C.M., S. Liu, and K.-C.K. Lee. 2013. Watching each other: Portrayals of gender and ethnicity in television advertisements. *Journal of Social Psychology* 153, no. 2: 175−95.

Sciglimpaglia, D., W.J. Lundstrom, and D.J. Vanier. 1979. Women's feminine role orientation and their attitudes toward sex role portrayals in advertising. *Current Issues and Research in Advertising* 2, no. 1: 163−75.

Shavitt, S., P. Lowrey, and J. Haefner. 1998. Public attitudes toward advertising: More favorable than you might think. *Journal of Advertising Research* 38, no. 4: 7−22.

Shavitt, S., P. Vargas, and P. Lowey. 2004. Exploring the role of memory for self-selected ad experiences: Are some advertising media better liked than others. *Psychology & Marketing* 21, no. 12: 1011–32.

Sheehan, K.B. 2014. *Controversies in contemporary advertising*. Thousand Oaks, CA: Sage.

Sveriges Kvinnolobby. 2013. *Ad watch*. Stockholm: Swedish Women's Lobby.

Tan, S.J., and L. Chia. 2007. Are we measuring the same attitude? Understanding media effects on attitude towards advertising. *Marketing Theory* 7, no. 4: 353–77.

Theodoridis, P.K., A.G. Kyrousi, A.Y. Zotou, and G.G. Panigyrakis. 2013. Male and female attitudes towards stereotypical advertisements: A paired country investigation. *Corporate Communications* 18, no. 1: 135–60.

Treise, D., M.F. Weigold, J. Conna, and H. Garrison. 1994. Ethics in advertising: Ideological correlates of consumer perceptions. *Journal of Advertising* 23, no. 1: 59–69.

Van Hellemont, C., and H. Van den Bulck. 2012. Impacts of advertisements that are unfriendly to women and men. *International Journal of Advertising* 31, no. 3: 623–56.

Veloutsou, C., and S.R. Ahmed. 2005. Perceptions of sex appeal in print advertising by young female Anglo-Saxon and second generation Asian-Islamic British. *Journal of Promotion Management* 11, no. 2/3: 91–111.

Waller, D.S. 2005. A proposed response model for controversial advertising. *Journal of Promotion Management* 11, no. 2–3: 3–15.

Wolin, L.D. 2003. Gender issues in advertising: An oversight synthesis of research 1970–2002. *Journal of Advertising Research* 43, no. 1: 111–29.

Wyllie, J., J. Carlson, and P.J. Rosenberger III. 2014. Examining the influence of different levels of sexual-stimuli intensity by gender on advertising effectiveness. *Journal of Marketing Management* 30, no. 7/8: 697–718.

Zimmerman, A., and J. Dahlberg. 2008. The sexual objectification of women in advertising: A contemporary cultural perspective. *Journal of Advertising Research* 48, no. 1: 71–9.

Stereotypical or just typical: how do US practitioners view the role and function of gender stereotypes in advertisements?

Kasey Windels

There is a long and diverse literature on gender stereotypes in advertising; however, US practitioners' perspectives on the role and function of stereotypes in advertising remain unknown. Understanding professionals' views on whether and how stereotypes communicate is important for anyone who believes it beneficial to reduce future stereotypical representations. Using qualitative interviews with 42 practitioners, this study detailed seven themes concerning professionals' perceptions of the role and function of stereotypes in advertising, including beliefs that stereotypes are based in truth, are attractive to audiences, communicate quickly, simplify processing, prevent distraction, prevent thinking, and are the obvious solution. Practitioners felt stereotypes were used most appropriately when they were subverted or challenged in advertising messages. Stereotypes were most inappropriate when they reinforced negative perceptions. Four factors believed to drive the use of stereotypes in advertising are discussed.

Introduction

The undomesticated husband, the super mom, the woman as sex object: all are examples of common gender stereotypes found in advertising. But why do they exist? What roles and functions do they serve? What, if anything, do stereotypes communicate?

Marketers and advertisers use segmentation methods to learn about their target audience's attitudes, opinions, and interests. Target audience gender is a frequently used segmentation tool in advertising, historically and today, due to three key factors; gender segments are (1) easily identifiable, (2) easily accessible through media data, and (3) large enough to be profitable (Darley and Smith 1995).

Studies generally find that advertising uses gender stereotypes. A meta-analysis of studies from 1974 to 2007 found women were more likely than men to have non-speaking roles, to be presented in a role dependent on others, to be presented in a domestic environment and role, and to give a non-scientific opinion on a product (Eisend 2010).

Stereotypical representations in advertising are often of interest due to concern that they can shape consumers' attitudes and worldview (e.g. Giaccardi 1995; Pollay and Gallagher 1990; Richins 1991). Advertisements provide perspectives on reality, and consumers can draw upon these perspectives to understand themselves and make sense of the world (Giaccardi 1995). Advertising has been implicated as creating and maintaining impossible beauty standards for women (Stephens, Hill, and Hanson 1994). Seeing idealized images in advertising can lower women's satisfaction with their own attractiveness (Richins 1991). Children's attitudes can also be impacted by advertisements with gender-related content (Bakir and Palan 2010).

To understand how to reduce gender stereotyping in advertisements, researchers much first understand why practitioners use stereotypes. However, to the author's knowledge, there has been no research to examine US practitioners' perceptions of why gender stereotypes are used in advertising campaigns. Understanding this perspective is important, since practitioners are responsible for developing creative strategies and ideas and executing those ideas in the form of advertisements. This study addressed the following research questions: Why do practitioners stereotype? What are the roles and functions of stereotypes? In which situations are stereotypes believed to be appropriate?

There has been a long tradition of consulting practitioners to examine their perceptions of the advertising industry and its practices (e.g. Kelly, Lawlor, and O'Donohoe 2005; Kover 1995; Mallia 2009; Taylor, Hoy, and Haley 1996). Drumwright and Murphy (2004) interviewed 51 practitioners to discern how they viewed ethics within the industry. Nyilasy and Reid (2009) interviewed 28 senior-level practitioners to determine their theories of how advertising works. This study used interviews with 42 US advertising practitioners to examine their perspectives on why gender-role stereotypes were used in advertising.

Literature review

Stereotypes

Gender-role stereotypes are general beliefs about the characteristics, behaviors, and appropriate activities of men and women (Browne 1998). Stereotypes serve a variety of purposes. They can ease informational processing and simplify cognitive demands on the receiver (Bodenhausen, Kramer, and Sussen 1994). They can also enrich perception by allowing the perceiver to generalize and attribute additional information to a person based on other stereotypical features (Hilton and von Hippel 1996).

Gender stereotyping is seen as a normal cognitive process that helps individuals categorize what it means to be male and female (Martin and Halverson 1981). Stereotypes are not necessarily negative, but even stereotypes containing positive information can cause oversimplified perceptions, incorrectly applied evaluations, and a failure to see individual differences (Eisend 2010; Hilton and von Hipel 1996). Stereotypes warrant attention because they influence the way individuals interact with each other and perceive themselves (Macklin and Kolbe 1984).

Potential effects of gender-role stereotypes in advertising

Stereotypes have been found in advertisements targeting adults and children. In children's advertising, male characters tend to appear in greater numbers, have dominant roles, and be more active and aggressive (Browne 1998; Macklin and Kolbe 1984). Female characters tend to be 'shyer, giggly, unlikely to assert control, and less instrumental' (Browne 1998, 93). Because of advertising's prevalence, it is seen as one potential source of gender-role socialization for children. Gender-related content, in which male characters are more likely to be active, dominant and in control than female characters, can perpetuate gender-role stereotypes (Bakir and Palan 2010; Macklin and Kolbe 1984). The gender-role stereotypes children acquire can influence their perceptions of themselves and others (Macklin and Kolbe 1984) and can affect their roles, choices, and behaviors.

Regarding adults, women are more likely to be passive and deferent in advertising portrayals, while men are portrayed as powerful, autonomous, and knowledgeable (Eisend 2010). A meta-analysis revealed women were four times more likely than men not to have a speaking role and to have a role dependent on others (Eisend 2010). Women were over three times more likely to be shown in a domestic environment and two times more likely to be associated with domestic products (Eisend 2010).

Rather than serve as a faithful mirror, many scholars believe advertising distorts, magnifies, and selects (Giaccardi 1995). Pollay (1986) and Pollay and Gallagher (1990) advanced the idea that advertising does not reflect all of culture, but rather certain attitudes, behaviors, and lifestyles that serve the seller's interests. Advertising is said to reflect only those values that 'are more readily linked to the available products, that are easily dramatized in advertisements, and that are most reliably responded to by consumers who see the advertisements' (Pollay and Gallagher 1990, 360). A potentially troublesome outcome occurs since consumers can draw upon the representations in advertising to understand themselves and make sense of the world (Giaccardi 1995).

In the aggregate, advertising messages have the potential to substantially impact people and society. Potential cultural consequences for advertising and commercialization include materialism, selfishness, dissatisfaction, anxiety, conformity, cynicism, and distrust (Pollay and Gallagher 1990; Richins 1991).

Researchers have contrasted changing gender roles in society with the relative stability of advertising representations of men and women. Eisend (2010) found women were most likely to be stereotyped with regard to occupational status, which contrasts with the reality of women attending college at unprecedented levels. Tsai (2010) found that while gender roles are rapidly changing in society, with men taking a greater role with children and household duties, advertising has been slower to change. In this way, 'advertising may work to maintain status quo in terms of family gender norms and resist social changes towards gender neutrality' (Tsai 2010, 437).

Advertising practitioners as creators of cultural meaning

Advertising practitioners are seen as cultural intermediaries who construct symbolic meaning for goods (Kelly, Lawlor, and O'Donohoe 2005). 'Cultural meaning flows continually between its several locations in the social world, aided by the collective and individual efforts of designers, producers, advertisers and consumers' (McCracken 1986, 71). Practitioners both are producers and consumers of culture (Kelly, Lawlor, and O'Donohoe 2005). They draw on 'shared repertoires of contents' from a cultural system (Giaccardi 1995, 113) to create advertising that is novel and resonates with consumers (Csikszentmihalyi 1999; Vanden Bergh and Stuhlfaut 2006). Creatives watch innovative movies, listen to new music, read magazines and novels and photography books, and draw from cultural affairs as raw material to construct meaning (McCracken 1989; Kelly, Lawlor, and O'Donohoe 2005). They then '[filter] these cultural interests and identifications into the generation of symbolic ideas for advertising campaigns' (Kelly, Lawlor, and O'Donohoe 2005, 514).

Creatives know they can only solve the problem by making a connection with consumers (Hackley 2002). Consumers, who are constantly searching for meaning in the culturally constituted world (McCracken 1987), can draw upon the representations in advertising to understand themselves and make sense of reality (Giaccardi 1995).

'[Consumers] are looking for something they can use in their construction of new version of the self, of the family, of a community' (McCracken 1987, 122). Advertising is a potential source of new meaning for consumers.

'Gender is probably the social resource that is used most by advertisers' (Jhally 1987, 135). Gender roles naturally become integrated into practitioners' cultural knowledge. Frequently and recently activated constructs are more readily accessible in memory, and gender roles are easily and automatically activated in virtually all situations (Eagly and Karau 2002). Thus, it is likely that gender roles are part of the meaning-making process for practitioners.

Advertising practitioners' perspectives on gender portrayals

After calls to strengthen research into practitioners' perspectives, researchers are increasingly interested in examining professionals' perspectives on ethics (Zayer and Coleman 2015), mental models of creativity (Nyilasy, Canniford, and Kreshel 2013), and theories of how advertising works (Nyilasy and Reid 2009). Understanding practitioners' cultural models of advertising helps to understand the two-sided relationship between consumers, who select products and appropriate their values, and practitioners, who use their knowledge of culture and market systems to develop adverting messages (Nyalisi, Canniford, and Kreshel 2013). Understanding the knowledge contained within advertising agencies is important because it helps us understand how advertisers create cultural meaning (Hackley 2002).

Though no research has addressed practitioner perspectives on the roles and functions of stereotypes, two recent studies have examined practitioner perspectives on gender portrayals in advertising. Zayer and Coleman(2015) found that many US practitioners did not believe that the gendered messages they might create could be problematic for consumers. Further, some professionals believed men were immune to media's influence, while women were particularly vulnerable to it. Advertising professionals were found to conceptualize gender in ways that largely mirrored societal discourses of men as stoic and powerful and women as sensitive and vulnerable.

Similar results were found in a study of Chinese advertising practitioners (Shao, Desmarais, and Weaver 2014). The practitioners associated women with nurturing roles, a subordinate position, and beauty, while they associated men with status and power. The practitioners saw their role as reflecting or mirroring societal norms rather than developing or distorting cultural norms. They felt their use of these stereotyped roles was acceptable, because they did not want to challenge the 'perceived patriarchal conservatism of the audience' (343).

The current study

The literature has established that advertising often employs stereotypical gender representations, which in the aggregate can affect consumers' attitudes, behaviors, and worldview. Further, advertising practitioners are thought of as creators of cultural meaning, who draw from the cultural systems of society to connect brands with particular meanings. Practitioners have been shown to associate men and women with stereotypical representations, often neglecting their own role in perpetuating the stereotypes.

While there is much research analyzing the stereotypical advertising content in magazines and on television, to the author's knowledge there is no research to examine why practitioners use stereotypes. This study examines practitioners' own knowledge schemas about whether and how stereotypes communicate (Nyilasy and Reid 2009). It further examines what roles and functions practitioners believe stereotypes serve in advertising, as well as the most appropriate uses for stereotypes. In exploring these issues, it examines which factors exert influence on the decision to use stereotypical representations.

Methods

In-depth interviews with 42 practitioners in advertising agencies were conducted to understand their perceptions of why stereotypes were used in advertising. Qualitative research was deemed to be appropriate because it allows for the in-depth understanding of participants' perspectives in their own words. Advertising practitioners were chosen because they are responsible for the strategic and creative development and creation for advertisements. This study included perspectives from many roles within the advertising agency, including partners, creative directors, copywriters, art directors, graphic designers, account executives, digital strategists, account planners, and media planners.

To select the sample for round one of interviews, the Standard Directory of Advertisers (Advertising Redbooks) was used to find all agencies that met the following criteria: 30 or more employees, $25 million or more in revenue, responsible for creation of advertisements, and within 3.5 hours driving distance from the researcher. The size and distance requirements allowed the researcher to ask for multiple, in-person interviews with practitioners in their own space, which helped develop a rapport. Eight agencies met the criteria. The highest ranking executive at each agency was contacted via email to request a day of 30−60-minute interviews with various agency personnel. Of those, five agreed to allow interviews. An agency representative from each agency developed a half- to full-day schedule of 30−60-minute interviews, depending on the needs and considerations of the agency and its personnel. In each agency, the researcher visited the agency and interviewed people in a conference room or in offices.

The interview protocol moved from general to specific questions to provide context for each participants' answers and allow the conversation to develop based on the point of view of the participant (Morrison et al. 2011). To develop a rapport, participants were first asked how they got into the industry. They were then asked a very general question about how target audience gender influenced their creative or strategic process. The conversation then moved into the role of stereotypes in advertising, specifically, why do advertisers use stereotypes? What role or function do they serve? How are stereotypes useful to practitioners? Finally, they were asked whether they ever considered how stereotypes might affect consumers' worldview. Each question used laddering to further probe perceptions (Reynolds and Gutman 1988). Participants were asked if they had any additional thoughts to share before the interview was concluded.

To provide greater balance to the sample and increase the validity of the findings, round two of the data collection focused on practitioners who worked in larger markets, such as New York, Chicago, and Los Angeles. In the second phase of the research, in addition to probing the questions above, a qualitative repertory grid method was used. The repertory grid method allows for the examination of gender stereotypes in advertising by allowing practitioners to generate constructs based on their own particular experiences or exemplars of stereotypical and non-stereotypical advertising (Tan and Hunter 2002). It is based on Kelly's (1955) personal construct theory, which argues that people interpret reality based upon their own constructs and experiences. Practitioners were asked to share and compare examples of past campaigns they worked on in which the use of stereotypes

Table 1. Characteristics of informants and agencies.

Pseudonym	Department	Level	Sex	Agency size	Market size
C1	Creative	Mid-level	M	30–50	Small
C2	Creative	Senior	M	30–50	Small
C3	Creative	Mid-level	F	30–50	Small
C4	Creative	VP/Director/ECD	M	30–50	Small
C5	Creative	Senior	F	50–100	Small
C6	Creative	VP/Director/ECD	F	50–100	Small
C7	Creative	VP/Director/ECD	M	50–100	Small
AE1	Account Service	Senior	F	30–50	Small
AE2	Account Service	Mid-level	F	30–50	Small
AE3	Account Service	VP/Director/ECD	F	30–50	Small
AE4	Account Service	VP/Director/ECD	F	30–50	Small
AE5	Account Service	Senior	F	30–50	Small
AE6	Account Service	Partner/President/CEO	M	50–100	Small
AE7	Account Service	Partner/President/CEO	M	50–100	Small
AP1	Strategy/Planning	Partner/President/CEO	M	30–50	Small
AP2	Strategy/Planning	Partner/President/CEO	F	30–50	Small
AP3	Strategy/Planning	VP/Director/ECD	F	30–50	Small
AP4	Strategy/Planning	Partner/President/CEO	F	50–100	Small
AP5	Strategy/Planning	Partner/President/CEO	M	50–100	Small
M1	Media	VP/Director/ECD	F	30–50	Small
M2	Media	Mid-level	F	50–100	Small
D1	Digital/Social	Senior	F	50–100	Small
C8	Creative	VP/Director/ECD	M	30–50	Medium
C9	Creative	Mid-level	F	100–150	Medium
C10	Creative	Senior	M	100–150	Medium
AE8	Account Service	VP/Director/ECD	F	30–50	Medium
AP6	Strategy/Planning	VP/Director/ECD	F	100–150	Medium
AP7	Strategy/Planning	Mid-level	F	100–150	Medium
AP8	Strategy/Planning	Senior	M	100–150	Medium
D2	Digital/Social	VP/Director/ECD	M	30–50	Medium
D3	Digital/Social	Mid-level	F	100–150	Medium
D4	Digital/Social	Senior	M	100–150	Medium
C11	Creative	Partner/President/CEO	M	30–50	Large
C12	Creative	VP/Director/ECD	M	50–100	Large
C13	Creative	Mid-level	M	150–500	Large
C14	Creative	Senior	M	150–500	Large
C15	Creative	Mid-level	M	500+	Large
C16	Creative	Mid-level	M	500+	Large
C17	Creative	Mid-level	F	500+	Large
C18	Creative	Freelance	F	N/A	Large
AP9	Strategy/Planning	Freelance	F	N/A	Large
D5	Digital/Social	VP/Director/ECD	F	500+	Large

was appropriate and was not appropriate. Practitioners were asked to detail the differences in developing the campaigns from the two categories.

The data were analyzed in the tradition of interpretive, empirical research that has its interest in understanding the experiences and meanings of participants, as suggested by Spiggle (1994). All interviews were transcribed, printed, and analyzed. The data were cut apart and separated into loose categories that developed organically based on the coherent meaning of each chunk of data (Nyilasy and Reid 2009). The data from each category were then analyzed in detail both separately and as it compared to other categories to dimensionalize the category. One major analysis took place after round one of interviews, and a second major analysis took place after round two of interviews.

In phase one of data collection, 32 interviews were conducted in five agencies. The agencies ranged in size from 30 employees to 140 employees. All agencies were regional agencies located in small- to mid-sized markets in the Southeastern United States. Two agencies arranged 30-minute interviews, one agency arranged 45-minute interviews, and two agencies arranged 1-hour interviews. The interviews lasted for 38 minutes on average, and they ranged from 21 to 66 minutes in length. The shorter interviews occurred because the interviews were conducted at the agency, which meant some practitioners arrived late or had to leave early due to meetings. This is a potential weakness of the study, since the shorter interviews may not have allowed for sufficient depth of exploration. In phase two of data collection, 10 participants were interviewed via telephone from large markets in the United States, such as New York, Chicago, and Los Angeles. These participants were chosen to provide greater balance to the sample and to increase the validity of the findings. Phase two interviews lasted for 40 minutes on average, and they ranged from 24 to 51 minutes in length. Data collection ended when saturation was achieved (Morse 1995). To allow for open and honest communication, all participants and their agencies and clients were ensured confidentiality (Table 1) (Drumwright and Murphy 2004).

Findings

Does advertising use stereotypes?

When asked whether advertising uses stereotypes, many practitioners reluctantly agreed:

> Yes, and I hate to say the word stereotypical because I don't like that word. I don't like to stereotype people, but when you're in this industry, you kind of feel like you have to stereotype people. It is not comfortable for me, but yes there are certain ways we default to speaking if we are speaking to a young mother or a senior man. (C10)

AE6 echoed the sentiment, 'The phrase that you're using is now a negative connotation, but we use that technique to bridge gaps by people identifying with that problem.' D5 preferred the term typecasting. 'I think that what we see with the male female stereotypes, we are typecasting more so than stereotyping – that typecasting being that men behave in this way and women in that way.' D5 felt typecasting was different than stereotyping, because typecasting did not take 'a negative aspect of it and put that front and center as to disparage or denigrate.'

This data suggested a difference in how advertising practitioners versus the advertising literature viewed stereotypes. The advertising literature, for example, might analyze a sample of advertising in which women are found to be more often portrayed in domestic roles and consider holistically the potential implications of that overrepresentation.

Practitioners, instead, compartmentalized advertising representations by placing roles and behaviors that were not inherently negative representations into a subcategory. While D5 understood that representations were not balanced, she did not feel they were stereotypical. She reserved the term stereotype for representations that were negative or disparaging. This suggests a form of moral myopia (Drumwright and Murphy 2004), where practitioners downplayed their own responsibility or culpability for the effects of advertising (Zayer and Coleman 2015).

Practitioners felt advertising today used fewer stereotypes than in the past. C4 compared the current environment with that of the 1980s. 'If we were in the '80s I think your paper would have much more obvious damning pronouncements to make.' C4 continued, 'Because of my age, I would have to say that over time, I see less and less gender bias inherent in the work.' In the 1980s and 1990s, everyone was trying to target the busy mom. 'There was this idea that busy mom needed to be celebrated, busy mom needed to be soothed, busy mom needed to be this and that. And there was this sameness to the work.' C4 said he saw many more psychological subgroups and nuances in today's target audience research and descriptions.

Social media sites were believed to be one reason for decreased stereotypes. Clients in the 1980s did not hear as often from angry consumers when they aired campaigns that featured stereotypes. However, social media sites have allowed consumers to voice their concerns directly to clients, resulting in more sensitivity to the issue both for clients and practitioners. 'You put something out there now, everyone sees it, everyone has a voice and everyone can talk back to you. [...] So you have to be careful about your messaging' (C13). AE5 said, 'The world is digital, and we get to talk back. Before, advertisers might not have heard how annoying I find it for you to always have the ditsy blonde as the secretary and the middle-aged Caucasian guy as the authority figure. Now, I can get on your website or your Facebook page and say, "stop with the stereotypes."'

While practitioners agreed that stereotypes seemed to be decreasing over time, C4 believed that today's biases were more subtle and harder for practitioners to see:

> The fact that as a group, we could still have biases that we're both participating in and agreeing with, both men and women, both agency and client, is probably something that needs to explored. It's probably something that we are blissfully unaware of. We're patting ourselves on the back at our progressiveness and our ability to rise above, not realizing that we really haven't risen above. We just, maybe – we're better than our parents. (C4)

Both C14 and C11 agreed that there were certain taken-for-granted stereotypes and social roles practitioners used without awareness or questioning. 'We do tend to perpetuate stereotypes that really do need to be rethought, that are accepted without thinking' (C11).

Practitioners believed that advertising stereotyped less now than in previous generations, yet they also acknowledged that they do sometimes use stereotypes. The following findings address three main questions: Why do practitioners stereotype? When is stereotyping appropriate and not appropriate? What outside or structural factors contribute to the use of stereotypes?

Why do practitioners stereotype?

Stereotypes are based in truth

Practitioners believed that stereotypes were based in truth. 'I believe that any stereotype has a basis in at least, like, general population acceptance. So in other words, there has to be some really general acceptance that it is the truth in some way' (AP6). The bumbling dad stereotype, AP6 believed,

> developed over that period of time when there were very distinct roles, and where mom runs the house. Mom basically is the order giver in the house, like—go take out the trash. She is the one giving tasks to everybody. So there is some truth to that in terms of how society developed.

Stereotypes were thought to be representations of 'qualities that society agrees with' (C4), and thought to be commonly recognized and instantly understood. C17 felt stereotypes 'resonate well with everybody. Everybody has a general sense of stereotypes, good and bad. I think when you utilize the most general ones in advertising, they resonate on such a broad level.' C16 said, 'I think sometimes you're safer going with something that might be more stereotypical. Because you almost feel like the stereotype will reach more people.' In calling stereotypes, 'part of our consciousness,' AP5 felt stereotypes meant speaking to the target audience in their own language. 'Why is it a stereotype? It's a stereotype because it represents a broad swath of the population. It is representative of some segment. So that's my audience. So why shouldn't I speak to them in a language that they can understand?' (AP5). C14 said, 'Those are the tropes, the ways that society sees those roles.'

Just as gender stereotypes have been defined as general beliefs about the characteristics and behaviors of men and women (Browne 1998), practitioners also recognized and utilized general societal beliefs in their messaging. Practitioners drew from the tropes and roles in society to develop campaigns that resonated with and generated meaning for consumers (Giaccardi 1995; McCracken 1986; Kelly, Lawlor, and O'Donohoe 2005). C16 felt it was better to use any knowledge of a consumer group to try to relate to them, and sometimes stereotypes were the only knowledge creatives had. 'You want to find something that connects with them, and if you have this preconceived notion of what they are like, you are going to put that in the advertising' (C16).

When D2 needed to talk to homemakers, he developed a persona of a motherly mom, a baker in an apron, who could serve as a credible resource for the brand.

> They really wanted to appeal to homemakers, and so I jumped and was like we need a woman, she needs to be in an apron, she needs to be cute as all get out cutsie, I mean very motherly mom, a baker. And that's who we need to put out there, because that's who needs to represent us; and it worked. It was who people wanted, they wanted to connect with her because she was a credible resource. (D2)

D2 believed homemakers would trust a motherly mom in an apron as a credible resource. Thus, stereotypes were one way to communicate the credibility of the brand image or personality.

D1 said she had seen research to support the effectiveness of using stereotypical representations. 'We had seen research that supports the numbers. So if I'm in a meeting with the creative director and they say, "Well, what sells?" I have the numbers to prove that a man is perceived in a much more positive light if he's in a board room versus if I switch the pictures.' Stereotypes were believed to be based in truth and backed up not only by the practitioners' own lived experiences, but also by consumer research.

Stereotypes are attractive to audiences

Practitioners thought people were attracted to stereotypical images of their ideal selves.

People are attracted to images of themselves or who they want to be. And I learned that in 1976 in undergraduate school; I never forgot, and it's never failed. It's never failed me. So if you're showing that stereotype for certain client or certain age group, then they're going to be attracted to it. (AP5)

Advertisers felt it was smart to show consumers a representation of themselves in advertisements, or to 'default to those stereotypical ways of speaking or what we think they might like' (C10). C1 talked about creating a message for a gym. While the client wanted to showcase the typical consumer they were trying to attract, C1 argued for showing someone who had achieved results:

When we show people ripped and really in good shape, [clients] don't want too much of that. My argument is – do you want us to show old people that are really out of shape working out? You want to show the end product, you don't want to show the beginning product. (C1)

This finding is supported in the literature (Chang 2002; Sirgy 1982), which shows consumers find brands to be appealing when the brand's image matches their own ideal self-concept. This includes a consumer preference for advertisements with characters similar to their self-concept (Chang 2002).

AP5 pointed to the difference between the people in Payless Shoes advertisements versus the Lexus for Christmas campaign with the bow on the car. Both advertisements showed people dressed in the style and status of the brand's typical consumers, which he believed was a smart advertising decision. AP5 elaborated on the choice of actors in the Lexus ads:

That Lexus always kills me with their Lexus for Christmas campaign. Here is this is perfect family with a beautiful, well-off blonde woman with her three kids. And this woman's like— this woman doesn't have three kids. She looks like she's about 40 years old. She's about big as that [holding up his pinky finger]. And you know, smiling, good-looking husband with the hair back and is tall. And these perfect children, perfect children. Even the dog looks good. And there's the key to a Lexus for Christmas. Well that's who's going to give each other a Lexus, somebody in this big house and all that. So they're attracted to that, or they want a Lexus. (AP5)

He believed that the family, house, and dog in the Lexus advertisement represented the ideal version of the type of family who might buy a Lexus for a Christmas gift. Choosing this perfect family tied the Lexus brand image to this particular and especially ideal vision of a family.

Practitioners thought people looked for communities to which they belonged, looked for people like them. So while not everyone identifies with the Lexus for Christmas family and campaign, there were other cars and campaigns with which others could identify. Brand communication helped consumers understand whether a brand fit within their lifestyle:

[Branding] is just everywhere. It's just all around. […] I think it sets an expectation or standard that we find our place in. So while I might not see myself as a Lexus person who's going to live in that big mansion, who's going to have the perfect children or the perfect spouse and the perfect dog; for one I'm aware that there are people like that, and that I'm not. So I might look more at a Toyota or Hyundai and identify with those people. (AP5)

There was a belief that advertising showcased a particular lifestyle and consumer likely to buy the brand. Advertising representations served as a source from which consumers could draw meaning for their identities (McCracken 1987). Consumers in a certain segment of the population were believed to identify with the lifestyle represented in the advertising, allowing the brand potentially to become integrated into the consumers' lifestyle perceptions.

Stereotypes communicate quickly

Stereotypes were believed to communicate quickly. 'You have a lot to convey in 30 seconds or less' (C4). Stereotypes were seen as a 'shorthand' way of communicating quickly (AP4). The goal of using stereotypical people in advertisements was for the audience to think, 'I know the type' (C4). Once this was accomplished, the message 'can move on to the situation, story, product usage, and you've saved these precious seconds in a 30-second commercial' (C4). C11 called this 'economy of storytelling.'

C14 said stereotypes could play against 'cultural clichés' and provide 'a quick way of setting up a story; you don't have to do a lot of explanation.' C9 provided an example of employing the ideal beauty stereotype when developing an ad for a beauty product. 'That's a really quick, easy shorthand. [...] It's a quick way to communicate my product *equals* ideal beauty.' Similarly, C12 understood that women did not typically wear 8-inch heels, but he felt their use in an advertisement offered 'instant identification or quick recognition' to communicate 'stylish, chic and very glamorous.' M2 said, 'it's really about making it easy for that person' to understand the message. These examples offer evidence of practitioners drawing on 'shared repertoires of contents' from culture (Giaccardi 1995, 113), such as perceptions of ideal beauty, to construct brand meaning (McCracken 1989).

Practitioners believed stereotypical or two-dimensional characters helped the consumer quickly understand the person in the advertisement, then have the mental capacity to focus on the message of the advertisement, which was typically about a problem and a solution (Table 2):

> We have two-dimensional characters often in short format things. This person is angry, or confused, or happy, or has a problem and needs a solution. We know that they are constipated. We don't know that there are also ten other qualities that will be fascinating if you know them for longer. They're constipated, they need ex-lax, and then they're better. She has a pimple, she needs this spray, and then she's better. Well, there a hundred others things about her that we should know. But we have 15 seconds or 30 seconds, and we've got to dumb things down a little bit. (C4)

Without the use of stereotypical representations, advertisers could spend 30 seconds just trying to explain 'the nuances of this person's life' (C4).

Stereotypes simplify processing and categorization

Practitioners believed stereotypes communicated simply. C17 said, 'I think it's the simplest. I think it gets a message across very simply. And it talks to your demographic very simply. So I think in terms of communication, it's just a simpler message.' C18 agreed that 'simplicity' was the key. The time constraints of a 30-second spot meant stereotypes were sometimes 'a smart way to talk to people in terms they are familiar with' (C18).

The stereotyping literature has shown that gender stereotypes can simplify message processing through categorization (Martin and Halverson 1981). Some practitioners also discussed the brain and humans' natural tendency to put objects, behaviors, and people into categories. AE6 recognized that the brain needed shortcuts because of the immense

Table 2. Why do practitioners use stereotypes?

	Description
Stereotypes are based in truth	Stereotypes are perceived as general knowledge with which society agrees.
Stereotypes are attractive to audiences	Consumers are attracted to and identify with images of their ideal selves in advertisements.
Stereotypes communicate quickly	A lot to convey in 30 seconds. Stereotypes communicate scene and characters quickly and allow a focus on the message.
Stereotypes simplify processing and categorization	Many brands in marketplace. Stereotypes allow consumers to categorize and quickly make decisions. Stereotypes help practitioners communicate with diverse audiences.
Stereotypes prevent distraction	Consumers expect typical situations and roles. Consumers are distracted by and question the motivation for atypical representations. Stereotypical situations and representations encourage a focus on the selling message.
Stereotypes prevent thinking	Consumers react emotionally to stereotypes or accept them without thinking rationally.
Stereotypes are the obvious solution	Stereotypes are the typical or obvious solution to a problem. Stereotypes are the safe solution and are often ignored by consumers.

amount of choices in the world. 'You've got 50,000 grocery store brands versus what used to be 10,000. And you're bombarded with so many messages, thousands and thousands everyday. The brain needs some shortcut helpers along the way and a stereotype is a shortcut to, "Oh, I get that."'

AP5 explained it as an evolutionary trait:

I'm going to explain to you as it's been explained to me. It makes more sense than anything. That's evolutionary because our ancient ancestors, whatever they were, whoever they were, they had to generalize. They had to know, okay that animal with the mask and the ring tail is not going to hurt me. But that thing over there with the big old fangs, I better get away from him. So that you can quickly make decisions, and you don't have to sit there and ponder every one. And so we try to lump things in a category. (A5)

Just as the literature on stereotypes notes that categorization is natural but can have negative consequences (Hilton and von Hippel 1996; Eisend 2010; Martin and Halverson 1981), AP5 also recognized that this evolutionary need to categorize and segment potentially could be beneficial or harmful. 'Now it's what causes prejudice and some other things like that. So it's a good thing, but it can be a bad thing.'

Stereotypes also simplified processing and categorization for practitioners as they developed advertisements. C16 felt stereotypical thinking occurred in advertising because 'human beings use stereotypes' and 'ads are written by human beings.' C18 agreed:

As a creative you are given a brief that says you are talking to males or to females. [...] You are taught to think in the voice of the person you are talking to. And unfortunately, if you are not that person, which you are generally not, [...] people don't know how to get into another person's shoes. And I think the closest thing they have are things they have seen. They have seen other ads. I think stereotypes push other stereotypes because we learn from each other.

For this creative, one tactic for trying to resonate was to draw upon stereotypes from other advertising campaigns and media representations. She said this happened 'because you are trying to get into the shoes of a very specific person, without knowing them' (C18). Thus, stereotypes simplified processing both for consumers bombarded by messages and for practitioners trying to communicate with diverse audiences.

Stereotypes prevent distraction

The professionals in this study believed stereotypes used established conventions to prevent distraction. C12 said, 'a large part of what is seen as stereotyping is just typical – a typical situation.' Practitioners believed meeting consumers' expectations with typical situations and roles allowed consumers to focus on the message. 'There are certain things they expect to be there' (C11). C11 continued, 'Part of it is to not let people get distracted by side issues […] In order to stay on the story, the conventions are used, the clichés are used, the stereotypes are used – to not let people get distracted.'

In using established conventions, practitioners felt they were speaking in a language the audience understood. D2 felt consumers were 'more comfortable with stereotypes.' C13 believed consumers were confused by and questioned the motives for representations that went against conventions. C13 said, 'The expectation is to always see a normal family. If you suddenly make the family mixed race or two dads or two moms, they are going to say, "Why are there two moms? Is the commercial about two moms?"' C14 had a similar example when dad was in the kitchen, rather than mom. 'If you put a man in the role of the homemaker pouring cereal, then the questions may arise. Is he out of work? Is he between jobs? Why is he putting stuff on the table instead of the mother?' When consumers spent cognitive effort questioning the choices in the advertisement, they were thought to be distracted from the selling message.

Using a typical family or an average mom was thought of as a template or background for the creative twist in the advertisement. In working with fast casual food brands, C13 said, 'We want to show that typical mealtime moment; and with that, the stereotyping works. Because, we go "OK, what does a typical family look like?" And it's a mom and a dad and two kids, and the kids are probably a boy and a girl.' He continued:

> And I think, in that instance, you're not really making any kind of statement. You're kind of using them as a template. As like, "We open on this average family of four eating burgers." Then we think, how can that scenario be different, what's funny about that scenario, what could be interesting? The casting and stereotyping of the family become a background element for a funny joke you put in there.

C13 felt that each ad could communicate one main message, and a non-traditional family would distract from that message. 'If you were to, say, make that family untraditional, then that, as a viewer, might take away from whatever your creative gag or creative twist is.' C13 continued, 'As a viewer, when you see something out of the stereotype, you're immediately going to go, "There must be a reason that this is different." And that would take the legs out from whatever your gag is.'

In order to prevent consumers from questioning the decisions within advertisements, advertisers and marketers often ensured that every cue within the advertisement met consumers' expectations. C13 said, 'Even in terms of the clothes, we've had issues on shoots, where the clothes seemed too hip. [Clients] worried the clothes weren't what the average mom in Ohio would be wearing.' Similarly, C15 talked about a bank client targeting the ultra-affluent. 'And we will get feedback on a print ad like, "Oh, I don't think someone that wealthy would wear this kind of watch." Or, "If her net worth were this much, she would be wearing pearls."' He continued, 'It's just an interesting thing to have to think about, you know, does this person look rich enough to sell an investment account to another rich person?'

A similar concern for meeting consumers' expectations was at play as C13 described a beer commercial. He talked about casting for a dad and 'hot girls' in the commercial several years back:

> At this casting literally every single woman in the room was attractive. And then the client would be like, "No, we need this kind of attractive versus this kind of attractive." And you're thinking, gosh. It felt ridiculous. And you end up with the stereotyped version of what an attractive woman looks like. (C13)

Since consumers questioned elements that were out of the ordinary, there may have been a special interest in using typical representations in this instance to avoid having consumers question the use of 'hot girls' in the advertisement.

Thus, practitioners thought consumers expected stereotypical representations, while representations that went against established conventions were thought to confuse consumers and distract from the selling message. Stereotypical roles were believed to help people assign reason. This meant that much effort went into ensuring that every cue within the message – such as casting, clothing and jewelry – met consumers' expectations. This ties closely with the next theme, which is that stereotypes prevent thinking.

Stereotypes prevent thinking

Stereotypical representations were said to be tools that get consumers to react emotionally rather than rationally. 'We want [consumers] to not think, but click and take an action' (D1). C11 believed, 'Thinking is vexatious. People will avoid it whenever they can.' C11 said, 'Stereotypes exist to stop thinking, to prevent thinking, to prevent consideration.' He continued:

> The girl is wearing glasses, so she is intellectual or bookish […] That sort of shorthand is useful if you want people to not think and just respond. We are much more often after an emotional response that we can evoke rather than some rational process.

C11 used political candidates as an example. 'Voters don't vote rationally. They think, "Here's a guy I'd like to have a beer with. He says the things I want to hear."'

C11 said politicians were especially likely to use stereotypes and emotional clichés so that consumers would react emotionally rather than rationally. 'Rick Perry puts on glasses so he can be smarter, using a stereotype to influence low information voters, who are numerous in the swing voter category' (C11). 'The audience he is trying to reach is likely to believe that on a very visceral level. Oh, look how intelligent he looks' (C11). He continued, 'Tactically that's a very smart move. Because fundamentally he's not a very bright man, and anything he can do to disguise that is good.' He believed this tactic was especially effective for low-knowledge voters and impulse purchases. The use of cues, such as glasses to signify a person who is bookish or smart, is an example of communicators drawing on meanings and clichés from culture, such as people who wear glasses are smart, and using these to connote brand meaning (e.g. McCracken 1986).

Stereotypes are the obvious solution

Finally, stereotypes were said to be the easy or obvious solution. 'They're top of mind. They're like a lot of clichés. That's just the first thing in your mind; that's where your mind goes. And that's why they are stereotypes. I guess I have to think past that' (C7). C11 said, 'It's a matter of having the restraint to reject the easy idea, the stereotype, the cliché.' Stereotypical representations were the easy way out for practitioners and clients. 'I would say, sometimes as marketers, people get lazy' (D5). 'They don't want to fight for "let's rethink this." It's so much easier to say, "I am going to get to a yes by taking the path that is already travelled, because that path is cleared already"' (D5). C17 said in this way, 'stereotypes can be a crutch.'

Practitioners felt advertisements containing stereotypes were middle of the road, bland, or ordinary. Stereotypical representations represented 'the status quo' and were 'invisible and bland' (C14). 'It's just safe,' said C14. He believed consumers were not usually offended by stereotypical advertising because they did not really notice it. 'It just floats by' (C14). Stereotypical representations were thought to be unsurprising to consumers, even expected. 'You disappear into the background of ordinary just by obeying every stereotype' (C11).

C11 contrasted ordinary stereotypical communication with breakthrough communication. 'To really have breakthrough communications, sometimes the best thing is to smash stereotypes in a very visible and obvious way.' The Dove Campaign for Real Beauty was an example of a campaign that challenged advertising norms for the beauty industry. When trying to persuade consumers, 'you can't simply make an argument out of pure rationality' (C11). Instead, practitioners first had to challenge consumers' acceptance of their current brand, then convince them to purchase the challenger brand instead:

> You don't just have to persuade them, you have to win them over. You have to disrupt their thinking. It's necessary to blow up their perception of what they are doing now, in that you have a much better model. You can't do that by adhering to convention and adhering to stereotypes. You have to have some sort of breakthrough, and that often calls for blowing up the stereotype and working very hard against it. (C11)

When is stereotyping appropriate and not appropriate?

Another key question of this study was when are stereotypes appropriate and inappropriate? Qualitative repertory grid analysis was used to probe practitioners for specific examples from their experiences. Several insights were revealed.

Appropriate uses of stereotypes

Practitioners believed the most effective use of stereotypes was stereotype subversion. C14 said, 'Lazy or weak communication plays into clichéd stereotypes and doesn't do anything with them. You have to question the roles when you put them in there and see if you want to subvert the stereotype and play with it.' The subversion of stereotypes took more energy and effort than using stereotypes. 'It takes a little extra work and a little extra thought' (C14). C14 continued, 'If you just play along with that gender stereotyping, you are not thinking deep enough about it.'

Sometimes, advertising flipped the stereotype on its head, and used an obvious 'wink' to let consumers in on the joke. D5 said, 'It needs to come across very clearly that we are all winking at this, or we are all laughing together. I am not laughing at you.' Several practitioners used the example of the Old Spice Man Your Man Could Smell Like. 'If you look at the Old Spice campaign, they take the stereotype of the arrogant male. They do a really good job with that and just turn it upside down and really exaggerate it to where it's funny' (AP3). D5 also referenced the ad, 'It is done in such an exaggerated fashion that we all get that is done tongue and cheek and it's a wink wink.'

Other times, advertising changed the discussion around a particular cultural norm, such as the Always 'Like a Girl' campaign. 'There are certain clients that are ahead of the curve in terms of stereotyping and using it to their advantage. Like the Always Like a Girl thing' (C13). C13 continued:

> It took this cultural notion or cultural insight – of why do you use this language? [...] They positioned it as almost a discussion or a dissertation on the topic. And people were able to join in on that discussion on social media. The thing about that is it resonated because it was a discussion, let's talk about this and bring this issue to resolution.

Stereotypes also were thought to be appropriate when the message respected and rang true to the consumer. C12 discussed an ad he made in which a new dad was carrying a baby, and it said, 'From the moment she was born, you never wanted to let go.' C12 felt this used a stereotype of the tender dad, but also resonated with consumers.

Finally, representations that allowed consumers to laugh at themselves rather than feel laughed at were seen to be appropriate. C14 said there were several examples of spots that used people from India running an electronic store. 'In some of them, they made the people heroic and funny and self-aware. They made it work so the group that was being stereotyped could kind of laugh at themselves and not feel they were being put down.' C14 felt this use of stereotypes was more appropriate than examples in which 'you would make fun of someone's Bollywood accent in a way that makes that seem the butt of the joke. You have to be sensitive to making people seem like clowns.'

Inappropriate uses of stereotypes

Stereotypes were particularly inappropriate when they reinforced negative perceptions. 'I think anything that puts down a gender, anything that says that one sex isn't as good at something as another, that's where stereotypes come into being a problem' (C18). 'You should never say that someone is stupid or not smart or not as athletic or not as career-oriented' (C18). D5 talked about making a video series for the IT space, in which the typical employee is a white, middle-aged man:

> And, of course, the star is always a man. And I have no problem with that. However, they did want to put a woman in, but they wanted to make her his assistant. And what is wrong with that? Well number one, in the land of IT, no one has assistants anymore. No one is getting him coffee. Nobody is checking his mail. There is no such thing. Not only do I not understand why the woman has to be that, but that job no longer exists.

D5 made some suggestions to improve the video series:

> So this person may be junior, and I am OK with that. But she is not going to be less knowledgeable. In the context of the series of videos, at some point, she is going to do something technical. At some point, even though she is not the star, we are going to clearly establish that women are not the dumb blondes of the technology industry. That they are capable. And more importantly, that they are on the come up.

Stereotypical messages that did not ring true to consumers also were thought to be inappropriate. C12 discussed an advertisement for that Motrin targeted moms. It sarcastically discussed the trend of wearing your baby in a sling or wrap and lamented the pain and strain associated with it. Moms, who enjoyed using slings and wraps, 'just went crazy' (C12). C12 felt the campaign missed the mark because 'that was a guy's interpretation of a stereotype that wasn't accurate. They projected themselves saying, "I wouldn't want to do that, therefore women don't want to do that."'

Representations that conjured up negative connotations or made a segment of the population into a clown or the butt of the joke were also thought to be particularly inappropriate. C12 discussed the Budweiser Super Bowl ad in which it was revealed that the referee was so good at ignoring coaches who yelled in his face because his wife did the same thing at home. In this case, 'Women think, "That could be me. They are making fun of me"' (C12).

The antidote to creating stereotypical ads that represented the consumer in a negative light, AP1 said, was 'a high degree of respect for the consumer. And coming at it from a perspective of – how can I best get to know you: your wants, your needs, your psychographics, in such a way that it helps us create a conversation with you?'

Other factors contributing to stereotypical representations

While this study took an individualized route to explaining stereotypical representations, probing practitioners for their own perceptions on the topic, practitioners' answers sometimes pointed to external or structural factors that contributed to stereotypical representations. Four key factors are outlined here, including the 30-second time constraint, the nature of segmentation research, the masculine culture of the creative department, and clients' risk aversion.

Thirty-second constraint

The structural constraints of the 30-second commercial were thought to contribute to the use of stereotypes in advertising (Giaccardi 1995). 'We're talking about a 30-second commercial, which is not a lot of time' (C13). Because practitioners had to accomplish a lot in 30 seconds – including gaining attention, communicating a brand message, gaining interest, and sometimes even prompting action – they relied on stereotypes as a device to communicate quickly with consumers. 'If I feel like this stereotype is going to convey this so that my viewer gets it [snaps fingers] just like that, and I can go on with what I have to say, it's just a shorthand. For better or for worse, that can still work very effectively' (AE5). Practitioners believed stereotypes allowed for quick communication under tight time constraints.

Segmentation research

The segmentation research commonly employed in marketing and advertising also promoted the use of stereotypes. D5 said good marketing began with segmentation research, but it could also lead to stereotyping:

> As a good marketer you are always starting with an insight, and what did the demographics and the psychographics of the target audience look like. And I think where stereotypes come in is where you take those averages and try to create a picture of that as a norm, without realizing that there are going to be some things on the fringe with outliers, and that we also have to put those images in front of us. (D5)

D5 discussed the example of IT, in which white men were overrepresented in the industry and in marketing messages. However, she believed the research supported the representation. 'I think if you stepped inside the company and said, "Why are we always using the same thing?" Someone is going to inevitably pull out a piece of paper that says, "Here's the research."' D5 continued, 'They are going to pull out the piece of paper from the research that shows it skewed male and it skewed middle aged and Caucasian.' Thus, the common practice of segmenting consumers and detailing a prototypical consumer, which is seen as an important part of communicating effectively, may also promote stereotypical representations in advertisements.

Masculine culture of the creative department

The masculine culture of the creative department and creative award shows was another factor that contributed to stereotypical representations. 'We are a traditional, heterosexual, male-oriented society, though it's changing' (C14). This extended to the creative department as well. 'For a long time, advertising has been a boys' club. There just aren't that many female creatives' (C18). C12 said, 'Because men are creating the ads to please other men, mostly the judges at shows, they can't get away from it.' The underrepresentation of women in the creative department, as well as its boys' club culture and masculine sensibility, has been detailed elsewhere (e.g. Alvesson 1998; Gregory 2009; Mallia 2009; Windels and Lee 2012). Similar to findings by Windels and Lee (2012), the masculine culture was so pervasive, according to C12, that women 'have to think like guys to succeed.' C12 felt the culture was one in which women did not feel comfortable challenging the norms. 'And if men are laughing, women are polite and they don't speak up.' This likely resulted from status inequities in the department (Windels and Lee 2012).

Practitioners believed that stereotypes stemmed from a lack of awareness or cultural sensitivity. 'I think most stereotypes come from just ignorance. [...] I don't mean ignorance in an intellectual level, but just the lack of awareness' (C7). D5 added, 'What happens with cultural sensitivity is that if you are not of that culture, you don't understand what you are saying and what you are doing.' That lack of knowledge and diversity could contribute to unintentional use of stereotypes. 'I think that if a guy is working on a female product, he probably isn't trying to be stereotypical, but he probably doesn't know that many things about women' (C18). D5 said companies and agencies needed to do better:

> Are companies doing enough to ensure that the company and the people making these communication decisions are reflective of what is actually in the marketplace today? So if you don't have a woman in technology helping with the ads, then you potentially step into a pile of something when it comes to women, because you're just not as sensitive. (D5)

Clients are risk averse

A key factor driving the use of stereotypes was clients' risk aversion (Nyilasy, Canniford, and Kreshel 2013). 'It's more dictated by clients than anything else' (C1). Clients wanted to avoid offending any consumers. 'Clients don't want their advertising to be offensive, that's the last thing they want. They want it to be appealing, and appealing to as many people as possible' (C13). C13 continued, 'With clients, there's this fear; they don't want to offend. Fear of — they want everyone to like what they put out there.'

In trying to appeal to as many consumers as possible, clients tended to push toward a perception of consumers that was average in every way. 'If our target is a mom in her 40s, what does the average mom in her 40s look like. Or is this person too attractive or not attractive enough?' (C13). There was also a push toward representations commonly seen in advertising and representations that fit clients' expectations of the target audience (C16).

Clients were not comfortable using actors or ideas that pushed the boundaries or differed from established conventions. 'I think there's a bit of fear from certain clients that pushes you to the middle of the road and pushes you to a stereotype' (C13). When messages were 'different than the norm, [clients] don't want to take a chance' (D1). Clients' risk aversion contributed to stereotypical representations in advertisements. 'Where you end up getting stereotypes is because that might feel safe. It's something they've seen before. It's safe. It matches their idea of something' (C13).

Discussion and implications

Practitioners reluctantly agreed that advertising sometimes used gender stereotypes. However, they believed that the term stereotype was too negative to describe what they perceived as the benign use of consumers in typical social roles. This provided further evidence for moral myopia among practitioners, who generally rationalized away or did not see their own role in contributing to gender stereotypes (Drumwright and Murphy 2004; Shao, Desmarias, and Weaver 2014; Zayer and Coleman 2015).

A key contribution of this study is that it was the first to detail why practitioners used stereotypes or what they believed to be the communication functions of stereotypes in advertising. Practitioners viewed stereotypes as useful tools that worked quickly and were based in truth. Stereotypes were said to be a part of our consciousness as a society, or representations of how society sees certain roles. Further, practitioners felt people were attracted to images of their ideal selves in advertising, including certain stereotypical ideals and roles. As such, practitioners used stereotypes quickly to communicate about a character, get the consumer to think, 'I know the type,' and move on to the more important, message-based aspects of the advertisement.

Professionals in this study believed stereotypes played on consumers' expectations, and thus helped to avoid distraction from the brand message. In using stereotypical norms and roles, practitioners were communicating messages they knew the audience understood. Stereotypes helped consumers assign reason or categorize the elements in the message. C13 referred to stereotypical characters as a background element in the message, as a template used to set up the actual creative twist or brand message. Practitioners went through great lengths to ensure that all elements of the campaign, such as clothing and casting, met consumers' expectations – except that one creative twist. Atypical gender representations were believed to prompt questions. Consumers might wonder why the unconventional roles were there or what they communicated. These questions distracted consumers from the selling message.

Using the proper cues or cultural clichés was important to several themes in this study. In addition to preventing distraction, it also prevented thinking. Through the use of cues, such as glasses to denote intelligence, practitioners hoped consumers would respond or accept the cue (and its implied meaning) rather than questioning or rationally thinking through the message. They wanted low-knowledge consumers to respond viscerally or emotionally and to associate the brand with a particular meaning without considering whether the brand actually delivers on it.

While simply using stereotypes was lazy, practitioners believed subverting stereotypes could be very effective. When advertising subverted stereotypes – such as the Old Spice Man Your Man Could Smell Like or the Dove Campaign for Real Beauty – it was seen to shape rather than reflect cultural norms. Alternatively, practitioners believed advertising was at its worst when it used stereotypes to reinforce negative perceptions of a particular group.

This study examined practitioners' perceptions on what and how stereotypes communicate; it extended a line of research that emphasizes practitioners' theories on how advertising works (e.g. Kover 1995; Nyilasy and Reid 2009; Nyilasy, Canniford, and Kreshel 2013). Similar to Nyilasy and Reid (2009), practitioners believed that advertisements that purposefully broke the rules, in this case by subverting stereotypes, were more successful. Practitioners had a theory on why stereotypes worked, as well. They attributed it to humans' natural tendency to categorize in order to simplify the environment. Their theory was in line with the psychological research on stereotypes, which found stereotypes make information processing easier for the receiver (Bodenhausen, Kramer, and Sussen 1994). Further, practitioners believed that stereotyping was not necessarily harmful or negative, but could help communicate quickly and effectively. This, too, was in line with psychological research on the topic (Hilton and von Hippel 1996; Martin and Halverson 1981).

Stereotypes as cultural meaning

This research contributed to the literature on advertisers as creators of cultural meaning. Cultural categories, such as gender, are the basic units used to segment the world (McCracken 1986). This study provided evidence that stereotypes were a part of the cultural resources practitioners drew upon to create meaning. Practitioners believed that stereotypes were based in truth. They understood that consumers put people into categories. They understood that brands could draw on stereotypical representations to position the brand and its values. They understood that consumers were drawn to representations of themselves and who they wanted to be. They also believed that stereotypes communicated quickly and allowed consumers more time and cognitive space to process brand-related information. Practitioners then used this knowledge to communicate with certain segments of the population in the audiences' own voice using a representative from their own group.

Practitioners understood their role as cultural intermediaries constructing meaning for goods, and they viewed stereotypes as a tool to use in the creation of cultural meaning for brands (e.g. Giaccardi 1995; Kelly, Lawlor, and O'Donohoe 2005; McCracken 1986). Stereotypes allowed practitioners to draw on well-known representations of a motherly baker or a busy mom as a cultural resource to communicate brand values. Practitioners drew on the cultural meaning associated with certain representations to create advertising that resonated with consumers.

It was hard for practitioners to recognize how the simple act of using those roles could affect consumers' worldview. Some norms and roles went unquestioned by advertising as a whole. They became taken-for-granted as the norm. The beauty industry, for example, developed norms over the years that included representations of thin, beautiful women with smooth skin and white teeth (Jhally, Kilbourne, and Rabinovitz 2010). However, practitioners who recognized these norms could subvert them, to great effect; such as Dove's subversion of the stereotypes used in the beauty industry.

Managerial implications

There was a belief among practitioners that stereotypes were based in truth, communicated quickly, and simplified processing – all beliefs are backed up in the stereotyping literature. Additionally, clients felt more comfortable with things they had seen and experienced before (C13). This suggests a difficult task for agency leaders and managers who wish to challenge those conventions and prevent the use or overuse of stereotypical representations.

While there were many themes related to the reasons stereotypes might communicate with consumers, one theme detailed why stereotypes might be ignored. Stereotypes were thought to be typical, ordinary, or obvious message solutions. Stereotypical representations were thought to be invisible to consumers. Practitioners believed breakthrough advertising smashed stereotypes rather than playing on them.

Creative practitioners 'believe there is only one rule for advertising to work effectively: It has to be creative' (Nyilasy and Reid 2009, 88). Advertising that does not take any risks often gets lost in the clutter (Windels and Stuhlfaut 2014). Managers who want to counteract or dissuade practitioners from using stereotypes must blow up existing perceptions of stereotypes as fast, effective tools based in truth or as reflections of reality that connote meaning to consumers. They must subvert practitioners' existing perceptions of stereotypes. One way to do this is to position stereotypical advertising as typical, commonplace or formulaic. Creatives want to create breakthrough work (Nyilasy and Reid 2009), not work that is formulaic. By positioning work that includes stereotypes as work that is not creative, managers might convince creatives to break the habit of using stereotypical representations.

Equally important is convincing clients that typical and stereotypical representations largely are ignored by consumers. Advertising practitioners must do a better job of educating clients on the value of breakthrough creative work and the risks associated with typical or expected work. Managers must find examples of campaigns that have broken through the clutter; they must detail to clients how and why these breakthrough campaigns succeeded. Breakthrough campaigns challenge conventions and change the discussion. They must also warn of the invisibility of expected campaigns.

The practitioners in this study referred to stereotypical communication as relevant and expected, but never as novel or creative. Creative advertising takes a risk. It does something new. Taking that risk is uncomfortable for the account executives, clients, and creatives who create it and sign off on it. Taking that risk can lead to greater chance of impact, but also greater chance of failure (Windels and Stuhlfaut 2014). For those wishing to make an impact above a baseline performance, framing stereotypical representations as safe or expected may help persuade clients and others to take a chance on a riskier solution. To push creative boundaries, that's part of a larger education that agency leaders must provide to others. Creativity cannot come from comfort. Truly creative work causes fear and discomfort for practitioners and clients alike (Nyilasy, Canniford, and Kreshel 2013; Windels and Stuhlfaut 2014). To break new ground, people have to get comfortable with being uncomfortable. Agency managers must communicate the value of discomfort to all involved in the campaign development process.

Limitations and future research

One potential limitation of this research was its overrepresentation of practitioners from small- to mid-sized regional agencies on the Gulf Coast. About half of the practitioners interviewed from the small- to mid-sized markets had worked in larger markets such as New York, Chicago, and Los Angeles, before moving to their current agencies, which does provide some geographic diversity to the data. Additionally, phase two of data collection focused specifically on practitioners who currently worked in larger markets to provide further validity for the results. Future research could examine advertising agencies that target specific ethnic populations, such as Latino or African-American consumers, to determine if their use of stereotypes differs from general market practitioners.

This study asked for individuals' perceptions of why stereotypes were used in advertising. It asked them to talk about and provide examples from their own experiences, to discuss their own perspectives on why advertising uses stereotypes or what stereotypes help communicate. Thus, this study does not directly address the institutional or cultural structures that also exert pressure on practitioners. In discussing their perspectives, practitioners did detail some external factors that contributed to stereotyping, such as clients' risk aversion and the boys' club culture of the creative department. Given that practitioners draw from culture to create meaning for brands in advertising campaigns, it is likely that sociocultural issues such as institutionalized sexism and societal gender norms greatly impact the use of stereotypes in advertising. As C4 noted, practitioners may be 'blissfully unaware of' the subtle forces and biases that shape practitioners' work. Future research might examine more deeply the greater institutional and cultural influences.

Another potential limitation of the paper is practitioners' desire to be seen as professional and effective, yet also caring and ethical. This might have affected their responses. They may have focused more on positive reasons for stereotyping to defend the practice and its validity. Finally, the shorter length of some of the interviews was a limitation. The shorter interviews were likely a feature of interviewing practitioners during the business day, when they had meetings and client calls in which to attend. Future research might consider interviewing practitioners on their own time.

This study filled a gap in the literature by examining practitioners' perspectives on the roles and functions of stereotypes in advertising. This research found that practitioners find stereotypes to be a quick and easy way to meet baseline performance levels. Unlike researchers' perceptions that stereotypes are offensive to consumers or shape their worldview negatively, practitioners felt consumers were comforted by seeing representations of themselves or who they aspired to be. The kind of stereotypical advertising practitioners felt they did today was advertising that was risk averse. This offers one possible way to move practitioners beyond the use of stereotypes. By framing stereotypes as typical solutions, solutions that, as C9 said, 'are things that frustrated creative say when they don't have any ideas,' perhaps we can influence practitioners' representations of stereotypical solutions. Because if there's one thing advertising practitioners don't want to be, it's typical.

Acknowledgements

The author wishes to thank the practitioners who volunteered their time and expertise for this study. Thanks also to the anonymous reviewers who provided comments that improved this manuscript. Finally, thanks to the Manship School of Mass Communication for its continued support.

Disclosure statement

No potential conflict of interest was reported by the author.

References

Alvesson, M. 1998. Gender relations and identity at work: A case of masculinities and femininities in an advertising agency. *Human Relations* 51, no. 8: 969–1005.
Bakir, A., and K.M. Palan. 2010. How are children's attitudes toward ads and brands affected by gender-related content in advertising. *Journal of Advertising* 39, no. 1: 35–48.

Bodenhausen, G.V., G.P. Kramer, and K. Susser. 1994. Happiness and stereotypic thinking in social judgment. *Journal of Personality and Social Psychology* 66, no. 4: 621–32.

Browne, B.A. 1998. Gender stereotypes in advertising on children's television in the 1990s: A cross-national analysis. *Journal of Advertising* 27, no. 1: 83–96.

Chang, C. 2002. Self-congruency as a cue in different advertising-processing contexts. *Communication Research* 29, no. 5: 503–36.

Csikszentmihalyi, M. 1999. Implications of a systems perspective for the study of creativity. In *Handbook of creativity*, ed. R.J. Sternberg, 313–335. Cambridge: Cambridge University Press.

Darley, W.K., and R.E. Smith. 1995. Gender differences in information processing strategies: An empirical test of the selectivity model in advertising response. *Journal of Advertising* 24, no. 1: 41–56.

Drumwright, M.E., and P.E. Murphy. 2004. How advertising practitioners view ethics: Moral muteness, moral myopia, and moral imagination. *Journal of Advertising* 33, no. 2: 7–24.

Eagly, A.H., and S.J. Karau. 2002. Role congruity theory and prejudice toward female leaders. *Psychological Review* 109, no. 3: 573–98.

Eisend, M. 2010. A meta-analysis of gender roles in advertising. *Journal of the Academy of Marketing Science* 38, no. 4: 418–40.

Giaccardi, C. 1995. Television advertising and the representation of social reality: A comparative study. *Theory, Culture and Society* 12, no. 1: 109–31.

Gregory, M.R. 2009. Inside the locker room: Male homosociability in the advertising industry. *Gender, Work and Organization* 16, no. 3: 323–437.

Hackley, C. 2002. The panoptic role of advertising agencies in the production of consumer culture. *Consumption, Markets and Culture* 5, no. 3: 211–29.

Hilton, J.L., and W. von Hippel. 1996. Stereotypes. *Annual Review of Psychology* 47, no. 1: 237–71.

Jhally, S. 1987. *The codes of advertising*. New York: St. Martin's Press.

Jhally, S., J. Kilbourne, and D. Rabinovitz. 2010. *Killing us softly 4: Advertising's image of women*. Northampton, MA: Media Education Foundation. http://www.worldcat.org/title/killing-us-softly-4-advertisings-image-of-women/oclc/606852641?page=citation

Kelly, G.A. 1955. *The psychology of personal constructs*. New York: W.W. Norton & Company.

Kelly, A., K. Lawlor, and S. O'Donohoe. 2005. Encoding advertisements: The creative perspective. *Journal of Marketing Management* 21, no. 5–6: 505–28.

Kover, A.J. 1995. Copywriters' implicit theories of communication: An exploration. *Journal of Consumer Research* 21, no. 4: 596–611.

Macklin, M.C., and R.H. Kolbe. 1984. Sex role stereotyping in children's advertising: Current and past trends, *Journal of Advertising* 13, no. 2: 34–42.

Mallia, K.L. 2009. Rare birds: Why so few women become ad agency creative directors. *Advertising and Society Review* 10, no. 3. DOI:10.1353/asr.0.0032

Martin, C., and C. Halverson. 1981. A schematic processing model of sex typing and stereotyping in children. *Child Development* 52, no. 4: 563–75.

McCracken, G. 1986. Culture and consumption: A theoretical account of the structure and movement of the cultural meaning of consumer goods. *Journal of Consumer Research* 13, no. 1: 71–84.

McCracken, G. 1987. Advertising: Meaning or information. In Vol. 14 of *Advances in consumer research*, eds. M. Wallendorg and P. Anderson, 121–24. Provo, UT: Association for Consumer Research.

McCracken, G. 1989. Who is the celebrity endorser? Cultural foundations of the endorsement process. *Journal of Consumer Research* 16, no. 3: 310–21.

Morrison, M.A., E. Haley, K.B. Sheehan, and R.E. Taylor. 2011. *Using qualitative research in advertising: Strategies, techniques and applications*. Thousand Oaks, CA: Sage Publications.

Morse, J.M. 1995. The significance of saturation. *Qualitative Health Research* 5, no. 2: 147–9.

Nyilasy, G., R. Canniford, and P.J. Kreshel. 2013. Ad agency professionals' mental models of advertising creativity, *European Journal of Marketing* 47, no. 10: 1691–710.

Nyilasy, G., and L.N. Reid. 2009. Agency practitioner theories of how advertising works. *Journal of Advertising* 38, no. 3: 81–96.

Pollay, R.W. 1986. The distorted mirror: Reflections on the unintended consequences of advertising. *Journal of Marketing* 50, no. 2: 18–38.

Pollay, R.W., and K. Gallagher. 1990. Advertising and cultural values: Reflections in the distorted mirror. *International Journal of Advertising* 9, no. 4: 359–72.

Reynolds, T.J., and J. Gutman. 1988. Laddering theory, method, analysis, and interpretation. *Journal of Advertising Research* 28, no. 1: 11–31.

Richins, M.L. 1991. Social comparison and idealized images of advertising. *Journal of Consumer Research* 18, no. 1: 71–83.

Shao, Y., F. Desmarais, and C.K. Weaver. 2014. Chinese advertising practitioners' conceptualisation of gender representation. *International Journal of Advertising* 33, no. 2: 329–50.

Sirgy, M.J. 1982. Self-concept in consumer behavior: A critical review. *Journal of Consumer Research* 9, no. 3: 287–99.

Spiggle, S. 1994. Analysis and interpretation of qualitative data in consumer research. *Journal of Consumer Research* 21, no. 3: 491–503.

Stephens, D.L., R.P. Hill, and C. Hanson. 1994. The beauty myth and female consumers: The controversial role of advertising. *Journal of Consumer Affairs* 28, no. 1: 137–53.

Tan, F.B., and M.G. Hunter. 2002. The repertory grid technique: A method for the study of cognition in information systems. *MIS Quarterly* 26, no. 1: 39–57.

Taylor, R.E., M.G. Hoy, and E. Haley. 1996. How French advertising professionals develop creative strategy. *Journal of Advertising* 25, no. 1: 1–14.

Tsai, W.S. 2010. Family man in advertising? A content analysis of male domesticity and fatherhood in Taiwanese commercials. *Asian Journal of Communication* 20, no. 4: 423–39.

Vanden Bergh, B., and M.W. Stuhlfaut. 2006. Is creativity primarily an individual or social process? *Mass Communication and Society* 9, no. 4: 373–97.

Windels, K., and W. Lee. 2012. The construction of gender and creativity in advertising creative departments. *Gender in Management: An International Journal* 27, no. 8: 502–19.

Windels, K., and M.W. Stuhlfaut. 2014. Confined creativity: The influence of creative code intensity and risk taking in advertising agencies. *Journal of Current Issues and Research in Advertising* 35, no. 2: 147–66.

Zayer, L.T., and C.A. Coleman. 2015. Advertising professionals' perceptions of the impact of gender portrayals on men and women: A question of ethics? *Journal of Advertising* 44, no. 3: 1–12.

A longitudinal analysis of the changing roles of gender in advertising: a content analysis of Super Bowl commercials

Leonidas Hatzithomas, Christina Boutsouki and Paschalina Ziamou

Although the prevalence of gender stereotypes in advertising is well established, relatively little research has examined gender stereotypes in the context of Super Bowl that is arguably the most important event in US television advertising. This study systematically examines gender representations across various product categories in Super Bowl commercials over a 20-year period (1990–2009). Our findings detect and discuss shifts in the cultural notions of gender constructed in advertising messages targeting the largest and the most demographically diverse audience in US television. The paper concludes with a discussion of the theoretical and managerial implications of our findings.

1. Introduction

Despite the growth of social media, television advertising is still the dominant form of advertising in the USA. In 2014, advertising spending on television reached $68.54 billion (Statista 2015) and recent research suggests that TV advertisements drive consumers' brand perceptions (Jin and Lutz 2013). Within advertising in general, and television advertising in particular, no single event underscores the centrality of advertising in US culture like the Super Bowl, the final game of the American football season (e.g., Kelley and Turley 2004; Kim and Cheong 2011; King 2012). Commercial time during the Super Bowl is the most expensive in the world (King 2012) and the cost of a 30-second commercial reached $4.5 million in 2015 (Tadena 2015). Furthermore, the 2015 Super Bowl was the most watched broadcast in the US TV history with an audience of 114.4 million viewers (Pallotta 2015), and recent research suggests that the audience is as interested in watching the commercials as they are in watching the game (Siltanen 2014; Tadena 2015).

Because of the importance of Super Bowl advertising to marketers and consumers alike, prior research has primarily focused on understanding the effectiveness of Super Bowl advertising (e.g., Chung and Zhao 2003; Jeong, Kim, and Zhao 2011; Newell and Wu 2003; Yelkur et al. 2013). Although the proliferation of cable and satellite channels has resulted in audience fragmentation, Super Bowl is the only TV program that has defied media fragmentation (Kelley and Turley 2004; Monteiro 2015). As recent data suggest, the event now attracts a 46% female audience, and more women watch the game than the Oscars, Grammys and Emmys combined (Brazile 2014). However, there is limited research on the cultural notions of gender that are constructed through the ads (King 2012), and how these cultural notions of gender have evolved (or not) over time (Verhellen, Dens, and Pelsmacker 2016). The purpose of this research is to conduct a longitudinal study, over a 20-year period (1990–2009), to examine how the depiction of female and male stereotypes in Super Bowl commercials has changed over time for the most advertised product categories.

The importance of cultural notions of gender in advertising has been highlighted on a number of occasions (Gulas, McKeage, and Weinberger 2010; Gentry and Harrison 2010; Kilbourne 1999), and the shifts in gender portrayals is the key to understanding potential shifts in power, in status quo and in socially accepted gender roles and trends (Gulas, McKeage, and Weinberger 2010). An important gap in prior research is the lack of longitudinal studies that examine shifts in gender portrayals in Super Bowl advertising. A longitudinal investigation of Super Bowl advertising is important in understanding changing gender stereotypes. Sports represent a site where gender ideologies are articulated (Messner 2010), and television coverage of sports events in general, and Super Bowl in particular, plays a crucial role in the social construction of gender roles (Buysse and Embser-Herbert 2004; Kane and Parks 1992).

A second gap in prior research on Super Bowl advertising is the absence of a systematic and comprehensive framework that includes a variety of female and male stereotypes. A study by Messner and Montez de Oca (2005) was a first step in this direction. This study, however, examined only a limited number of stereotypes, a single product category, and was conducted at a time when the Super Bowl audience consisted primarily of men – i.e., 2002 and 2003. A comprehensive framework, however, has been developed and used in several studies investigating gender stereotypes in print (e.g., Lysonski 1985; Plakoyiannaki and Zotos 2009; Zotos and Lysonski 1994) and online advertisements (e.g., Plakoyiannaki et al. 2008) and has enabled a systematic investigation of gender stereotypes in advertising.

A third gap in prior research on Super Bowl advertising is the lack of studies that examine how specific stereotypes have changed over time and across different product categories. Several studies have suggested that female and male stereotypes in advertising vary across product categories (e.g., Ganahl, Prinsen, and Netzley 2003; Plakoyiannaki and Zotos 2009; Verhellen, Dens, and Pelsmacker 2016). However, none of the aforementioned studies examined if the longitudinal changes in the use of gender stereotypes vary across different product categories. Managerially, a longitudinal investigation will help in understanding changing ideals of gender-related behavior and will provide useful guidelines for managers' advertising decisions.

The remainder of the paper is organized as follows: the first section discusses prior research on Super Bowl advertising that is relevant to the purpose of this study, our framework and the research questions. The second section describes the methodology used in this study. In the results section, we describe how gender stereotypes have evolved over time and across different product categories in the context of Super Bowl. The paper concludes with a summary of the findings, their theoretical and managerial contributions and directions for future research.

2. Theoretical background and research questions

2.1. Super Bowl advertising

Given the importance of Super Bowl advertising to marketers and consumers alike, several prior studies have examined the effectiveness of Super Bowl commercials (Newell and Wu 2003; Kelley and Turley 2004; Jeong, Kim, and Zhao 2011; Yelkur et al. 2013).

A great deal of research has focused on brand recall. For example, Jeong, Kim, and Zhao (2011) have examined the effects of TV clutter on brand recall in Super Bowl commercials. Their results suggest that TV clutter, such as other ads, on-air promos and TV billboards have a negative impact on the recognition and recall of the advertised brand. In another study, Chung and Zhao (2003) have examined the effects of humor on memory and attitude towards the ad. They found that the degree of perceived humor of a Super Bowl commercial is positively related to brand recall and attitude towards Super Bowl commercials. Newell, Henderson, and Wu (2001) have investigated whether arousal levels of Super Bowl viewers affect advertising recall. The results of their study suggest that programs that evoke strong emotional reactions, such as the Super Bowl, inhibit the recall of advertisements. Prior research has also examined the effect of the placement of commercials during Super Bowl and has found lower levels of brand recall for services (Newell and Wu 2003), and higher levels of effect for products rather than services (Kelley and Turley 2004).

Lastly, in a series of studies, Tomkovick and his colleagues examined predictors of likeability of Super Bowl commercials (e.g., Tomkovick, Yelkur, and Christians 2001; Yelkur et al. 2013). The results of these studies suggest that humor and the amount of product information are significant predictors of ad likeability. Specifically, there is a positive relationship between humor and Super Bowl advertisement likeability, whereas, the amount of information provided in the commercials is inversely related to ad likeability. These studies have also found that the presence of children and the presence of animals significantly impacted the likeability of Super Bowl commercials. Furthermore, commercials for food, beverages and restaurants scored the highest on Super Bowl ad likeability (Tomkovick, Yelkur, and Christians 2001; Yelkur et al. 2013).

While there has been extensive analysis of the effectiveness of Super Bowl advertising on a variety of metrics such as advertising recall and liking, there is a limited number of studies that have examined the construction of gender identities in Super Bowl commercials and how these cultural notions of gender have evolved (or not) over time. Prior research, however, has highlighted the importance of studying gender representation in Super Bowl commercials (e.g., King 2012; Green and Van Oort 2013). A thorough examination of female and male stereotypes in Super Bowl commercials is important for two reasons: first, sports represent a site where gender ideologies are always contested, negotiated and articulated (Messner 2010), and television coverage of sports events plays a significant role in the social construction of gender roles and gender relations (Kane and Parks 1992; Buysse and Embser-Herbert 2004). Furthermore, for many years, sports and especially football were considered as a 'male preserve', in which women were marginalized (Dundes 1978; Dunning 1986; Dunning, Birrell, and Cole 1994). American football players have been regarded as exemplars of hegemonic masculinity (Anderson and Kian 2012). As a result, in popular culture, Super Bowl has been considered as a site for the transmission and reproduction of masculinity (Green and Van Oort 2013). Prior research suggests that masculinity is the product of historical, social and cultural processes and a response to changing roles of femininity (Kimmel 1987). Hence, an examination of gender representation in advertisements requires the consideration of both female and male stereotypes (Hanke 1990).

Second, Super Bowl has evolved into the most watched broadcast in US television and the only event that defies media fragmentation (Kelley and Turley 2004; Monteiro 2015). The event has now reached a 46% female audience (Brazile 2014). Given the changing nature of the demographics of the Super Bowl audience, and specifically the increasing number of women who watch the event, a longitudinal investigation of female and male stereotypes in Super Bowl commercials is timely.

In the following section, we review the studies that have examined gender stereotypes in Super Bowl commercials and identify a series of issues that are yet to be addressed.

2.2. Gender stereotypes in Super Bowl commercials

One of the early studies that examined gender representations in Super Bowl commercials was conducted by Drewniany (2003). In this longitudinal study – from 1989 to 2002 – Drewniany (2003) reports an overrepresentation of men compared to women in Super Bowl commercials. Out of the 585 commercials with gender stereotypes analyzed in her study, 349 commercials portrayed a male stereotype, while only 94 commercials featured a female stereotype. In addition to the overrepresentation of men in the commercials, Drewniany (2003) has noted the persistence of traditional stereotypes such as 'men as voices of authority.'

In a more recent study, King (2012) presented a comparative content analysis of Super Bowl commercials over a 10-year period. Specifically, King (2012) examined how gender and race are depicted in Super Bowl commercials and how this depiction has changed over time. The results of this study show that women continue to be underrepresented. However, women seemed to gain ground since they are depicted more and more frequently in business settings and as frequently as men in promoting high-value products.

Although these two studies offer important insights on gender representations in Super Bowl commercials, they focus on the frequency with which women and men are depicted and do not use a systematic and comprehensive framework that incorporates a variety of female and male stereotypes. A comprehensive framework, however, has been developed and extensively used in prior research on gender representations in print and online advertisements and can provide valuable insights on the type of female and male stereotypes used in Super Bowl commercials (e.g., Lysonski 1985; Plakoyiannaki et al. 2008; Plakoyiannaki and Zotos 2009; Tsichla and Zotos 2014; Zotos and Lysonski 1994). Furthermore, the studies on gender stereotypes in Super Bowl commercials discussed earlier have not examined how gender representations may vary across product categories, although prior research has suggested that gender stereotypes are likely to vary across product categories (e.g., Ganahl, Prinsen, and Netzley 2003; Plakoyiannaki and Zotos 2009; Verhellen, Dens, and Pelsmacker 2016).

An attempt in this direction is a study by Messner and Montez de Oca (2005) that examined beer and liquor commercials in Super Bowl commercials and *Sports Illustrated* advertisements in a two-year period – i.e., 2002–2003 – to explore tropes of masculinity that prevail in these ads. The results of their research show that male portrayals in beer and liquor Super Bowl ads are situated within a larger historical context, where social changes have led to shifting patterns in male representations in Super Bowl commercials, such as the depiction of men as losers. Building on this study, Green and Van Oort (2013) examined the changing construction of masculine identities in Super Bowl commercials during the 2010 Super Bowl. Their findings suggest that the loser depiction is still present, but instead of being lovable and happy, he is depicted as pitiful and stupid.

Although these two studies examine various types of female and male stereotypes in Super Bowl commercials, they focus on a single product category – i.e., beer and liquor– (Messner and Montez de Oca 2005) or a very limited number of commercials – i.e., three commercials – (Green and Van Oort 2013). Further, their analysis is limited to a subset of the gender stereotypes that have been identified in the broader literature.

In sum, although these studies offer important insights on gender representations in Super Bowl commercials, one can highlight a number of issues that merit further investigation:

(1) The need for longitudinal studies that will allow us to understand the evolution of gender stereotypes in Super Bowl commercials over time.
(2) The need for a systematic and comprehensive framework that will identify various types of male and female stereotypes.
(3) The need to investigate how female and male stereotypes vary across product categories.

In the present study, we address these gaps by building on prior research on gender stereotypes in print and television advertisements.

2.3. Framework for gender stereotypes in advertising and research questions

Researchers have studied gender stereotypes in advertising since the early 1970s (e.g., Belkaoui and Belkaoui 1976; Courtney and Lockeretz 1971) with an emphasis on the portrayals of women (Gentry and Harrison 2010). Initially, female stereotypes focused on women's working roles (Courtney and Lockeretz 1971), but they evolved over the years to include a variety of representations. Male stereotypes were studied systematically for the first time in a study by Lysonski (1985).

Our study adopts a framework that has identified a comprehensive list of female and male stereotypes and has been extensively used in prior research to examine gender stereotypes in print advertisements (e.g., Lysonski 1985; Zotos and Lysonski 1994; Plakoyiannaki and Zotos 2009; Tsichla and Zotos 2014) and online advertisements (Plakoyiannaki et al. 2008). The stereotype of the 'man as loser' was added to the pre-existing framework, given its important role in prior research on gender stereotypes in Super Bowl commercials (Green and Van Oort 2013; Messner and Montez de Oca 2005). Tables 1 and 2 list the stereotypes examined in the present research.

Several important findings have emerged from this framework and help us to understand the differences in gender stereotypes. Research on female stereotypes in advertising (Lundstrom and Sciglimpaglia 1977; Belkaoui and Belkaoui 1976; Plakoyiannaki and Zotos 2009; Zotos and Tsichla 2014) suggests that the images of women have changed very modestly over time. Advertisers have been largely portraying women in traditional roles (Klassen, Jasper, and Schwartz 1993), in non-working roles and as having limited purchasing power. Women are portrayed mainly in decorative non-functional capacities and are predominantly shown as housewives or concerned with their physical attractiveness (Lysonski 1985). Sexism is prevailing not only in traditional media (Theodoridis et al. 2013; Zimmerman and Dahlberg 2008) but also in the context of online advertisements (Plakoyiannaki et al. 2008).

The framework also identifies a variety of male stereotypes and helps us to gain insights in the depiction of male stereotypes. For example, male stereotypes in advertising portray men as 'authority figures', using non-domestic products outside of the home (Knoll, Eisend, and Steinhagen 2011). The theme of 'authority figure' seems to prevail in early studies in print advertisements (Lysonski 1983, 1985). Furthermore, there is a focus on the occupational roles of men (Klassen, Jasper, and Schwartz 1993; Wiles, Wiles, and Tjernlund 1995; Wolheter and Lammers 1980) and emphasis is given on physical characteristics (Kolbe and Albanese 1996). Overall, men are portrayed as authoritative and

Table 1.   Categories for female stereotypes*.

Stereotypes	Description
Dependency	• Dependent on male's protection • In need of reassurance • Making unimportant decisions
Housewife	• Women's place is in the home • Primary role is to be a good wife • Concerned with tasks of housekeeping
Women concerned with physical attractiveness	• To appear more appealing (e.g., youthful) • Concerned with cosmetics and jewelry products • Concerned with fashion
Women as sex objects	• Sex is related to product • Sex is unrelated to product
Women in non-traditional activities	• Engaged in activities outside the home (e.g., buying a car) • Engaged in sports (e.g., golf, tennis, skiing, swimming)
Career-oriented	• Professional occupations • Entertainer • Non-professional (e.g., clerical, bank teller) • Blue collar
Voice of authority	• The expert
Neutral	• Woman shown as equal to man
None of the above categories	

*Adapted from Lysonski (1985). This table is reproduced with permission of Professor Lysonski.

Table 2.   Categories for male stereotypes*.

Stereotypes	Description
The theme of sex appeal	• Macho man (e.g., physical strength, prowess, 'cool') • Womanizer (e.g., physical attractiveness, active seeker)
Dominant over women	• Man protects woman • Man is in control • Man offers reassurance to woman
Authority figure (product representative)	• Provides the expertize (i.e., the expert) • Celebrity • Voice of authority
Family man	• Activities at home • Conventional activities
Frustrated male	• Frustrated in work • Frustrated in life
Activities and life outside the home	• Concerned about his own needs • Shown in activities and sports (e.g., golf, hunting) • Seeking gratification outside the home
Career-oriented	• Professional career orientation
Non-traditional role	• Showing women in non-traditional activities (e.g., washing dishes, changing baby's clothes)
Neutral	• Man shown as equal to woman
None of the above categories	

*Adapted from Lysonski (1985) . This table is reproduced with permission of Professor Lysonski independent in both professional and recreational roles (Furnham and Mak 1999; Eisend 2010). Masculinity is represented via discourses concerning physical appearance (strength), behaviors (violent and assertive) and occupations (subordination of women) (Ricciardelli, Clow, and White 2010). Recent studies in the USA report that men are increasingly portrayed in decorative roles (Paek, Nelson, and Vilela 2011) and in suggestive poses (Mager and Helgeson 2011).

Building on prior research on gender stereotypes, we investigate the various types of female and male stereotypes depicted in Super Bowl commercials and how these stereotypes vary across product categories. We consider a 20-year period (1990–2009), 10 years before and 10 years after the millennium. Our goal is to detect shifts in the cultural notions of gender constructed in advertising messages targeting the largest and the most demographically diverse TV audience in US television. Our research questions are formulated as follows:

RQ1: How do female and male stereotypes in Super Bowl commercials before the millennium (1990–1999) compare with those after the millennium (2000–2009)?

RQ2: How do these stereotypes vary for the five most advertised product categories?

3. Methodology

3.1. Sample of Super Bowl commercials

A content analysis approach was adopted as it is widely accepted for the scientific, quantitative and generalizable analysis of advertising messages (Kassarjian 1977). The primary strength of content analysis is that it provides a concise and replicable coding scheme with explicit coding rules and allows for systematic coding and analysis (Treadwell 2014). Furthermore, content analysis is a suitable method for reflecting cultural patterns of societies and describes trends in advertising content (Weber 1990), and as recent research suggests, a useful tool for investigating gender roles in advertising (Fields, Swan, and Kloos 2010; Neuendorf 2011). In addition, content analysis was the method of investigation in prior research on gender stereotypes (e.g., Plakoyiannaki and Zotos 2009; Zotos and Lysonski 1994).

The Super Bowl commercials were content-analyzed for two time periods, 1990–1999 and 2000–2009. These Super Bowl commercials were retrieved from Adland, an independent organization that hosts the world's largest collection of Super Bowl ads (Adland 2014). At the beginning of this research, we identified several product categories based on prior research in the area (e.g., Plakoyiannaki and Zotos 2009) and the types of product categories that were featured in the Super Bowl commercials. We adopted Kim, Cheong, and Kim's (2012) approach and excluded movie trailers and network show promos from our sample since they reflect stereotypes conveyed by the films and TV programs, and their analysis has little to add to our understanding of cultural changes. Our sample consists of the five most advertised categories. The ads in these five product categories accounted for 74% of the total number of ads retrieved. The product categories selected for this study are (1) food and drinks (non-alcoholic), (2), alcoholic beverages, (3) services, (4) auto and related products and (5) financial services. Our sample consisted of a total of 447 commercials that included at least one female or/and a male stereotype. Of the 447 commercials, 408 commercials featured a male stereotype and 215 featured a female stereotype.

3.2. *Coding procedure*

The content analysis instrument used in this study is based on the typologies of gender stereotypes described and validated by prior studies (Lysonski 1985; Zotos and Lysonski 1994; Plakoyiannaki and Zotos 2009). The coders were trained to content analyze the commercials and assign them into specific categories of analysis and product categories. All coders received a list of all gender stereotypes with their definitions, a list with all product categories, and written instructions on how to perform the categorization procedure. Prior to the main study, each coder was trained on a sample of 200 non-Super Bowl commercials to ensure the reliability of the coding process. In the main study, each one of the coders analyzed approximately 210 commercials. Each commercial was analyzed by two coders (a male and a female). The coders worked independently in order to determine whether each commercial involved one or more gender stereotypes. Each coder watched each commercial twice. Inter-coder agreement was estimated based on Cohen's conditional Kappa (Cohen 1960). Inter-coder reliability coefficients ranged between 80% and 89%. Discrepancies amongst the coders were resolved by the authors. Female and male stereotypes were coded as dichotomous variables with values 0 (absence of the stereotype) or 1 (presence of the stereotype). Because the variables were binary in nature, a series of chi-square tests were conducted to examine whether the proportions of female and male stereotypes have changed before vs. after the millennium. A Fisher's exact test of independence was used instead of a chi-square test when a cell's expected value was less than five.

4. Results and discussion

Our main objective was to investigate how the depiction of female and male stereotypes in Super Bowl commercials has changed before vs. after the millennium and how these changes vary across different product categories. Although not predicted by our research questions, our data show that male stereotypes are more frequently used than female stereotypes in both time periods. Specifically, 90% male vs. 47% female stereotypes were used during 1990–1999 and 92% male vs. 49% female stereotypes were used during 2000–2009 (Table 3). These findings are consistent with prior studies in Super Bowl advertising (Drewniany 2003; King 2012) that pointed out the underrepresentation of women in Super Bowl commercials. It appears that Super Bowl is still considered to be a male territory (Duncan and Hasbrook 2002), despite the fact that female Super Bowl viewership has significantly increased in the last decade (Nielsen 2009). In the following section, we discuss our findings as they apply to our research questions.

4.1. *Female stereotypes in Super Bowl commercials: comparing 1990–1999 to 2000–2009*

In our study, an analysis of female stereotypes shows that before the millennium (1990–1999), women were mainly portrayed as 'career-oriented' (23%), as being equal

Table 3. Sample description.

	1990–1999	2000–2009	Total
Number of ads including at least one female or male stereotype in all five product categories	186	261	447
Number of female stereotypes	87 (47%)	128 (49%)	215
Number of male stereotypes	167 (90%)	241 (92%)	408

Table 4. Female stereotypes across years.

Female stereotypes	1990–1999% $N = 87$	2000–2009% $N = 128$
(1) Dependency	5.7	2.3
(2) Housewife	11.5	5.5*
(3) Women concerned with physical attractiveness	3.4	4.7
(4) Women as sex objects	8.0	11.7
(5) Women in non-traditional activities	16.1	28.9**
(6) Career-oriented	23.0	15.6
(7) Voice of authority	10.4	4.7*
(8) Neutral	17.3	21.9
(9) None	4.6	4.7

*$p < .1$, **$p < .05$.

to men – 'neutral' stereotype– (17.3%) and as 'women in non-traditional activities' (16.1%). The same stereotypes seem to prevail after the millennium (2000–2009) (Table 4). Specifically, women are depicted 'in non-traditional activities' (28.9%), as being equal to men – i.e., 'neutral' stereotype– (21.9%) or as 'career-oriented' (15.6%).

Furthermore, the results show that the 'women in non-traditional activities' stereotype significantly increased after the millennium (16.1% before vs. 28.9% after the millennium; $X^2 = 4.70$, df $= 1$, $p < .05$). For instance, in a Super Bowl commercial (2006) for Michelob Ultra Amber, a group of male and female friends play a game of touch football, a typically male game. A young woman is trying to get the ball into the touchdown zone, when one of the men lays a monster hit on her. However, hours later, she takes her revenge by hitting him back, while he is having a beer with a male friend. The commercial clearly portrays the woman as the winner. Since the early 2000s, several commercials similar to this one have appeared during Super Bowl, indicating a shift from traditional representations of women. In contrast, the 'housewife' stereotype showed a marginally significant decrease from 11.5% before the millennium to 5.5% after the millennium ($X^2 = 2.58$, df $= 1$, $p < .1$).

These findings are consistent with prior research suggesting that women are more likely to be depicted in non-traditional roles in advertisements featured in magazines (Tsichla and Zotos 2014; Zotos and Lysonski 1994) and websites (Plakoyiannaki et al. 2008) targeting a male audience. One could also suggest that the observed changes in the depiction of women coincide with National Football League's (NFL) increasing focus on women as sports fans, fostering a new culture for women in Super Bowl (Nielsen 2009). Nevertheless, it is important to note that the definition of 'non-traditional' originates from the early studies of gender stereotypes (Lysonski 1983, 1985). It referred to women engaged in activities outside the home or women engaged in sports, behaviors that in the early 1980s were not considered to be the norm for women. Our results also suggest that the 'voice of authority' stereotype (i.e., women as experts) shows a marginally significant decrease, from 10.4% before the millennium to 4.7% after the millennium ($X^2 = 2.55$, df $= 1$, $p < .1$). This finding may be due to the gradual reduction in the use of experts in Super Bowl commercials in recent years (Hatzithomas, Outra, and Zotos 2010).

4.2. Male stereotypes in Super Bowl commercials: comparing 1990–1999 to 2000–2009

An analysis of male stereotypes shows a shift in the depiction of men as authority figures. Specifically, our results show that the most frequently used male stereotypes, in both time periods examined in this study, were 'authority figure' (30.5% before vs. 16.6% after the millennium), 'career-oriented' (23.4% before vs. 21.6% after the millennium) and 'activities and life outside the home' (15.6% before vs. 20.7% after the millennium) (Table 5). They reflect traditional masculine images that have been used for a long time in Super Bowl advertising (Nelson 1994). The results are consistent with prior research in gender stereotypes in print advertising which has shown that men are primarily portrayed as authority figures (Lysonski 1983), as career-oriented and as being involved in outdoor activities (Lysonski 1985; Zotos and Lysonski 1994). It is also consistent with more recent research suggesting that although male roles have significantly changed since the millennium, advertising continues to portray men in their traditional stereotypical roles (Gentry and Harrison 2010).

It is interesting, however, to note a statistically significant decrease in the representation of men as 'authority figures', from 30.5% before to 16.6% after the millennium ($X^2 = 11.06$, df $= 1$, $p < .005$). It seems that despite the prevalence of traditional stereotypical roles, men lose their status as authority figure. This finding is consistent with prior research that highlights the diminishing power of men in several Super Bowl commercials in recent years (Green and Van Oort 2013).

4.3. Female stereotypes in Super Bowl commercials per product category: comparing 1990–1999 to 2000–2009

Table 6 displays the percentages of female stereotypes by product category in the two time periods examined in this study.

The stereotype of 'dependency' declined in most product categories after the millennium. In the alcoholic beverages category, the decrease was marginally significant (25% before vs. 3.1% after the millennium; $p < .1$, Fisher's exact test). In contrast, the theme

Table 5. Male stereotypes across years.

Male stereotypes	1990–1999% $N = 167$	2000–2009% $N = 241$
(1) The theme of sex appeal	4.8	6.6
(2) Dominant over women	1.2	2.5
(3) Authority figure	30.5	16.6***
(4) Family man	3.6	4.6
(5) Frustrated male	3.6	1.7
(6) Activities and life outside the home	15.6	20.7
(7) Career-oriented	23.4	21.6
(8) Non-traditional role	0	0.8
(9) Man as loser	7.8	10.0
(10) Neutral	9.0	11.6
(11) None	.6	3.3

***$p < .005$.

Table 6. Female stereotypes across years and product categories.

Female stereotypes	Food and drinks		Alcoholic beverages		Services		Auto and related products		Financial services	
	1990–1999 % N = 35	2000–2009% N = 40	1990–1999% N = 8	2000–2009% N = 31	1990–1999% N = 19	2000–2009% N = 16	1990–1999% N = 13	2000–2009% N = 17	1990–1999% N = 12	2000–2009% N = 24
(1) Dependency	5.7	0	25.0	3.1*	0	0	0	5.9	8.3	4.2
(2) Housewife	5.7	2.5	0	3.2	26.3	6.2	7.7	11.8	16.7	8.3
(3) Women concerned with physical attractiveness	2.9	7.5	0	6.5	5.3	6.2	7.7	0	0	0
(4) Women as sex objects	14.3	15.0	0	16.1	0	12.5	0	5.9	16.7	4.2
(5) Women in non-traditional activities	17.1	22.5	25.0	29.0	10.5	12.5	15.4	47.1*	16.7	37.5
(6) Career-oriented	25.7	15.0	12.5	6.5	36.8	37.5	15.4	5.9	8.3	20.8
(7) Voice of authority	17.1	15.0	0	0	0	0	15.4	0	8.3	0
(8) Neutral	11.4	22.5	25.0	22.6	15.8	25.0	30.8	17.6	16.7	20.8
(9) None	0	0	12.5	12.9	5.3	0	7.7	5.9	8.3	4.2
Total	100%	100%	100%	100%	100%	100%	100%	100%	100%	100%

*p < .1.

of 'women in non-traditional activities' increased in all product categories. In the auto and related products category, there was a marginally significant increase (15.4% before vs. 47.1% after the millennium; $p = .1$, Fisher's exact test). This may be attributed to the growing role and participation of women in decision-making surrounding non-domestic product categories such as auto and related products. For instance, the target audience of many automobile Super Bowl commercials in recent years was the so-called soccer mom (Ghizoni 2014; Carter 2013), a North American middle-class suburban woman who drives an SUV or a mini-van and spends a great deal of her time transporting her children to different sporting activities (MacFarquhar 1996).

4.4. Male stereotypes in Super Bowl commercials per product category: comparing 1990–1999 to 2000–2009

Table 7 displays the percentages of male stereotypes by product category in the two time periods examined in this study.

The 'authority figure' theme significantly decreased in both the food and drinks category (from 45.2% before to 20.3% after the millennium; $X^2 = 9.66$, df $= 1$, $p < .005$) and the alcoholic beverages category (26.5% before vs. 11.1% after the millennium; $X^2 = 4.04$, df $= 1$, $p < .05$). This finding is consistent with earlier research suggesting that before the millennium several celebrities starred in Super Bowl commercials (Drewniany 2003). In this study, this was mainly apparent in the food and drinks and the alcoholic beverages categories, with brands such as Pepsi Diet (with Shaquille O'Neal) and Doritos (with Jay Leno) using celebrity endorsements in their Super Bowl commercials.

Our results also show a marginally significant decrease in the 'career-oriented' theme in the auto and related products category (28% before vs. 7.1% after the millennium; $p = .1$, Fisher's exact test). Since the millennium, men have been often depicted driving cars through urban and rural landscapes, shifting the focus from a career-oriented environment to leisure-oriented activities and life outside the home (Thompson 2006). Another marginally significant decrease was observed in the theme of 'frustrated male' in the alcoholic beverages category (5.9% before vs. 0% after the millennium; $p = .1$, Fisher's exact test).

In contrast, the representation of men in 'activities and life outside the home' significantly increased in the food and drinks category (11.3% before vs. 24.3% after the millennium; $X^2 = 3.82$, df $= 1$, $p < .05$). After the millennium, many advertisements in the category of food and drinks portrayed 'average Americans' engaging in activities outside the home. For instance, a 2009 Coca Cola Super Bowl commercial featured a male picnicker taking a nap in a park on a sunny day (Zmuda 2009). These two findings are consistent with recent research which suggests that in recent years, men's frustration with the corporate world is only hinted at and contrasted with the portrayal of men in activities outside the home (Green and Van Oort 2013).

Although we did not find any changing pattern over time, it is interesting to point out that the stereotype of 'man as loser' appeared with relatively high frequency especially in the commercials in the alcoholic beverages category. As stated earlier, this stereotype was not accounted for in the initial typology introduced by Lysonski (1985) and adopted by subsequent studies (e.g., Plakoyiannaki and Zotos 2009; Zotos and Lysonski 1994). However, previous studies in gender stereotypes in Super Bowl have extensively discussed the presence of men as losers, behaving stupidly and being publicly humiliated (Green and Van Oort 2013; Gulas, McKeage, and Weinberger 2013; Messner and Montez de Oca 2005).

Table 7. Male stereotypes across years and product categories.

Male stereotypes	Food and drinks		Alcoholic beverages		Services		Auto and related products		Financial services	
	1990–1999% N = 62	2000–2009% N = 74	1990–999% N = 34	2000–2009% N = 72	1990–1999% N = 24	2000–2009% N = 37	1990-1999% N = 25	2000–2009% N = 28	1990–1999% N = 22	2000–2009% N = 30
(1) The theme of sex appeal	3.2	5.4	5.9	5.6	0	2.7	8.0	7.1	9.1	16.7
(2) Dominant over women	0	2.7	2.9	4.2	0	0	0	3.6	4.5	0
(3) Authority figure	45.2	20.3***	26.5	11.1**	12.5	18.9	24.0	14.3	22.7	20.0
(4) Family man	4.8	4.1	0	2.8	8.3	5.4	0	10.7	4.5	3.3
(5) Frustrated male	0	0	5.9	0*	4.2	5.4	4.0	0	9.1	6.7
(6) Activities and life outside the home	11.3	24.3**	20.6	22.2	16.7	13.5	16.0	28.6	18.2	10.0
(7) Career-oriented	19.4	24.3	17.6	20.8	45.8	29.7	28.0	7.1*	13.6	20.0
(8) Non-traditional role	0	0	0	0	0	2.7	0	0	0	3.3
(9) Man as loser	8.1	5.4	14.7	19.4	0	2.7	4.0	14.3	9.1	3.3
(10) Neutral	6.5	12.2	5.9	9.7	12.5	10.8	16.0	10.7	9.1	16.7
(11) None	1.6	1.4	0	4.2	0	8.1	0	3.6	0	0
Total	100%	100%	100%	100%	100%	100%	100%	100%	100%	100%

*p < .1, **p < .05, ***p < .005.

5. Conclusions and implications

Despite ample evidence on the importance of studying gender representations in advertising (e.g., Eisend 2010), there has been limited research on gender representation in Super Bowl commercials (e.g., King 2012). The present study attempts to fill this gap by providing a longitudinal investigation of gender stereotypes based on a systematic and comprehensive framework that has been used in several studies investigating gender stereotypes (e.g., Lysonski 1985; Mitchell and Taylor 1990; Plakoyiannaki and Zotos 2009; Zotos and Lysonski 1994). Although prior research has highlighted the need for a systematic framework that includes a variety of gender roles when examining gender stereotypes in advertising (Zotos and Tsichla 2014), such a systematic approach is virtually non-existent in Super Bowl studies examining gender stereotypes. More specifically, this study investigates the types of female and male stereotypes depicted in Super Bowl commercials and how these stereotypes vary across product categories over a 20-year period. Our goal was to detect shifts in the cultural notions of gender constructed in advertising messages targeting the largest and the most demographically diverse TV audience in US television.

Consistent with previous studies (Drewniany 2003; King 2012), we found that women are underrepresented in Super Bowl commercials. Specifically, male stereotypes are more frequently used than female stereotypes in both time periods. Despite the fact that female Super Bowl viewership has significantly increased in the last decade (Nielsen 2009), it appears that Super Bowl is still considered, by advertisers, to be a male territory. Our results did identify shifts in the representation of female and male stereotypes that have occurred after the millennium. Both female and male stereotypes are becoming less traditional and begin to shift away from traditional patriarchal norms towards a somewhat more egalitarian depiction.

The first research question of the present study compared female and male stereotypes in Super Bowl commercials before the millennium (1990–1999) with those after the millennium (2000–2009). The findings indicate that, after the millennium, women are more frequently represented in 'non-traditional activities.' These changes coincide with NFL's increasing focus on women as sports fans (Nielsen 2009). The findings also show that the portrayal of men as 'figures of authority' has significantly decreased after the millennium. This sharp reduction is consistent with the loss of male dominance in family decisions and in several professional areas in American society (Peterson 2012).

A second research question examined by the present study is whether female and male stereotypes in Super Bowl commercials have changed over time across five major product categories. Significant changes are detected in three out of five product categories that were examined, namely, in food and drinks, alcoholic beverages and auto and related products. Both alcoholic beverages and auto and related products are considered to be traditionally 'male' product categories. According to Brennan (2009), however, when launching new products in these categories, companies develop advertising campaigns targeting women because of their growing purchasing power. The findings of the present study are consistent with this approach. After the millennium, in the commercials of alcoholic beverages, women are depicted less often as 'dependent' upon men, while men are portrayed less frequently as 'authority figures.' In addition, in the commercials of auto and related products, women are more often depicted as involved in 'non-traditional activities', while men are less frequently portrayed as 'career-oriented.' In the food and drinks product category, after the millennium, men are more frequently portrayed in 'activities and life outside the home' and less frequently portrayed as 'authority figures.'

The study findings have important implications for academic researchers and advertisers. First, the present study provides a longitudinal investigation of gender stereotypes across product categories in Super Bowl commercials. To the best of our knowledge, this is the longest time period of systematic monitoring of gender stereotypes in Super Bowl commercials recorded so far. As advertisements in general and Super Bowl advertisements in particular are slow in adapting to social changes, a longitudinal approach is necessary in order to identify how cultural notions of gender are constructed in Super Bowl commercials (e.g., King 2012) and how these cultural notions of gender have evolved (or not) over time (Verhellen, Dens, and Pelsmacker 2016).

Second, this research investigates gender stereotypes across five product categories over a 20-year period. Although prior research suggested that gender stereotypes do vary across product categories (e.g., Ganahl, Prinsen, and Netzley 2003; Plakoyiannaki and Zotos 2009; Verhellen, Dens, and Pelsmacker 2016), prior research on Super Bowl commercials has neglected to examine whether gender stereotypes vary across different product categories. Our results suggest that shifts in gender stereotypes are more likely to occur in certain product categories and highlight the importance of considering several product categories over several years in order to identify shifts in the cultural notions of gender in Super Bowl advertising.

Given the large expense and the magnitude of impact of Super Bowl commercials, understanding shifts in gender representation is critical for advertisers. Our results suggest that advertisers might lag in terms of responding to the changing audience mix as well as to cultural trends. Understanding shifts in gender representation will enable advertisers to better adapt to the current environment and create more effective advertising messages (Gentry and Harrison 2010, Weinberger, Gulas, and Weinberger 2015). Advertisers should also take into consideration the product context since, as our result suggests, shifts in gender portrayals vary across product categories.

6. Future research directions

This study provides us with important insights into gender representations across product categories in Super Bowl commercials and suggests several avenues for future research. First, future research could examine additional product categories and a longer time period. This study focused on the most advertised product categories in a 20-year period. It is, however, possible that other product categories become more prominent in a different time frame. Second, Dhar and Wertenbroch (2000) refer to consumer choice between hedonic and utilitarian products indicating that hedonic products might be of greater value than utilitarian products when making forfeiture choices. Extending prior research (Plakoyiannaki and Zotos 2009), it would be interesting to examine whether the hedonic or utilitarian nature of a product affects gender representation in Super Bowl commercials. Third, future research could enhance the existing framework by refining the definitions of the existing gender stereotypes and perhaps the addition of new stereotypes, in order to address changes in the current socioeconomic and cultural environment. Fourth, it would be interesting to replicate this study in the context of other major sports events that attract worldwide attention such as the Olympics, in order to identify potential differences in gender representations in TV advertising.

Acknowledgements

The authors would like to extend a special acknowledgement and thank you to Professor Lysonsky for his permission to use his original typology on gender stereotypes. The authors would also like to thank the three anonymous reviewers for their helpful comments.

Disclosure statement

No potential conflict of interest was reported by the authors.

References

Adland. 2014. *Super Bowl: World's largest archive of Super Bowl commercials.* http://adland.tv/ SuperBowlCommercials (accessed January 10, 2014).

Anderson, E., and E.M. Kian. 2012. Examining media contestation of masculinity and head trauma in the National Football League. *Men and Masculinities* 15, no. 2: 152–73.

Belkaoui, A., and J. Belkaoui. 1976. A comparative analysis of the roles portrayed by women in print advertisements: 1958, 1979, 1972. *Journal of Marketing Research* 13, no. 2: 168–72.

Brazile, D. 2014. Gladiator sport or a family thing: Why are women so into the Super Bowl? *CNN*, February 2, http://www.cnn.com/2014/02/02/opinion/brazile-super-bowl-women/index.html (accessed January 10, 2015).

Brennan, B. 2009. *Why she buys: The new strategy for reaching the world's most powerful consumers.* New York: Crown Business.

Buysse, J.A.M., and M.S. Embser-Herbert. 2004. Constructions of gender in sport. An analysis of intercollegiate media guide cover photographs. *Gender & Society* 18, no. 1: 66–81.

Carter, K. 2013. Super Bowl ads play to women. *ESPN*, January 30, http://espn.go.com/espnw/ news-commentary/article/8895041/espnw-super-bowl-ads-play-women (accessed January 10, 2015).

Chung, H., and X. Zhao. 2003. Humour effect on memory and attitude: Moderating role of product involvement. *International Journal of Advertising* 22, no. 1: 117–44.

Cohen, J. 1960. A coefficient of agreement for nominal scales. *Educational and Psychological Measurement* 20, no. 1: 37–46.

Courtney, A.E., and S.W. Lockeretz. 1971. A woman's place: An analysis of the roles portrayed by women in magazine advertisements. *Journal of Marketing Research* 8, no. 1: 92–5.

Dhar, R., and K. Wertenbroch. 2000. Consumer choice between hedonic and utilitarian goods. *Journal of Marketing Research* 37 (February): 60–71.

Drewniany, B. 2003. We've come a long way maybe: An analysis of the portrayal of women in Super Bowl commercials from 1989 to 2002. In *Images that injure*, ed. P.M. Lester and S.D. Ross, 149–56. Westport: Praeger Publishers.

Duncan, M.C., and C.A. Hasbrook. 2002. Denial of power in televised women's sports. In *Gender and Sport: A Reader*, ed. S. Scraton and A. Flintoff, 83–93. London: Routledge.

Dundes, A. 1978. Into the endzone for a touchdown: A psychoanalytic consideration of American football. *Western Folklore* 37, no. 2: 75–88.

Dunning, E. 1986. Sport as a male preserve: Notes on the social sources of masculine identity and its transformations. *Theory, Culture and Society* 3, no. 1: 79–90.

Dunning, E., S. Birrell, and C.L. Cole. 1994. Sport as a male preserve: Notes on the social sources of masculine identity and its transformations. In *Women, sport, and culture*, ed. S. Birrell and C.L. Cole, 163–79. Champaign, IL: Human Kinetics Publishers.

Eisend, M. 2010. A meta-analysis of gender roles in advertising. *Journal of the Academy of Marketing Science* 38, no. 4: 418–40.

Fields, A.M., S. Swan, and B. Kloos. 2010. What it means to be a woman: Ambivalent sexism in female college students' experiences and attitudes. *Sex Roles* 62, no. 7–8: 554–67.

Furnham, A., and T. Mak. 1999. Sex-role stereotyping in television commercials: A review and comparison of fourteen studies done on five continents over 25 years. *Sex Roles* 41, no. 5–6: 413–37.

Ganahl, D.J., T.J. Prinsen, and S.B. Netzley. 2003. A content analysis of prime time commercials: A contextual framework of gender representation. *Sex Roles* 49, no. 9–10: 545–51.

Gentry, J., and R. Harrison. 2010. Is advertising a barrier to male movement toward gender change? *Marketing Theory* 10, no. 1: 74–96.

Ghizoni, J.M. 2014. Identification and the 2013 Hyundai Team Super Bowl commercial. *Celebrating Scholarship & Creativity Day.* Paper 14. Minessota: College of Saint Benedict and Saint John's University. http://digitalcommons.csbsju.edu/elce_cscday/14 (accessed January 10, 2015).

Green, K., and M. Van Oort. 2013. We wear no pants: Selling the crisis of masculinity in the 2010 Super Bowl commercials. *Signs* 38, no. 3: 695–719.

Gulas C.S., K.K. McKeage, and M.G. Weinberger. 2010. It's just a joke. *Journal of Advertising* 39, no. 4: 109–20.

Hanke, R. 1990. Hegemonic masculinity in thirty something. *Critical Studies in Media Communication* 7, no. 3: 231–48.

Hatzithomas L., E. Outra, and Y. Zotos. 2010. Postmodern advertising: A longitudinal study of Super Bowl commercials. In *39th Annual Conference of the European Marketing Academy (EMAC)*. Copenhagen.

Jeong, Y., Y. Kim, and X. Zhao. 2011. Competing for consumer memory in television advertising: An empirical examination of the impacts of non-editorial clutter on brand memory in mega-event broadcasts. *International Journal of Advertising* 30, no. 4: 617–40.

Jin, H., and R.J. Lutz. 2013. The typicality and accessibility of consumer attitudes toward television advertising: Implications for the measurement of attitudes toward advertising in general. *Journal of Advertising* 42, no. 4: 343–57.

Kane, M.J., and J.B. Parks. 1992. The social construction of gender difference and hierarchy in sport journalism – few new twists on very old themes. *Women in Sport & Physical Activity Journal* 1, no. 1: 49–83.

Kassarjian, H.H. 1977. Content analysis in consumer research. *Journal of Consumer Research* 4, no. 1: 8–18.

Kelley, S.W., and L.W. Turley. 2004. The effect of content on perceived affect of Super Bowl commercials. *Journal of Sport Management* 18 (October): 398–420.

Kilbourne, J. 1999. *Deadly persuasion: Why women and girls must fight the addictive power of advertising*. New York: Free Press.

Kim, K., and Y. Cheong. 2011. Creative strategies of Super Bowl commercials 2001–2009: An analysis of message strategies. *International Journal of Sports Marketing & Sponsorship* 13, no. 1: 7–20.

Kim, K., Y. Cheong, and H. Kim. 2012. Information content of Super Bowl commercials 2001–2009. *Journal of Marketing Communications* 18, no. 4: 249–64.

Kimmel, M.S. 1987. The contemporary 'crisis' of masculinity in historical perspective. In *The Making of Masculinities*, ed. H. Brod, 121–53. Boston, MA: Allen & Unwin.

King, B. 2012. Images of gender and race in Super Bowl advertising. *Media Report to Women* 40, no. 1: 6–11 and 18–9.

Klassen, M.L., C. Jasper, and A. Schwartz. 1993. Men and women images of their relationships in magazine advertisements. *Journal of Advertising Research* 33, no. 2: 30–9.

Knoll, S., M. Eisend, and J. Steinhagen. 2011. Gender roles in advertising. *International Journal of Advertising* 30, no. 5: 867–88.

Kolbe, R.H., and P.J. Albanese. 1996. Man to Man: A content analysis of sole – male images in male – audience magazines *Journal of Advertising* 25, no. 4: 1–20.

Lundstrom, J.W., and D. Sciglimpaglia. 1977. Sex role portrayals in advertising. *Journal of Marketing* 41, no. 3: 29–72.

Lysonski, S. 1983. Female and male portrayals in magazine advertisements – a re-examination. *Akron Business and Economic Review* 14, no. 2: 45–50.

Lysonski, S. 1985. Role portrayals in British magazine advertisement. *European Journal of Marketing* 19, no. 7: 37–55.

MacFarquhar, N. 1996. What's a soccer mom anyway? *The New York Times*, October 20, http://www.nytimes.com/1996/10/20/weekinreview/what-s-a-soccer-mom-anyway.html (accessed January 10, 2015).

Mager, J., and J.G. Helgeson. 2011. Fifty years of advertising images: Some changing perspectives on role portrayals along with enduring consistencies. *Sex Roles* 64, no. 3–4: 238–52.

Messner, M. 2010. *Out of play: Critical essays on gender and sport*. New York: Suny Press.

Messner, M.A., and J. Montez de Oca. 2005. The male consumer as loser: Beer and liquor ads in mega sports media events. *Signs: Journal of Women in Culture & Society* 30: 1879–909.

Mitchell, P.C.N., and W. Taylor. 1990. Polarising trends in female role portrayal in UK advertising. *European Journal of Marketing* 24, no. 5: 41–9.

Monteiro, C. 2015. Infographic: Things Super Bowl viewers love (besides the big game): A closer look at their behaviors and interests. *Adweek*, January 25, http://www.adweek.com/news/television/things-super-bowl-viewers-love-besides-big-game-162514 (accessed January 30, 2015).

Nelson, M.B. 1994. *The stronger women get, the more men love football: Sexism and the American culture of sports*. New York: Harcourt Brace.

Neuendorf, K.A. 2011. Content analysis — a methodological primer for gender research. *Sex Roles* 64 no. 3—4: 276—89.

Newell, S.J., K.V. Henderson, and B.T. Wu. 2001. The effects of pleasure and arousal on recall of advertisements during the Super Bowl. *Psychology & Marketing* 18, no. 11: 1135—53.

Newell, S.J., and B. Wu. 2003. Evaluating the significance of placement on recall of advertisements during the Super Bowl. *Journal of Current Issues & Research in Advertising* 25, no. 2: 57—67.

Nielsen. 2009. Women increasingly Super Bowl fans. Media and Entertainment, January 26, http:// www.nielsen.com/us/en/insights/news/2009/women-increasingly-super-super-bowl-fans.html (accessed January 10, 2015).

Paek, H.J., M.R. Nelson, and A.M. Vilela. 2011. Examination of gender-role portrayals in television advertising across seven countries. *Sex Roles* 64, no. 3—4: 192—207.

Pallotta, F. 2015. Super Bowl XLIX posts the largest audience in TV history. *CNN*, February 2, http://money.cnn.com/2015/02/02/media/super-bowl-ratings (accessed February 10, 2015).

Peterson, J. 2012. The great crisis and the significance of gender in the U.S. economy. *Journal of Economic Issues* 46, no. 2: 277—90.

Plakoyiannaki, E., K. Mathioudaki, P. Dimitratos, and Y. Zotos. 2008. Images of women in online advertisements of global products: Does sexism exist? *Journal of Business Ethics* 83: 101—12.

Plakoyiannaki, E., and Y. Zotos. 2009. Female role stereotypes in print advertising: Identifying associations with magazine and product categories. *European Journal of Marketing* 43, no. 11/ 12: 1411—34.

Ricciardelli, R., K.A. Clow, and P. White. 2010. Investigating hegemonic masculinity: Portrayals of masculinity in men's lifestyle magazines. *Sex Roles* 63, no. 1—2: 64—78.

Siltanen, R. 2014. Yes, a Super Bowl ad really is worth $4 million. *Forbes*, January 29, http://www. forbes.com/sites/onmarketing/2014/01/29/yes-a-super-bowl-ad-really-is-worth-4-million/ (accessed January 10, 2015).

Statista. 2015. *TV advertising spending in the United States from 2011 to 2018 (in billion U.S. dollars).* http://www.statista.com/statistics/272404/tv-advertising-spending-in-the-us/ (accessed January 30, 2015).

Tadena, N. 2015. Super Bowl ad prices have gone up 75% over a decade. *The Wall Street Journal* (January 12): 1, http://blogs.wsj.com/cmo/2015/01/12/super-bowl-ad-prices-have-gone-up-75-over-a-decade/ (accessed January 20, 2015).

Theodoridis, P., A. Kyrousi, A. Zotou, and G. Panigyrakis. 2013. Male and female attitudes towards stereotypical advertisements: A paired country investigation. *Corporate Communications: An International Journal* 8, no. 1: 135—60.

Thompson, S. 2006. Super Bowl advertisers finally notice women: Anheuser-Busch eyes female beer drinkers; unilever runs 'real beauty' spots. *Advertising Age*, January 31, http://adage.com/ article/news/super-bowl-advertisers-finally-notice-women/48303/ (accessed January 10, 2015).

Tomkovick, C., R. Yelkur, and L. Christians. 2001. The USA's biggest marketing event keeps getting bigger: An in-depth look at Super Bowl advertising in the 1990s. *Journal of Marketing Communications* 7, no. 2: 89—108.

Treadwell, D. 2014. *Introducing communication research.* 2nd ed. California: Sage.

Tsichla, E., and Y. Zotos. 2014. Snapshots of men and women in interaction: An investigation of stereotypes in print advertisement relationship portrayals. *Journal of Euromarketing* 23, no. 3: 446—54.

Verhellen, Y., N. Dens, and P. de Pelsmacker. 2016. A longitudinal content analysis of gender role portrayal in Belgian television advertising. *Journal of Marketing Communications* 22, no. 2: 170—88.

Weber, R.P. 1990. *Basic content analysis.* London: Sage.

Weinberger, M.G., C.S. Gulas, and M.F. Weinberger. 2015. Looking in through outdoor: A socio-cultural and historical perspective on the evolution of advertising humour. *International Journal of Advertising* 34, no. 3: 447—72.

Wiles, J.A., C.R. Wiles, and A. Tjernlund. 1995. A comparison of gender role portrayals in magazine advertising: The Netherlands, Sweden and the USA. *European Journal of Marketing* 29, no. 11: 35—49.

Wolheter, M., and L.B. Lammers. 1980. An analysis of males' roles in print advertisements over a 20-year span. In *Advances in consumer research* (7th ed.), ed. Olson, J.C., 760—61. Ann Arbor: Association for Consumer Research.

Yelkur, R., C. Tomkovick, A. Hofer, and D. Rozumalski. 2013. Super Bowl ad likeability: Enduring and emerging predictors. *Journal of Marketing Communications* 19, no. 1: 58–80.

Zimmerman, A., and J. Dahlberg. 2008. The sexual objectification of women in advertising: A contemporary cultural perspective. *Journal of Advertising Research* 48, no. 1: 71–9.

Zmuda, N. 2009. Coca-Cola gives Coke Zero a Super Bowl spot. Ad stars Pittsburgh Steeler Troy Polamalu. *Ad Age*, January 22, http://adage.com/article/media/coca-cola-coke-a-super-bowl-spot/134040/ (accessed January 10, 2015).

Zotos, Y., and S. Lysonski. 1994. Gender representations. *Journal of Euromarketing* 3, no. 2: 27–47.

Zotos, Y., and E. Tsichla. 2014. Female stereotypes in print advertising: A retrospective analysis. *Proceedia – Social and Behavioral Sciences* 148: 446–54.

Is there gender bias when creative directors judge advertising? Name cue effect in ad evaluation

David Roca, Daniel Tena, Patrícia Lázaro and Alfons González

A lack of women in creative departments has been documented in previous research. These departments are seen as a male fraternity subculture in advertising agencies, where women experience many difficulties in their career progress. One of these drawbacks is gender bias in the selection of ideas' process. Male creative directors are believed to promote ideas created by men within a homosocial environment. This female perception emerged from previous qualitative research is studied experimentally for the first time. Almost 90 advertising creative directors and higher level positions assessed ads created by students in an advertising university course. In the current study, we explore the effects of ad gender authorship. Results revealed an absence of gender bias based on ad name cues, neither the gender of the ad creators nor the creatives affected the evaluations. The findings are discussed and future research is proposed.

Introduction

Canary and Hause (1993) wrote an article based on a meta-analysis methodology entitled, 'Is There Any Reason to Research Sex Differences in Communications?' Their paper concluded that sex effects are negligible but encouraged the development of new practices to find them. This inquiry satisfies this purpose and also resonates with recent calls from 'women's perspective' studies to go deeper into the research of gender and creative departments (Mallia 2009; Grow and Broyles 2011; Mallia and Windels 2011) and specifically in 'the effect gender bias can have on the output and evaluation of women's creative work' (Windels and Lee 2012, 504). This research aims to investigate gender differences in the advertising creation process, specifically in the evaluation stage, to discover if there is gender bias when male professionals working in advertising agencies select ideas. Due to the complexity of gender bias research, this paper will only focus on name cues (male, female or unknown) shown on the ads. Other related factors will not be addressed in this experimental design. Previous qualitative research suggests that professional women feel their ideas are discriminated against by men in advertising agencies (Grow and Broyles 2011; Windels and Lee 2012). On the other hand, Hernández, Martín, and Beléndez (2012) argue that there is no relationship between a predominant creative male environment (Nixon 2003; Grow and Broyles 2011) and advertising sexism, despite the broad use of gender stereotypes in advertising (Shao, Desmarais, and Weaver 2014). In the same vein, Roca et al. (2013) gave voice to male creatives. Results show they do not perceive equality as a problem and feel discrimination is determined by a historically male chauvinistic society and not by creative department dynamics.

The main objective of this paper is to study if there is an unconscious bias towards advertising ideas from junior women. This can be understood as the hiring homogeneity that jeopardizes the minority which is women (Mallia 2009). Previous research regarding bias in the hiring processes in advertising has been studied by Sego (1999) in the account area and by Windels and Lee (2012) and Roca, Tena, and Lázaro (2012) in the creative field. All three investigations used students as judges. The topic of gender bias on ad ideas has never been studied experimentally with advertising professionals to date. A new element is the use of creative practitioners as evaluators of ads, as done in previous literature related to advertising creativity evaluation (Koslow, Sasser, and Riordan 2003; Sasser and Koslow 2008). Having the opinions of authentic creatives is very important, since young newcomers applying for entry-level positions in creative departments, are judged by their creative portfolio (Slayden, Broyles, and Kendrick 1998; McLeod, O'Donohoe, and Townley 2011) and not by university grades, selling experience or recommendation letters, as is the case within other departments and industries.

Some articles present extensive research regarding relationships among professionals in creative departments (Gelade 1997; Hackley 2003; Nixon 2003; Chong 2006; Hackley and Kover 2007; Stuhlfaut 2011), factors that have an effect on advertising creativity (Sasser and Koslow 2013), ad evaluations for awards (Kilgour, Sasser, and Koslow 2013), and by consumers (Rosengren, Dáhlen, and Modig 2013), and effects of advertising creativity (Dáhlen, Rosengren, and Törn 2008). However, little attention has been dedicated to gender influences on ad evaluation (Roca, Tena, and Lázaro 2012). This research is a new step towards studying gender bias during the selection of creative ads using experimental methodology with practitioners, as globally framed in Csikszentmihalyi's (1999) systems model of creativity. Transferred to the advertising domain, creative directors are the gatekeepers who allow newcomers to belong and progress in this field. If we refer to advertising creative outcomes, could gender be considered a barrier?

Literature suggests that women dominate advertising programs (Weisberg and Robbs 1997; Mallia 2008; Fullerton, Kendrick, and Frazier 2009) and account departments (Klein 2000; Pueyo 2010). The number of male and female students is equal in portfolio schools (Grow and Broyles 2011). However, the presence of women is limited in the creative departments of several western countries – Peru, Spain, Sweden, United Kingdom, and the USA – due to various factors (Weisberg and Robbs 1997; Alvesson 1998; Kelly 2000; Martín-Laguno 2007; Pueyo 2010; Grow and Broyles 2011; Hernández, Martín, and Beléndez 2012; Mensa and Grow 2015). Creative departments are considered as being a *laddish* creative environment, or what has been defined as men's club (Alvesson 1998; Nixon and Crewe 2004; Broyles and Grow 2008; Etayo and Del Río 2008; Fitzsimmons 2008; Mallia 2009; Gregory 2009). One of the reasons is male networking outside the agency (Ibarra 1992; Gregory 2009) which leads, for example, to male dominance in judgment committees (Grow and Broyles 2011; Roca, Alegre, and Pueyo 2011; Windels and Lee 2012). Women lack peer recognition since they do not participate in such networks (Cuneo and Petrecca 1997; Bosman 2005). In contrast, they appear to be trapped as *pink ghetto,* especially when limited to working on female products such as those, related with beauty, cleaning and children (Roca and Pueyo 2011; Windels and Lee 2012). Some other variables show that an absence of women in creative departments is related to managerial knowledge (Martín, Hernández, and Beléndez 2009), lower salaries in the advertising industry for women (Martín 2007), a lack of creative leadership positions (Pool 2001; Mallia 2009) and, especially, motherhood penalty (Mallia 2009;

Grow and Broyles 2011), which is not exclusive to the advertising sector (e.g., Correll, Benard, and Paik 2007). Industry interest to highlight the lack of women in creative departments is growing. Recently, several books by female practitioners have appeared: *Seducing the Boys Club: Uncensored Tactics from a Woman at the Top* (Di Sesa 2008); *Mad Women: A Herstory of Advertising* (Knight and Thorsell 2012); and *Mad Women: The Other Side of Life on Madison Avenue in the '60s and Beyond* (Mass 2013). Furthermore, the web page www.3percentconf.com developed by creative director Kate Gordon, points out that there is a lack of women in creative departments.

Thus, the question to answer is whether creative author gender influences the selection of best ideas and if creators experience unconscious bias and are, therefore, gender biased. Our research question is tested in an experimental study where creative directors evaluated students' ads where gender was visible for the evaluators by means of a perception test.

Literature review

Considering a gender perspective, the homosociability theory (1977), the similarity-attraction theory (1961) and the gender bias paradigm (1968) provide a framework for this paper.

Homosociability theory

Similarity plays a big role in homosociability. This can be defined as the 'non sexual attraction held by men for members of their own sex' without erotic attraction (Bird 1996, 121). This area of research started with Lipman-Blumen (1976) and Kanter (1977). The former introduced the concept 'homosociality' as a form of occupational segregation of women, where men are attracted to and interested in other men as a way of keeping the high level hierarchies, building what is known as men's club or 'old boy network.' The latter proposed the concept 'homosociability,' and explained the disadvantages for women of being in low proportion in skewed groups in organizations. Kanter named the phenomena 'tokenism': people are identified by ascribed characteristics such as sex, and a set of assumptions concerning culture, status and behavior. The approach to this theory in advertising has been developed mainly through qualitative methodology as now detailed. Homosociability was found in the construction of multiple networks, where men get better returns that women reinforcing gender inequalities (Ibarra 1992). These networks lead to two kinds of gender segregation (Grow and Deng 2014): vertical, when there are fewer women in senior positions (creative directors) and horizontal, with male domination within creative departments. Windels and Lee (2012) researched the construction of gender and creativity in advertising departments through female voices. They found gender had a strong negative impact in creative's ideas evaluation, credibility and quality of assignments. Their results were consistent with previous qualitative research where creative women were the informants (Mallia 2009; Grow and Broyles 2011; Grow, Roca, and Broyles 2012). From these accounts, women's ideas are considered less valuable to male creative directors, who award more merit to men's ideas, to the detriment of creative quality, and indirectly women. However, when men are interviewed gender is not considered a key factor in the choosing of ideas (Roca et al. 2013).

Theory of similarity

The theory of similarity is also known as *the similarity-attraction paradigm, similar-to-me effect, similarity effect* or *law of attraction* (Michinov and Michinov 2011). This theory states that there is a strong relationship between interpersonal similarity and attraction (Byrne 1997). Perceived similarity has been studied through different dimensions which are likely to play a key role in attraction judgments, be it in love or recruitment processes. A meta-analysis conducted by Montoya, Horton, and Kirchner (2008) studied 313 laboratory and field investigations in this topic. The *similarity effect,* used by the vast majority of studies, was operationalized as attitudes and personality traits, refusing to study other types of similarity. After their research, they concluded that: 'similarity leads to attraction in the laboratory setting' (907), when there is no previous interaction. However, results are not so clear in field studies with existing relationships.

The body of research related to recruiters' interpersonal attraction started with the Byrne's model in industrial-organization research in 1961. He suggested that 'when applicants present biographically similar information to a white middle-class interviewer, ratings of job suitability, intelligence, personal attributes, and attraction of candidate are increased' (cited in Rand and Wexley 1975, 541). In this area, these kinds of findings have been mainly developed with interviews through laboratory (simulated interview technique) or field experiments (real-life interviews). Orphen (1984) employed real-life selection interviews in four insurance companies. He discovered that actual and perceived similarity based on attitude scales was fairly strongly related to both attraction and the decision to accept candidates for these jobs. Rand and Wexley (1975) observed this phenomenon generally occurs regardless of the race of the applicant or the level of racial prejudice of interviewers, and similar attitudes are more important for the hiring process. Considering previous research, the question arises as to whether gender similarity is a key factor in recruitment. Graves and Powell (1988, 1995) examined the direct and indirect effects on applicant sex on real campus interview outcomes and tested whether the similarity-attraction paradigm mediated these effects, but their results revealed no significant effects of applicant sex on interview outcomes; for male recruiters, interview outcomes were not affected by sex similarity. These results did not lead to *similarity bias,* and consequently there is a need to look into the research undertaken using the *gender bias* paradigm (Goldberg 1968). In this paradigm, judges don't have any information of applicants; they just judge creative outcomes.

Gender bias paradigm

Prejudice against women can be generally examined with two kinds of studies. First, assessing attitudes toward some groups (e.g., women), by getting conscious answers through qualitative methods as described previously (Mallia 2009; Grow and Broyles 2011; Windels and Lee 2012; Roca et al. 2013) and by means of quantitative ones. In both cases, respondents are aware of examined attitudes towards gender. One survey (Hartman 1988) states that creative directors think they don't discriminate between men and women. Second, conducting studies with less information than that occurring in real sets where respondents are not aware that gender biases are being examined (unconscious answers). This methodology uses unobtrusive measures and usually employs student samples rather than engaging professional samples. These studies evaluate gender bias with respect to articles (Paludi and Bauer 1983; Levenson et al. 1975), paintings (Ward 1979), job applications (Halon Soto and Cole 1975), resumes (Bosak and Sczesny 2008), etc. Surprisingly, only three articles are related with advertising (Sego 1999; Windels, Lee, and Yeh 2010; Roca, Tena, and Lázaro 2012).

Goldberg (1968) was the first to experiment the concept of unconscious gender bias by changing the authors' names in academic articles. He tried to discover if women were prejudiced against women. Results of this research are known as the 'Goldberg paradigm.' His experiment assessed students' perceptions regarding six academic articles from various professional backgrounds written supposedly by men as well as women. The results indicated that identical articles signed by men were better evaluated, although bias against women's work was significant only for the two articles in traditionally masculine fields as city planning and law (gender incongruity) and one in a neutral field (linguistics). Women assessed women worse than men, even for feminine fields. Swim et al. (1989) conducted a meta-analysis of 123 'real world' settings using students. They reported hardly any gender bias related with the articles. Only a slight effect was observed when the work being judged consisted of a masculine domain. Eagly, Makhijani, and Klonsky (1992) drew conclusions from meta-analysis of studies regarding gender effects on evaluation of leaders. It was found that female leaders were evaluated slightly less favorably compared to males, particularly for stereotypical masculine styles. Earlier, Olian, Schwab, and Haberfeld (1988) examined job applications and found a considerable tendency for men to fare better than women ($d = 0.41$), but almost 80% of studies were based on 'male-type' positions.

The first investigation on gender bias in advertising was conducted much later than Goldberg's. Sego (1999) researched whether advertising professionals have negative beliefs when hiring women and black people in a laboratory setting. Results showed that sexist stereotypes did not modify the evaluations for advertising candidates in account services. Furthermore, the interaction of feminist beliefs and candidate sex were not significant. Male candidates were evaluated a little better than females. Windels et al. (2010) examined students' perceptions regarding gender norms associated with creative departments of advertising agencies. The experiment constituted an evaluation of fictitious text-based resumes from students for the position of creative director in the creative department of a student-run advertising agency. Gender perceptions did not influence decision-making when choosing a creative director for a student-run agency. A creative portfolio is, undoubtedly, a fundamental tool in accessing creative departments. Roca, Tena, and Lázaro (2012) researched gender bias when selecting creative ads in experimental conditions. They used advertising students as creators and about 800 undergraduate advertising students as judges of print ads created by the former group. Neither the gender of advertisement creators nor the judges affected the evaluations. These studies research gender bias in the hiring process in advertising, but none used practitioners as experimental subjects to judge creativity. The aim of this study is to present a closer perspective to reality introducing creative directors' evaluations.

Hypotheses

'Male-dominated jobs are thought to require characteristics stereotypically ascribed to men' (Eagly and Mladinic 1994, 2). Advertising creative departments are traditionally considered a masculine domain that impedes progress and job satisfaction for women (Windels and Lee 2012). Grow and Broyles (2011, 217) wrote in a cross-cultural qualitative study: 'Both Spanish and American women suggest that the Big Ideas of male creatives are often prioritized.' This study explores if gender bias is not only a female perception but also occurs in lab conditions. A real portfolio exercise was simulated based on this assumption. We analyze the influence of ad authorship on the professional appraisal of the level of creativity in print ads. Three hypotheses were established to measure gender bias name cues related with the evaluation of a creative portfolio in advertising.

H_1 Male authorship increases the probability of recommending the selection of an ad compared to female authorship of ads.

H_2 Male authorship increases the probability of recommending the selection of an ad compared to female authorship of ads when the creativity of the ad is taken into account (interaction effect).

H_3 Male authorship increases the probability of recommending the selection of an ad compared to female authorship of ads when the creative director's gender is taken into account.

Methods

This research aims to verify the extent to which there is gender bias based on name cues when creative directors judge ads. As a result an experimental design was selected where the independent variable was gender authorship of the ad. In contrast to previous studies, samples were practitioners working in creative departments in top advertising agencies, as opposed to students. Creative directors were selected from Spanish advertising agencies.

Participants sample and procedure

Names of advertising agencies were obtained from three different sources: *Infoadex,* a Spanish advertising database; *Independent Agencies Association*; and finally, a special issue of the magazine *El Publicista* (*Revista Especial Agencias de Publicidad y Medios 2013*). The final pool had 70 advertising agencies based in Spain, including mainstream (31) and creative hotshops (39). In the end, 45 agencies took part in the study. Data from a total of 87 creative directors including top positions (Executive Creative Director, General Creative Director...) were used for the study. This is a pleasing number considering the difficulty in reaching this population and the market size of Spain (10,406.3 million euros in 2013, *Estudio Infoadex de la inversión publicitaria en España* 2014). Professionals who had never taken part in new talent selection processes were discarded, and copywriters and art directors, as well. Most of the professionals were aged between 35 and 44 years old (56.3%). According to our sample data, 83.9% were male creatives ($n = 73$) and 16.1% were female creatives ($n = 14$). These figures coincide with previous studies of the advertising creative population in Spain (Martín 2007; Roca, Alegre, and Pueyo 2011). The sample was taken from Barcelona (45.2%) and Madrid (54.8%) since these cities represent 90% of the advertising business in Spain. The experimental test was available online from November 2013 to February 2014. The experiment could be completed on line in less than 15 minutes.

Ad sample and manipulation

In order to increase external validity (confidence in the generalizability) of the research, print ads were obtained from university students on a creativity course in their final years of advertising studies. They created and designed a print ad for a local winery to be included in their portfolio. Prior to the experiment, creativity professors selected the most creative ads based on criteria called 'subjective creativity' established in previous literature (Koslow, Sasser, and Riordan 2003). The measure defines a 'creative' advertisement as one that is 'both original and appropriate' (Sasser et al. 2013, 2). This first pool contained 29 print ads. In a second stage, 6 senior creatives, known by the researchers, rated the ads online based on a short creative brief. To reduce possible confound effects caused

Figure 1.   Online random set of ads and authors (male, female, unknown gender).

by screen variations, all ads were displayed in black and white. The final pool had the 9 most creative ads. Names and surnames of the authors were added and manipulated to present three variations, as used in previous literature: male (e.g., Ángel Lázaro), female (e.g., Ángela Lázaro), and first name initial (in order to avoid gender identification), expressed in this paper as unknown gender (e.g., A. Lázaro). In contrast to English, Spanish enables the delimitation of the gender of a name, so manipulation check was not necessary in this case. The resulting factorial design had a total of 27 combinations (3 gender authorship × 9 ads). The participants were randomly assigned to one of the 3 sets to guarantee internal validity. Nine different ads, with their authorship, appeared randomly in each one (see Figures 1 and 2). All participants evaluated the same nine ads but with a different name variation. The names used in the experiment were taken from previous research (Roca, Tena, and Lázaro 2012) in order to avoid Kasof's (1993) bias, which states that female names are usually less attractive than those of males, when minimal information is shown in gender-bias researches (see Table 1).

Figure 2.   27 combinations of the factorial design (3 gender authorship × 9 ads).

Table 1. Author name variations.

Female	Male	Unknown
Angela Lázaro	Angel Lázaro	A. Lázaro
Juana Campos	Juan Campos	J. Campos
María Cuesta	Mario Cuesta	M. Cuesta
Carla Hinojo	Carlo Hinojo	C. Hinojo
Sandra Gamir	Sandro Gamir	S. Gamir
Victoria Gascón	Víctor Gascón	V. Gascón
Alejandra Pascual	Alejandro Pascual	A. Pascual
Claudia Erquicia	Claudio Erquicia	C. Erquicia
Adriana Campoy	Adriano Campoy	A. Campoy

Measures

The administration of the stimuli consisted of five parts. The first part involved the presentation and general instructions. Creatives were told they formed part of an experiment which consisted in evaluating the level of creativity in students' ads applying for an entry-level position. The second part entailed the asking of demographic questions in order to know the profile of the respondents. In the third section, the experiment was explained. Following a short creative brief, participants were asked to 'evaluate the creative quality of the ads' according to their own criteria, based on the consensual assessment technique (CAT; see Amabile 1982, 1996; Baer, Kaufman, and Gentile 2004). To ensure validity of the instrument they were aware of authorship of the ad, because they had to type the name and surname of the author before evaluating. They could not continue the test without doing this step. Those ads where names were not well typed were not taken into account for the research.

Participants evaluated creativity of nine different ads based on the following dichotomous question (as recommended by Rossiter 2011), 'Would you recommend a student select this ad for their portfolio if they were looking for a creative job position?' Later, they had to evaluate each ad on an interval scale of 0–10, with 10 representing the highest value in creativity and 0 the lowest (this scale is broadly known in Spain because is used in school grading). At the end of the experiment, respondents were thanked for their collaboration in the research. They were never told that gender bias based on authorship was being tested in order to avoid this information being passed on to the other practitioners. All tests were done on line through Parc (www.parc-online.es). This Spanish web-based tool, similar to Qualtrix, allows the simultaneous viewing of stimuli and questions (Lázaro et al. 2014).

Findings

We conducted a randomized block design with nine ads and three different authorships (male, female, unknown gender). Each participant evaluated nine ads where the authorship was randomly assigned. The order of the ads was rotated. The reliability of the portfolio was evaluated using Cronbach's alpha ($\alpha = 0.87$). To test H_1 two models were adjusted: (1) A logistic regression model to analyze the variable 'Recommend the selection of an ad as a part of a junior portfolio' (yes or no). Ad gender authorship and their interaction were included as covariates, and the creative director as a random effect to

Table 2. Estimated probabilities of recommending the selection of an ad depending on the gender who signs it (male, female, unknown gender).

Surname	Campos	Campoy	Cuesta	Erquicia	Gamir	Gascón	Hinojo	Lázaro	Pascual	Total mean
Male	3.5%	26.2%	16.0%	7.4%	26.8%	16.1%	45.1%	58.2%	19.6%	25.8%
Female	20.1%	28.9%	19.6%	15.8%	26.2%	22.7%	55.7%	43.7%	14.7%	27.1%
Unknown	38.6%	14.7%	14.7%	10.8%	19.6.%	10.9%	37.1%	55.7%	26.2%	26.0%
Total mean	20.7%	23.3%	16,8%	11.3%	24.2%	16.6%	45.9%	52.5%	20.2%	26.3%

take into account for repeated measures. (2) A linear regression model to analyze the variable 'Score of a $0-10$ scale,' considering the same factors defined in the previous model. The analyses were carried out using the procedure PROC GLIMMIX of SAS version 9.3 (SAS Institute Inc., Cary, NC, USA). Contrary to that hypothesized (H_1), male authorship did not increase the probabilities of recommending the selection of an ad compared to female authorship of ads ($M_{mean} = 20\%$, $F_{mean} = 26\%$, $U_{mean} = 23\%$; $F = 0.99$; $p = 0.37$). The interaction between ad creativity and gender authorship was neither found statistically significant ($F = 0.91$; $p = 0.56$). Results of the estimated probabilities of recommending the selection of an ad depending on the gender who signs the authorship of the ad (male, female, unknown gender) are presented in Table 2. Although no statistically significant differences were found we may see some if we check authorship one by one (sometimes in favor of male names, sometimes in favor of female names). The biggest differences are found with the surname 'Campos,' but when performing pairwise comparisons, no statistically significant differences were found after applying Tukey's correction.

Similar results were obtained from the analysis of the quantitative response variable (score of $0-10$ interval scale), and it confirmed that gender authorship did not affect the evaluation ($M_{mean} = 3.29$, $F_{mean} = 3.45$, $U_{mean} = 3.38$; $F = 0.82$; $p = 0.44$). The interaction results ($F = 1.01$; $p = 0.44$) are presented in Table 3.

H_2 stated that 'Male authorship increases the probability of recommending the selection of an ad compared to female authorship of ads when the creativity of the ad is taken into account' (interaction effect). The creativity level of ads was based on the question 'Which is the best ad you have seen?' Lazaro and Hinojo's ads were recommended by 32% and 25% of the creative directors respectively. The recommendation of the rest of the ads did not reach 8%. To check H_2, the interaction between creativity of the ad and gender authorship was included in the logistic regression model. No statistically significant differences were found ($F = 0.30$, $p = 0.74$). Gender name cues did not influence the evaluations (see Table 4). Therefore, the findings did not support either H_1 or H_2, and hence demonstrate that gender is not a key factor in evaluating advertising creativity under lab conditions when taking into account the name cues of the author.

Table 3. Judges' interval mean rating ($0-10$) of creativity for each ad.

Surname	Campos	Campoy	Cuesta	Erquicia	Gamir	Gascón	Hinojo	Lázaro	Pascual	Total
Male	2.60	3.00	2.56	2.22	3.40	3.11	4.55	4.82	3.39	3.37
Female	3.10	3.70	3.48	2.48	3.48	3.55	4.14	4.16	2.96	3.44
Unknown	4.03	2.96	2.80	3.12	3.45	2.84	3.72	4.34	3.10	3.41
Total mean	3.24	3.22	2.95	2.61	3.44	3.15	4.14	4.44	3.15	3.41

Table 4. Interaction between the level of creativity and gender authorship (% of recommended pieces).

Author's name	Level of creativity	
	High creativity	Low creativity
Male	49.9%	17.2%
Female	53.3%	20.9%
Unknown	45.2%	20.0%
Mean	49.4%	19.3%

Finally, in order to check H_3, 'Male authorship increases the probability of recommending the selection of an ad compared to female authorship of ads when the creative
director's gender is taken into account.' The interaction between gender of the creative
director and authorship gender was included in the logistic regression model. No differences were found between these two variables ($F = 1.4$; $p = 0.25$). In contrast to the claim,
the probability of recommending the selection of an ad does not depend on the gender of
the creative director. The data obtained depict that unconscious bias, based on name cues,
does not prevail either in male or in female creative directors when they evaluate ads of a
junior portfolio created by future advertising professionals (see Table 5).

Discussion

Gender bias in creative departments is a multifactorial topic. This research did not aim to
give an answer to this phenomenon as a whole. The purpose of this study was to evaluate
one factor of gender bias through an experiment, where 87 creative directors assessed
print ads for a student's portfolio with different gender authorships. Thus, it is the first
time this topic is investigated with this methodology with advertising creative directors,
and contributes to the progress in gender and management research (see Broadbridge and
Simpson 2011).

A portfolio is essential for young advertising students to access creative careers
(McLeod, O'Donohoe, and Townley 2011). Gender bias was evaluated through the factor
of authorship (female, male and unknown gender). For the first time in academic literature, a sample composed of advertising creative practitioners was used for this purpose.
Although creative departments are highly male dominated, the results of this study reveal
that there is no gender bias with respect to the evaluation of the ads, considering the

Table 5. Interaction between the author's name and the creative
director's gender (% of recommended pieces).

Author's name	Gender of the creative director	
	Male	Female
Male	21.8%	10.2%
Female	26.6%	22.2%
Unknown	22.2%	25.8%
Mean	23.5%	18.3%

variable of gender authorship through name cues. Findings show that gender authorship of the ad was not a determining factor in recommending its selection for the student's portfolio, even when high creativity ads were studied separately. Creative advertising professionals, both men and women value ads equally, regardless of the gender of the author. Theories of homosociability (Lipman-Blumen 1976; Kanter 1977), similarity (see overview in Byrne 1997) and the Goldberg (1968) paradigm were not confirmed through our experiment set. Results show no pro-male bias of men in the evaluation of the work, and are congruent with earlier research regarding creativity in other fields (Kaufman et al. 2010) and advertising assessment of gender bias using students as judges (Sego 1999; Windels et al. 2010; Roca, Tena, and Lázaro 2012). They are also very similar to the results of the gender-bias research in other fields using name cues (Olian, Schwab, and Haberfeld 1988; Swim et al. 1989; Eagly, Makhijani, and Klonsky 1992). This is particularly significant in Spain, where culture is considered more male oriented than in other western countries (Grow and Broyles 2011). If Windels et al. (2010, 22) found that 'boys' club culture does not start in the classroom,' following this research we could suggest this biased culture, also does not start in creatives' minds as isolated individuals when they judge ads, and it appears to be born in the social dynamics of the creative departments themselves or other factors different to name cues studied here. Results complement previous research based on the social construction of creativity (e.g., Grow and Broyles 2011; Windels and Lee 2012), where women felt their ideas were discriminated against when evaluated by men. The question arises as to whether findings would vary if the evaluations were performed in a real-life ongoing assessment scenario, as opposed to the individual isolated decision-making conditions employed in the study. Female accounts claim women's ideas are devalued. In this sense, if we assume that there are no gender differences in creative outcomes (see Baer and Kaufman 2008), we might think devaluation is about social gender interaction and not about ideas. Under lab conditions, authorship is not a decisive factor for gender bias, but undoubtedly more research is needed along the lines of gender bias.

Managerial implications

The results of the study suggest that there is no gender bias among creatives when they judge students' print ads based on name cues. Previous qualitative research states that dynamics in creative departments provoke male discrimination by gender in a wider sense. This discrimination has been expressed with different concepts in literature: boys' club, pink ghetto, glass ceiling, etc. It may also include gender bias in the idea selection (Grow and Broyles 2011; Windels and Lee 2012).

However, this research indicates that this claim must be seen in context: gender bias related to idea evaluation was not found for the job entry-level positions (portfolio), although results could be different for creative women working in creative departments. If it were the case, some measures could be used to prevent evaluation bias: anonymity when presenting ideas, using external creative directors when working in networks, improving university education to support the defense of female work, etc. Likewise, a lack of gender bias in the factor of authorship is not sufficient to ensure a higher presence of females in entry-level creative job positions. Their ideas may be recommended to be included in a junior portfolio, but are they? More research is needed on these gender differences. Prior research suggests a lack of gender diversity in creative departments since subjectivity of creativity has a negative impact on women (Mallia 2009); however, our data show creatives would not undermine female ideas when represented by authorship.

Nonetheless, the industry should question not only why creative senior women complain about gender bias at work, but also why so few women reach creative junior positions. There are many other factors at play that can impact hiring besides an impressive portfolio. We might think about lack of women in junior positions for different reasons: (1) the self-selection done by white upper middle class men (boys' club); (2) the self-limitation of young women (future mother penalty, perception of being less creative, less tendency for risk taking...); (3) a minor female student preference for creative positions, as previous research suggest (Fullerton, Kendrick, and Frazier 2009); (4) a lack of professors at university level who teach about the male environment and how to be efficient there (use of humor, social abilities with men, sensitivity management...); (5) a male professor climate at university could already reproduce the actual dynamics of advertising agencies and girls may lack a mentor who encourages them to trust and believe in their own ideas; and finally (6) portfolio based mainly on *pink account* ideas. If diversity sparks creativity (Govendo 2005; Basset-Jones 2005), academy could help with new lines of research to understand the lack of gender diversity at entrance level. Prevailing professional male creative criteria about ideas does not seem to be one of the reasons, at least under lab conditions. More research is needed into the impact of creative director instinct and homosociability on candidates for creative positions.

Limitation and future research

This study has several limitations, some related to the phenomenon of gender bias and others with the methodology. This is a complex topic and the methodology used can only objectify one factor of gender bias (authorship based on name cues), gender bias is not activated by the name but could be by other gender cues. A second point of criticism of this paper is the use of the same product (wine) for all ads in the portfolio. A future improvement could be to consider using different products and brands. In this case, instead of assessing just one ad per author, creatives would be asked to evaluate a whole portfolio, thereby adding more realism to the evaluation process. Putting aside these considerations, the present experimental research did provide valuable information about the absence of gender discrimination in creative professionals' minds when judging students work under lab conditions. A third limitation could be the limited scope of the research since it involved only 87 creatives (despite around 80 hours of phone calls), and in just one country, Spain. In the future, this research could be extended to other countries with larger markets. Future research on gender bias could lead to different scenarios. First, the interviews could be performed under lab conditions (e.g., future creatives introducing their portfolios or actors playing different roles), and, in addition, through the ethnographic methodology (Cronin 2008), observing the hiring processes of juniors in creative departments. The latter could help identify if creative director instinct about the candidate and homosociability are more important than the portfolio. Second, replication of this study at a senior level would help to generalize findings, although at senior levels networking plays a key role (McLeod, O'Donohoe, and Townley 2011). Finally, researching the presence of young women in junior awards and the reasons for job preferences among advertising students would help the industry to ascertain whether creative female talent is lost at universities, as previous research claims (Grow and Broyles 2011), and what should be done to keep it. Social and cultural pressure could prevent females applying to creative departments, and self-exclusion or self-discrimination could already be present at a university level, prior to applying for positions with advertising agencies.

Acknowledgements

The authors gratefully acknowledge the *Ministerio de Economía y Competitividad* (The Spanish Ministry of Economy and Competitivity) for funding this research, Edu Bonet for database work and Olivier Grau for statistical advice.

Disclosure statement

No potential conflict of interest was reported by the authors.

References

Alvesson, M. 1998. Gender relations and identity at work: A case study of masculinities and femininities in an advertising agency. *Human Relations* 51, no. 8: 969–1005.

Amabile, T.M. 1982. Social psychology of creativity: A consensual assessment technique. *Journal of Personality and Social Psychology* 43, no. 5: 997–1013.

Amabile, T.M. 1996. *Creativity in context*. Boulder, CO: Westview.

Baer, J., and J.C. Kaufman 2008. Gender differences in creativity. *The Journal of Creative Behavior* 42, no. 2: 75–105.

Baer, J., J.C. Kaufman, and C.A. Gentile 2004. Extension of the consensual assessment technique to nonparallel creative products. *Creativity Research Journal* 16, no. 1: 113–7.

Basset-Jones, N. 2005. The paradox of diversity management, creativity and innovation. *Creativity and Innovation Management* 14, no. 2: 169–75.

Bird, S.R. 1996. Welcome to the men's club: Homosociality and the maintenance of hegemonic masculinity author(s). *Gender and Society* 10, no. 2: 120–32.

Bosak, J., and S. Sczesny 2008. Am I the right candidate? Self-ascribed fit of women and men to a leadership position. *Sex Roles* 58, no. 9–10: 682–88.

Bosman, J. (2005, 5 November). Stuck at the edges of the ad game: Women feel sidelined, in subtle ways. *New York Times* C.1.

Broadbridge, A., and R. Simpson 2011. Twenty five years on: Reflecting on the past and looking to the future in gender and management research. *British Journal of Management* 22: 470–83.

Broyles, S., and J. Grow 2008. Creative women in advertising agencies: Why so few 'babes in boyland'? *Journal of Consumer Marketing* 25, no. 1: 4–6.

Byrne, D. 1997. An overview (and underview) of research and theory within the attraction paradigm. *Journal of Social and Personal Relationships* 14, no. 3: 417–31.

Canary, D.J., and K. Hause 1993. Is there any reason to research sex differences in communication? *Communication Quarterly* 41, no. 2: 129–44.

Chong, M. 2006. How do advertising creative directors perceive research? *International Journal of Advertising* 25, no. 3: 361–80.

Correll, S., S. Benard, and I. Paik 2007. Getting a job: Is there a motherhood penalty? *American Journal of Sociology* 112, no. 5: 1297–1338.

Cronin, A.M. 2008. Gender in the making of commercials worlds: Creativity, vitalism and the practices of marketing. *Feminist Theory* 9, no. 3: 293–312.

Csikszentmihalyi, M. 1999. A systems perspective on creativity. In *Handbook of creativity*, ed. R. Sternberg, 313–35. Cambridge: Cambridge University Press. Available at: www.sagepub.com/upm-data/11443_01_Henry_Ch01.pdf (accessed 15 October 2014).

Cuneo, A., and L. Petrecca 1997. Women target boys club of ad creatives. *Advertising Age* 68, no. 45: 24.

Dáhlen, M., S. Rosengren, and F. Törn 2008. Advertising creativity matters. *Journal of Advertising Research* 48, no. 3: 392–403.

Di Sesa, N. 2008. *Seducing the boys club: Uncensored tactics from a woman at the top*. New York: Ballantines Books.

Eagly, A.H., M.G. Makhijani, and B.G. Klonsky 1992. Gender and the evaluation of leaders: A meta-analysis. *Psychological Bulletin* 111: 3–22.

Eagly, A.H., and A. Mladinic 1994. Are people prejudiced against women? Some answers from research on attitudes, gender stereotypes, and judgments of competence. *European Review of Social Psychology* 5, no. 1: 1–35.

Estudio Infoadex de la inversión publicitaria en España. 2014. Madrid: Infoadex. Available at: http://www.infoadex.es/resumen_estudio_2014.pdf (accessed 21 november 2014).

Etayo, C., and J. Del Río 2008. Influencia de los factores humanos sobre la creatividad en las agencias de publicidad. *Zer* 25: 197–219.

Fitzsimmons, E. (2008). Feature…Asian advertising's glass ceiling. *Media* 24–5. Available at: http://bit.ly/1wKiiUP (accessed 9 October 2014).

Fullerton, J., A. Kendrick, and C. Frazier 2009. Advertising student career preferences: A national survey. *Special Report for the Journal of Advertising Education* 13, no. 2: 70–4.

Gelade, G.A. 1997. Creativity in conflict: The personality of the commercial creative. *Journal of Genetic Psychology* 158, no. 1: 67–78.

Goldberg, P. 1968. Are women prejudiced against women? *Society* 5, no. 5: 28–30.

Govendo, J.A. 2005. Workforce, diversity and corporate creativity. *Handbook of Business Strategy* 6, no. 1: 213–8.

Graves, L., and G. Powell 1988. An investigation of sex discrimination in recruiters' evaluation of actual applicants. *Journal of Applied Psychology* 73, no. 1: 20–9.

Graves, L., and G. Powell 1995. The effect of sex similarity on recruiters' evaluations of actual applicants: A test of the similarity-attraction paradigm. *Personnel Psychology* 48, no. 1: 85–98.

Gregory, M.R. 2009. Inside the locker room: Male homosociability in the advertising industry. *Gender, Work and Organization* 16, no. 3: 323–47.

Grow, J.M., and S.J. Broyles 2011. Unspoken rules of creativity game: Insights to shape the next generation from top advertising creative women. *Advertising & Society Review* 12, no. 1: 1–16.

Grow, J.M., and T. Deng 2014. Sex segregation in advertising creative departments across the globe. *Advertising & Society Review* 14, no. 4: 1–16.

Grow, J.M., D. Roca, and S.J. Broyles 2012. Vanishing acts: Creative women in Spain and the United States. *International Journal of Advertising* 31, no. 3: 657–79.

Hackley, C. 2003. How divergent beliefs cause account team conflict. *International Journal of Advertising* 22, no. 3: 313–31.

Hackley, C., and A.J. Kover 2007. The trouble with creatives: Negotiating creative identity in advertising agencies. *International Journal of Advertising* 26, no. 1: 63–78.

Halon Soto, D., and C. Cole 1975. Prejudice against women: A new perspective. *Sex Roles* 1, no. 4: 385–93.

Hartman, J. 1988. *Assessing women in the creative department: What creative directors think.* Portland: Association for Education in Journalism and Mass Communication.

Hernández, A., M. Martín, and M. Beléndez 2012. La representación de la mujer en publicidad: (des)igualdad cuantitativa y cualitativa en la creatividad española [The representation of women in advertising: quantitative and qualitative inequality in spanish creativity]. *Estudios sobre el Mensaje Periodístico* 18: 521–30.

Ibarra, H. 1992. Homophily and differential returns: sex differences in network structure and access in an advertising firm. *Administrative Science Quarterly* 37: 422–47.

Kanter, R.M. 1977. Some effects of proportions on group life: Skewed sex ratios and responses to token women. *The American Journal of Sociology* 82, no. 5: 965–90.

Kasof, J. 1993. Sex bias in the naming of stimulus persons. *Psychological Bulletin* 113, no. 1: 140–63.

Kaufman, J.C., W. Niu, J.D. Sexton, and J.C. Cole 2010. In the eye of the beholder: Differences across ethnicity and gender in evaluating creative work. *Journal of Applied Social Psychology* 40, no. 2: 496–511.

Kilgour, M., S. Sasser, and S. Koslow 2013. Creativity awards; great expectations. *Creativity Research Journal* 25, no. 2: 163–71.

Klein, D. 2000. *Women in advertising. 10 years on.* London: Institute of Practitioners in Advertising.

Knight, C., and H. Thorsell 2012. *Mad women: A herstory of advertising.* Stockholm: Olika Publishing.

Koslow, S., S. Sasser, and E. Riordan 2003. What is creative to whom and why? Perceptions in advertising agencies. *Journal of Advertising Research* 43, no. 1: 96–110.

Lázaro, P., D. Tena, D. Roca, J.M. Blanco, and A. González. 2014. Prácticas epistémicas de la e-Research en comunicación: el caso PARC. In *Ciencias Sociales y Humanidades Digitales. Técnicas, herramientas y experiencias de e-Research e investigación en colaboración*, ed. E. Romeo & M. Sánchez, 195–214. Granada: Cuadernos Artesanos de Comunicació. Available at: http://grinugr.org/wp-content/uploads/libro-ciencias-sociales-y-humanidades-digitales-cap8. pdf (accessed 16 November 2014).

Levenson, H., B. Burford, B. Bonno, and L. Davis 1975. Are women still prejudiced against women? A replication and extension of Goldberg's study. *Journal of Psychology* 89, no. 1: 67–71.

Lipman-Blumen, J. 1976. Toward a homosocial theory of sex roles: an explanation of the sex segregation of social institutions. *Signs* 1, no. 3: 15–31.

Mallia, K.E. 2008. New century, same story: Women scarce when Adweek ranks 'best spots. *Journal of Advertising Education* 12, no. 1: 5–14.

Mallia, K.E. 2009. Rare birds: Why so few women become ad agency creative directors. *Advertising & Society Review* 10, no. 3. Retrieved from: http://bit.ly/1xGr4Du (accessed 6 September 2014).

Mallia, K.E., and K. Windels 2011. Will changing media change the world? An exploratory investigation of the impact of digital advertising on opportunities for creative women. *Journal of Interactive Advertising* 11, no. 2: 30–44.

Martín, M. 2007. La mujer en la industria publicitaria. La concentración horizontal en la comunicación comercial. *Anàlisi* 35: 95–136.

Martín, M., A. Hernández, and M. Beléndez 2009. Competencias directivas en el sector publicitario. Diferencias en la percepción por generación y por sexo. *Revista Latina de Comunicación Social* 12, no. 64: 228–37.

Mass, J. 2013. *Mad women: The other side on Madison Avenue in the '60s and beyond*. New York: Thomas Dunne Books.

Mensa, M., and J.M. Grow 2015. Creative women in Peru: Outliers in a machismo world. *Communication & Society* 28, no. 2: 1–18.

McLeod, C., S. O'Donohoe, and B. Townley 2011. Pot noodles, placements and peer regard: Creative career trajectories and communities of practice in the British advertising industry. *British Journal of Management* 22, no. 1: 114–31.

Michinov, E., and N. Michinov 2011. Social comparison orientation moderates the effects of group membership on the similarity-attraction relationship. *The Journal of Social Psychology* 151, no. 6: 754–66.

Montoya, R.M., R.S. Horton, and J. Kirchner 2008. Is actual similarity necessary for attraction? A meta-analysis of actual and perceived similarity. *Journal of Social and Personal Relationships* 25, no. 6: 889–922.

Nixon, S. 2003. *Advertising Cultures: Gender, Commerce, Creativity*. London: Sage.

Nixon, S., and B. Crewe 2004. Pleasure at work? Gender, consumption and work-based identities in the creative industries. *Consumption, Markets and Culture* 7, no. 2: 129–47.

Olian, J.D., D.P. Schwab, and Y. Haberfeld 1988. The impact of applicant gender compared to qualifications on hiring recommendations. *Organizational Behavior of Human Decision Processes* 41, no. 2: 180–95.

Orphen, C. 1984. Attitude similarity, attraction, and decision-making in employment interview. *The Journal of Psychology* 117, no. 1: 111–20.

Paludi, M., and W. Bauer 1983. Goldberg revisited: What's in an author's name. *Sex Roles* 9, no. 3: 387–90.

Pool, J. 2001. Quiet never gets you anywhere. *Advertising Age* 72, no. 23: 1–12.

Pueyo, N. 2010. Sex structure of occupations in the advertising industry: Where are the female ad practitioners? *Observatorio Journal* 4, no. 3: 243–67.

Rand, T.M., and K.N. Wexley 1975. Demonstration of the effect, 'similar to me' in simulated employment interviews. *Psychological Reports* 36: 535–44.

Roca, D., D. Tena, and P. Lázaro. 2012. Is there gender bias in the assessment of advertising creativity? *11th International Conference on Research in Advertising*. Stockholm: ICORIA.

Roca, D., I. Alegre, and N. Pueyo. 2011. The absence of creative women as judges in advertising awards: A case study of El Sol (1998-2008). *Trípodos* 31: 143–57.

Roca, D., and N. Pueyo. 2011. A Gendered view on account assignment in creative departments. *10th International Conference on Research in Advertising*. Berlin: ICORIA.

Roca. D., P. Lázaro, A. González, J.M. Blanco, and D. Tena. 2013. Creative departments: are they for women? *11th International Conference on Research in Advertising*. Zagreb: ICORIA.

Rosengren, S., M. Dáhlen, and E. Modig 2013. Think outside the ad: Can advertising creativity benefit more than the advertiser? *Journal of Advertising Research* 42, no. 4: 320–330.

Rossiter, J.R. 2011. *Measurement for the social sciences: The C-OAR-SE method and why it must replace psychometrics*. New York: Springer.

Sasser, S.L., and S. Koslow 2008. Desperately seeking advertising creativity: Engaging an imaginative '3Ps' research agenda. *Journal of Advertising* 37, no. 4: 5–19.

Sasser, S.L., and S. Koslow 2013. Passion, expertise, politics and support. *Journal of Advertising* 41, no. 3: 5–17.

Sasser, S.L., S. Koslow, and M. Kilgour 2013. Do clients really need highly creative advertising? *Journal of Advertising Research* 53, no. 3: 297–312.

Sego, T. 1999. The effects of sex and ethnicity on evaluations of advertising job candidates: Do stereotypes predict discrimination? *Journal of Current Issues and Research in Advertising* 21, no. 1: 63–74.

Shao, Y., F. Desmarais, and K. Weaver 2014. Chinese advertising practitioners' conceptualization of gender representation. *International Journal of Advertising* 33, no. 2: 329–50.

Slayden, D., S.J. Broyles, and A. Kendrick 1998. Content and strategy in the entry-level advertising portfolio. *Journalism & Mass Communication Educator* 53, no. 3: 13–27.

Stuhlfaut, M.W. 2011. The creative code: An organizational influence on the creative process in advertising. *International Journal of Advertising* 30, no. 2: 283–304.

Swim, J., E. Borgida, G. Marutama, and D. Myers 1989. Joan McKay versus John McKay: Do gender stereotypes bias evaluation? *Psychological Bulletin* 105, no. 3: 409–29.

Ward, C. 1979. Differential evaluation of male and female expertise: Prejudice against women. *The British Journal of Social and Clinical Psychology* 18, no. 1: 65–9.

Weisberg, L., and B. Robbs 1997. *A study of the under representation of women in advertising agency creative departments*. Chicago: Association for Education in Journalism & Mass Communication.

Windels, K., and W. Lee 2012. The construction of gender and creativity in advertising creative departments. *Gender in Management: An International Journal* 27, no. 8: 502–19.

Windels, K., W. Lee, and Y. Yeh 2010. Does the creative boys' club begin in the classroom? *Journal of Creative Education* 14, no. 2: 15–24.

Index

For Product Safety Concerns and Information please contact our EU
representative GPSR@taylorandfrancis.com
Taylor & Francis Verlag GmbH, Kaufingerstraße 24, 80331 München, Germany

www.ingramcontent.com/pod-product-compliance
Ingram Content Group UK Ltd.
Pitfield, Milton Keynes, MK11 3LW, UK
UKHW051831180425
457613UK00022B/1194